RUSSELL WINNOCK is a pseudonym, but the author is a real criminal barrister, called in 1999 and trying his best ever since.

RUSSELL WINNOCK

Confessions of a Barrister

THE
FRIDAY
PROJECT

The Friday Project
An imprint of HarperCollins*Publishers*
1 London Bridge Street
London SE1 9GF

www.harpercollins.co.uk

This edition published by The Friday Project in 2015

1

ISBN: 978-0-00-810034-6

Set in Minion by Palimpsest Book Production Limited, Falkirk, Stirlingshire

Printed and bound in Great Britain by
Clays Ltd, St Ives plc

Disclaimer

This book is dedicated to the Judges, barristers, solicitors, court staff, clients and criminals who have inspired the stories. All names and events have been changed, but each story and event has its genesis in some case or incident that has actually happened.

To my Dad, who taught me to always try to look after
those who struggle to look after themselves

Brian Fordyke

The buzzer. The buzzer of doom. The buzzer that indicates that the jury have reached a verdict and are now ready to come back into the courtroom to deliver it. Guilty or not guilty, that's what the buzzer means. And as soon as I hear it, the pace of my heart starts to quicken and I feel the prickle of sweat forming under my wig.

I look behind me to the dock where my client, a pockmarked and serially dishonest rogue and drug addict by the name of Brian Fordyke, sits, charged with shoplifting. The trial has not gone particularly well for him.

I'm in court sixteen of the City Crown Court. It's a court where odd things happen, far away from the gaze of the media and the high-profile cases. It is tucked away, ancient, dusty and largely ignored. It is where I ply my trade as a barrister. In court sixteen the buzzer is followed by the footsteps – heavy, foreboding footsteps on the wooden floor that leads from the jury room to the court-room: clomp, clomp, clomp.

And with every footstep, the verdict 'guilty' or 'not guilty', happiness or sadness, freedom or incarceration is brought a clomping step nearer.

The door from the jury room to the courtroom opens and in

they walk. The usual vengeful suspects: my jury, Brian Fordyke's jury. There's the little old lady who has sucked Everton Mints religiously throughout the trial; the bloke with the tattoos who sat and stared utterly oblivious to my attempts to persuade him of Brian Fordyke's innocence; the middle-class man who has worn a suit throughout; the hippy lady in the flowing blouse who chose to affirm rather than swear on the Bible (always nice to get a couple of liberals on the jury); and the pretty girl to whom I found myself paying far too much attention during my closing speech. These and the seven others clomp towards their place in the jury box and sit down.

At this point I watch them carefully. I know that if they look towards me or the dock then they will acquit my client, if they don't, it's curtains.

They look straight ahead, steely-faced. There isn't so much as a glimpse in my direction or towards the dock. This isn't good.

The foreman is the man with tattoos – for a second I try to persuade myself that this might be a good thing, that the man with the tattoos might have a bit of a colourful history himself, but I know I'm grasping at greasy straws. I know what is about to happen only too well.

The Clerk of the Court gets up and clears her throat: 'Will the foreman of the jury please stand.' Tattoo man gets up.

'Have the jury reached a verdict upon which you are all agreed?'

'Yes.' His voice is deep and gravelly without a hint of reasonable doubt.

'Do you find the defendant, Brian Fordyke, guilty or not guilty of the theft of a marital aid from Mr Nookies Adult Emporium?'

'Guilty.'

Damn.

'And that is the verdict of you all?'

'It is.'

I hear my client let out a little sigh from the dock as the Judge replaces his glasses and looks disapprovingly at me. Why is he looking at me? I didn't steal the bloody marital aid; and why do we have to call it a marital aid? I mean, who uses that term – no one! Why can't we just say dildo?

'Mr Russell Winnock,' says the Judge.

I rise obediently to my feet. 'Your Honour?' I reply.

'Your client has been found guilty on the most overwhelming of evidence.'

'Well . . . Yes.' I try to put up some kind of counter proposition to this, but the Judge, a ruthless and often confused old codger by the name of Marmaduke, is having none of it.

'In fact, Mr Winnock, this case shouldn't have even been in my court.'

'Well, Your Honour . . .' I'm stumbling now, looking for words, but nothing except air leaves my mouth.

'This is the type of case that should have been heard by . . .' he pauses '. . . the Magistrates.' His Honour, Judge Marmaduke, spits out the words 'the Magistrates' as though he were talking about a group of lepers.

'Who advised *this* man –' he points in the direction of the now guilty Brian Fordyke as he shouts at me – 'to elect to come to the Crown Court rather than,' another pause, '*the Magistrates*?'

'Er, me, Your Honour. That was me.'

'You, Winnock!'

'Yes, Your Honour.'

'Why the devil did you do that? You've wasted thousands of pounds of taxpayers' money.'

'Well, Your Honour, I believe that all men and women should have the chance to be tried by their peers.'

'Well, your client was tried by his peers.'

'Yes, Your Honour.'

3

'And they convicted him.'

'They did, Your Honour.'

'Of the theft of this, this . . .' he is gesticulating wildly, his eyes bulging. Finally, without finishing his sentence, and with his face a coronary shade of incensed purple, he turns to my client. 'Brian Fordyke, stand – you will go to prison for fifteen years.'

There is a gasp from around the courtroom – even the jury gasp. I jump up to my feet: 'Your Honour, fifteen years? The dildo was only worth eight quid.'

'Alright then, fifteen weeks,' spits Marmaduke, and with that he flounces out of the court.

The jury look at me, I look at them and the little old lady turns to the woman next to her and says in a loud stage whisper – 'God love him.'

I sigh, it wasn't meant to be like this, my life as a criminal barrister. I had imagined it so very differently. I had imagined that I would be revered in court, loved by clients and solicitors, respected by Judges and opponents. I had imagined a life of serious, headline-worthy cases, trials at the Old Bailey, interviews with Joshua Rosenberg, where I would effortlessly say things like, 'Joshua, no, bless you, your interpretation of the meaning of the decision in the case of Galbraith is quite wrong, let me help you out.' And then there's the money, I had always imagined that being a barrister would lend itself to having a few quid. I had imagined having a fast red sports car, a penthouse flat and an extensive fine wine collection. I imagined having handmade suits, a little place in France and a posh girlfriend who looked good in jodhpurs.

In short, when I decided to study law at Leeds University, some thirteen years ago, I imagined that I would become successful, powerful, rich, highly sexed and, yes, probably a bit of a tosser. Sadly, having been a barrister for nine years and having just turned

31, only one of those ambitions has come to fruition – and it isn't the sex bit.

Now, don't get me wrong, it's not that I don't enjoy being a barrister – I truly love my job (well, most of it) and there are parts of the job that I would never want to give up. I still see it as a privilege, I still see it as performing an important function; I quite like my clients, even the pervs and weirdos; I enjoy the cut and thrust of a trial and I even like the old-fashioned ways, the pomp and ceremony, wigs and gowns and bowing, and the peculiar language that is unique to courts. I like all that, but, in truth, being a criminal barrister today, after all the cuts and the changes and closures, is a bit like arriving at a party at the point when everyone is already getting into a taxi or passed out on the couch – fun's been had, but I ain't getting any of it.

This book is about all of it – the fun and the pomp, the seriousness and the stress. It is about the weirdos and Judges and clients, the opponents you respect and the opponents you despise. It is about, I hope, my attempts to do my best and let you into a few little secrets along the way. It is about being a barrister.

How do you defend someone who you know is guilty?

As a criminal barrister, the first question I get asked when people find out what I do for a living is 'How do you defend someone who you know is guilty?' It's probably the first question you thought of when you picked up this book. Well, I'll tell you.

After Brian Fordyke's trial, I went down to see him – it's what you do. He was sat alone in his cell. It was small and grey, with nothing in it but a table and two chairs – it is the place a person is put before a big part of their life is taken from them – their freedom – and it's every bit as soulless as you would imagine. On the table someone had scratched the words, 'Marmaduke is a Cock-Knocker' – which seemed entirely apposite. I sat down opposite my rather forlorn and puzzled-looking client; thankfully, I didn't detect any bitterness being directed towards me – which was something at least. I considered cracking a little joke – maybe, suggesting that on the occasion of him being convicted of his fiftieth offence of shoplifting, the police and courts might commemorate the occasion and have a whip round and present him with a small engraved tankard to mark the occasion – but I thought better of it.

That is the worst part of the job: when someone has put their faith in you, entrusted you to maintain their liberty, defend their name, and you lose. Because you both lose – but the only difference is, you'll be going home tonight.

'Well, Brian,' I said, trying to muster up a bit of a smile, 'for a second there I thought the Judge had gone mad. Fifteen years, pfft.'

He smiled weakly at me. 'Do you know, Russ, on this occasion, I actually wasn't guilty.'

'I know, mate.' I added, 'But, the CCTV wasn't very good for us, was it?'

He shrugged in acknowledgement of the utterly damning Close Circuit Television footage that showed him in HD quality fiddling with his flies, before placing the offending marital aid down his trousers and making to leave the shop.

'And, I suppose, if you put yourself in the jury's position,' I continued, 'they were never going to believe that you were simply attempting to compare the, er, marital aid, to your own tackle.'

He shrugged again and it hit me that actually, if I had been a juror I would probably have convicted him as well.

But that isn't my job, I am not there to decide if someone is guilty or innocent. That is why the question 'How do you defend someone who you know is guilty?' – which every barrister is asked by everyone they ever speak to at every dinner party or family gathering they ever attend – is so perplexing. We don't know if the person is guilty or not, we only do what our clients tell us. And if they tell us that they were sticking a dildo down their trousers because they were buying a saucy present for the Mrs and wanted to compare the present to their own appendage to ensure that they didn't get anything too big, then that's the defence which we will place before a jury, even if it's probably a load of cobblers. Because all of us, whether we like it or not, are innocent until *proven* guilty. So it's not a dilemma at all, it's very simple – if someone tells us that they are not guilty, even after we've told them that the evidence is strong, even after we have told them that they will be making things far worse for themselves if they have a trial, then we have to take them at their word, our own feelings and opinions are irrelevant. We put forward the points as best we can, and let others decide about guilt or innocence, right or wrong. That is our job.

I shook hands with Brian Fordyke. He'd been to prison before, for him fifteen weeks offered no fear and no surprises. He would come out after about six weeks, his craving for whatever drug he had been using would probably return, his desire to go straight probably forgotten, and before long, he'd be back in court, waiting for the buzzer and the jury's verdict. And then, because it would almost certainly be 'guilty', he would be back in prison for another couple of months. That was his life.

And me, well, I limped back to chambers to prepare myself for the next brief, the next case – in the hope that, perhaps, it would be more exciting, more successful and more lucrative than the last one. Perhaps it would be the case that would make my name.

Chambers

I'm not proud of this, but by the time I get back to my chambers, Gray's Buildings, after a trial, I've usually forgotten about my client. I know that sounds callous and cold, but the brain of a barrister has a habit of jettisoning things quite quickly – it has to, otherwise we'd end up demented, our every thought haunted by the ghosts of cases long gone. Yes, okay, there are occasions when you wake up in the middle of the night, sit bolt upright and think – 'Why didn't I just ask that question?' or, actually, more likely, 'Why *did* I have to ask that one last stupid question?' But usually we go to court, we do our cases, we come back from court, and somewhere in between leaving court and arriving at our next destination, the gruesome details of the last client become lost in the canopy of our minds.

They're funny things, chambers. They don't really seem to belong to the modern age. Despite the desperate attempts of some of the big City sets to employ practice managers and IT consultants and PR gurus, they almost all still have a sniff of the eighteenth century about them, when a man could conduct a court case whilst simultaneously eating a hearty dinner and enjoying a flagon of ale before going on to enjoy the delights of Madame Pomfrey's girls on Petticoat Lane.

11

Gray's Buildings is tucked down a back street and about a ten-minute walk from the City Crown Court. It has seen better days and as a building is remarkable only for its 1970s pebble-dash and a massive oak door that is painted gallows black. Next door is a sandwich shop, across the road is the Erskine Pub and next door to that is the super-duper, ultra-modern Extempar Chambers – motto 'We Don't Judge, We Just Care.' Extempar Chambers is the future, or so we are told. They have about 150 members, all of whom have a First Class degree from Cambridge or come from a long line of High Court Judges. They have fifteen clerks who all appear to be former models and a liveried van to deliver briefs to your doorstep. They have corporate days out, hunting and white-water rafting, they even have a motion sensor espresso machine (whatever that is). They have contracts with multinational companies, an interactive website and a career plan for each member.

But, surely all of that counts for nothing when you're faced with the likes of Brian Fordyke – then, all the motion sensor espresso machines and smiley clerks in the world can't compensate for the ability to talk and act like a normal human being.

My chambers does not have a motto. We are what is termed a medium-sized traditional chambers. There are about 60 barristers and we are all strictly self-employed sole-trading businessmen (we are not allowed to take a wage), but we band together and pay an astronomically high percentage of our fees to our chambers to employ five clerks, two typists and one extremely bubbly Scottish girl whose role no one is quite sure of.

I have a desk in a room and a pigeonhole and a shelf upon which I keep my red-ribboned briefs.

My room is on the top floor down a dark and hidden corridor next to the toilet. It is home to four of us: me; Amir Saddique, a young and extremely intelligent Personal Injury (PI) and contract lawyer; Jenny Catrell-Jones, a criminal barrister in her fifties who swears like a trucker, wears frighteningly short skirts and scares the life out of most Judges; and Angus Tollman, who is a couple of years junior to me and already has a shelf bulging with cases involving serious frauds, gruesome violence and despicable sex – bastard, he probably has a red sports car as well.

Amir rarely goes to court, his practice is what we call a paper practice, every day he sits down with a pile of briefs about people who have tripped or slipped or been in car crashes or are refusing to be bound by some contractual agreement or other. For me, I would rather sit watching grass grow than do this kind of law, but Ammie has a wonderful ability to sit quietly at his desk, which is covered in Tottenham Hotspur memorabilia, and plough methodically through them.

Even though Amir has never been in the Crown Court in his life, I know that if I am going to moan about a case or a Judge or a jury, then he will feel my pain. He knows what it's like to lose (though I'd wager it doesn't happen very often to him).

I have always been pleasantly surprised by my relationship with other members of chambers. True, there are one or two who are stuck so firmly up their own arses that they are virtually impossible to speak to, but, on the whole, most members of my chambers are sound. We provide a service to one another, a warm, yet slightly disengaged comradeship – offering a word of advice here, a friendly ear to moan to there, and a feeling of solidarity that is important.

The names of each member of chambers appear on a copper-plated list above the black front door. We are listed in order of call, which is the date when our Inn (an ancient organisation that no one can quite remember the purpose of – more of which, later) deems that we are fit to be a barrister.

I have long concluded that there are really two types of people who become barristers – those whose parents were barristers and judges and those of us who, when we were children, watched a TV courtroom drama, probably involving an incredibly handsome advocate or a fascinating and flawed maverick genius advocate who either managed to get himself involved in an action-packed adventure that led to him 'solving the case', or cross-examined someone with such supreme skill that suddenly they broke down and confessed that 'Yes, you're right, *I* did it.' You know the ones.

Both scenarios are of course utter nonsense: no one ever breaks down and confesses to anything under cross-examination. The best you can usually hope for is that you manage to make someone look a little bit shifty, which hardly lends itself to good TV drama – '*In tonight's episode of* Courtroom QC, *rugged maverick genius Silk, Arthur Morse QC, manages to make someone look a bit shifty.*'

As for action-packed adventure, the nearest a barrister gets is when they have to get the night bus home after the annual Christmas drinks do.

My parents were not Judges or lawyers, they were teachers. Why did I come to the Bar? *Kavanagh QC*, ITV, 9pm, Thursday nights, that's why.

Do I regret it?

Well, the jury, as they say, is still out.

Wigs, gowns, three-piece suits and my blue bag

There are a few things about a barrister's appearance that will help you understand the life of a barrister and possibly a few things that will help you understand me. First, I wear a three-piece suit. You may have noticed that a lot of male barristers wear three-piece or double-breasted suits and you may have dismissed this as a sartorial throwback to a different age or that we have the fashion sense of a politician, but actually there is more to it than that. Barristers are, strictly speaking, not allowed to wear a single-breasted suit whilst in a Crown Court. True, some do, especially since more and more solicitors have taken up work in the Crown Courts, but they risk being admonished by a Judge. Indeed, I once saw a Judge bellow at a hapless and slightly unkempt solicitor advocate, screaming at him, 'Jones, I can see oceans of your shirt wallowing about under your robes – don't you know anything: single breasts are banned in the Crown Courts of England and Wales.' He then refused to hear the unfortunate advocate until he'd borrowed a waistcoat.

It could have been worse, mind, he could have been wearing the wrong type of shirt; woe betide you if you wore the wrong shirt – that would be catastrophic. All male barristers must wear a stiff court collar. And legend has it that a barrister who once

15

appeared before the High Court wearing a 'theatre dress shirt' – which is completely taboo – was taken out the back by the bins and flogged to within an inch of his life. As I say, probably a legend that one, but it works because none of us would dare to break that rule.

The women don't have it that much easier – being forced to wear a white stiff collar that looks suspiciously like a nun's wimple.

Is there any justification for these strict rules? Not really. I suppose the powers that be would say that if the standards of dress are maintained then the standards in court will also be kept up.

It's a bit of a pain because most shops don't sell three-piece suits, and the ones that do, sell them for extortionately high prices. Luckily, in the last couple of years, I've discovered Suits'R'Us.com of Bangkok, who, for under 200 quid, will sort you out something lovely with a brand new three-piece, just as long as you aren't too fussy about either the quality or the fit.

The next thing to notice about me is that over my shoulder I carry a blue, drawstring canvas bag, upon which you will find my initials embroidered in gold cotton – RW: Russell Winnock. Inside the bag are my robes and wig, my kit.

Now, the blue bag is important. You'll hear a lot about it. And, very nice you might think, but, in actual fact, the blue bag is a desperate sign of failure – *because* it's blue. You see, there are two types of bags used by barristers to carry their wigs and gowns, a blue one or a red one. Now, the blue one is the one you buy (or your parents buy) when you are first called to the Bar, in that moment when you proudly don your clobber for the first time, and the outfitter tells you how lovely you look and suggests that 'sir might be interested in a special bag to put it all in'. Next minute, you're parting with another 200 notes for a blue bag to go with the 700 you've just spent on a horsehair wig and nylon cape. At first, you're quite proud of your lovely blue bag and you confidently sling it over your shoulder. But after a while you realise that the blue bag is inferior in every way to the red bag. Now, apart from the colour, the red bag is exactly the same, except that you can't buy a red bag, someone has to buy it for you, and that someone is a Silk – or Queen's Counsel – the international star strikers in the world of the Bar. It's a sign that you have been involved in a 'big case', a case which has involved, more often than not, someone's death, a case which required leading Counsel, a Silk; and that the Silk was so pleased with your work as a junior that he's decided to buy you a red bag.

It is therefore a mark of success, and still having your blue bag – the one purchased by your loving mother and father in a moment of pride – means that you are a failure because you've never been deemed quite good enough to have a red bag.

I still have a bloody blue bag, and the pursuit of a red one has become an all-consuming passion in my professional life.

Pupilage and Ronnie Sherman

In the olden days, every chambers had a Senior Clerk. Now things are slowly changing. Extempar Chambers (you remember, 'We Don't Judge, We Just Care') have something called a Director of Advocacy Services.

My chambers still has a Senior Clerk. His name is Clem Wilson – and he scares the living daylights out of me.

Most people will have seen legal dramas on TV where the stereotypical depiction of barristers' clerks is as a ruthless former East End barrow boy blessed with the cunning of an especially cunning fox, who pit their crafty, working-class street wits against those of the lumbering toffs who pay their wages – I have to say that this is entirely realistic. The only difference between the fictional clerks of TV and my Senior Clerk is that mine isn't a cockney, he comes from Manchester, and this, somehow, makes him seem even more ferociously scary.

Most of the junior members of chambers are petrified of him. Occasionally, there is talk of a coup to oust him, but that is only after a few pints at the Erskine, when everyone is sure that he's nowhere to be seen.

On my first day in chambers as a pupil barrister, he called me into his room.

'You must be Russell Winnock,' he said.

'Yes, Mr Wilson,' I said, 'that's right.'

He then gazed up at me, in a way that a cunning fox might gaze at a particularly stupid hedgehog.

'Now, if one year from today you are lucky enough to be taken on by chambers and become a tenant, I shall cease calling you Russell Winnock and I shall call you Mr Winnock – but not until then, you understand that?'

'Yes,' I said, 'of course.'

'And if you're any good, then I shall be proud to do so. But, if you're rubbish and you make a tit out of me or chambers, I'll get rid of you, is that understood?'

I continued to nod.

'Now, you are a very lucky young man, Russell Winnock, because your pupil-master is going to be Mr Sherman.'

'Fantastic,' I said, with the enthusiasm of a collie dog, though I hadn't the first clue who Mr Sherman was.

'There are two things you need to know about Mr Sherman. First, he is a genius, second, like all geniuses, he has his particular foibles.' At this point he looked at me with a strange intensity, which I have come to realise is his way of trying to indicate that he is employing some euphemism and that he wanted to see if I understood. I didn't. I didn't have a clue what he was going on about.

'Alright?'

I nodded and my Senior Clerk continued, 'Now today, Mr Sherman is at the Bailey. I suggest you wait for him in the waiting area, he'll be around shortly to pick you up.'

'Thank you Mr Wilson,' I said, 'thank you.'

I went to leave – but before I did, Clem Wilson called out to me again, 'And Russell,' I turned around, 'some words of advice. For the next twelve months, don't even try to have a personality of your own; don't make any friends; and don't do anything stupid.'

'Right,' I said, beaming in a confused way like a half-wit, as bits of my personality flaked off there and then.

I took myself off to the waiting area and sat, patiently, until eventually my pupil-master arrived. I heard him before I saw him – his great baritone voice, oozing masculine power and confidence. He was talking to one of the clerks.

'What pupil?'

'Your new pupil, Mr Sherman, he's waiting for you in the foyer.'

'No one told me I was getting a bloody pupil. Whose idea was this?'

'Head of Chambers, Mr Sherman, he thought it would be a good thing.'

'Well I hope she's got big tits and makes good coffee.'

'It's a boy, Mr Sherman, his name's Russell Winnock.'

'A boy? What, like in short trousers?'

'No.'

'Oh for god's sake. The last thing I want is some young lad hanging around me – pupils are a bloody nuisance at the best of times.'

I soon realised what Clem Wilson meant by Ronnie Sherman's foibles: he was a hopeless chauvinist, misogynist and snob and an even more hopeless alcoholic. He had clearly been given me as an unwanted gift in a desperate attempt to re-invigorate his interest in a flagging career, because Ronnie Sherman had become one of those old barristers who spends more time talking about the great cases of the past than preparing the mediocre cases of the present.

My six months with Ronnie were indeed an education. I learnt how to do a bail application without having any clue what your case actually was; I learnt how to drink a bottle of wine and two pints of bitter during lunch, after which I would watch my pupil-master either swerve and sway on his feet as he embarked on a lengthy and meandering cross-examination, or engineer an adjournment because he was not actually capable of embarking upon any cross-examination at all. I learnt how to ignore Judges, solicitors and junior clerks; I learnt how to lie to a wife or loved one about my whereabouts and I learnt how I was entering the profession at the worst time ever. 'Russell,' he would tell me, 'you should have been doing this job twenty years ago – the money was great and everyone knew their place. Not like now.'

But amazingly, despite this reluctance to have me hanging round him, and despite the fact that he was mostly pissed after two o'clock, Ronnie Sherman did teach me some vital things about being a barrister: he taught me how to properly address a Judge, how to conduct yourself in court and about the strange rituals and customs of the Bar and the judicial system; but most of all, he taught me – and I'm not sure that he would admit to this – about how to treat your clients. You see, despite his bluff snobbery, pomposity and supposed antipathy towards most other sectors of society, when Ronnie Sherman was with his clients, he was transformed. When he entered a cell or a conference room, he would instantly change; he would listen gently and carefully, instinctively understanding and empathetic. Every client, regardless of the charge they faced, their background or history – tragic or stupid – would be treated with compassion and courtesy. In an instant he could put a young lad facing prison for the first time at ease, or coax a confession out of the worst kind of sex offender. And that ability – to build a trusting relationship with your client – is possibly the most important that a barrister can possess. Because the law isn't just about, well, laws and statutes and being learned or clever, it's about people. As a barrister you're becoming involved in a person's life at a time when that life has gone wrong.

And that, dear reader, is the beauty of the pupilage system. A young barrister, fresh from Bar School and totally wet behind the ears, spends the first six months of his or her career doing nothing but sitting behind their pupil-master, observing the right and wrong way to do things.

A couple of years after being my pupil-master, the Lord Chancellor's department decided to make Ronnie a Judge; surprisingly, considering his outward disapproval of most people's lives, they made him a family Judge.

What's the difference between a solicitor and a barrister?

One afternoon, I walked through the foyer of chambers, heading to the room where our pigeonholes are kept. There is one for each barrister, set out, like everything else in this job, strictly in order of seniority or call. I checked mine on the off-chance that there was either a massive cheque or a massive brief nestling inside it. There was neither, only a flier advertising the services of a company offering me a low-interest loan to pay my tax bill. I groaned and went to make my way up a back staircase to my room.

This was a mistake. The back stairs took me past the Senior Clerk's office – the office of Clem Wilson, and as I walked past his door, he spotted me.

'Mr Winnock.'

I considered pretending not to hear, but knew that that wouldn't make any difference: if Clem Wilson wanted to talk to me, then the conversation would happen one way or another.

'Hi Clem,' I proffered, 'everything okay?'

'Come in and sit down,' he suggested wearily. I felt like a piece of lettuce being addressed by a slug.

'I'm a bit worried, Mr Winnock,' he said.

'Worried?' I asked him. 'Why?'

Now, at this stage, it's worth noting that I had lost a trial earlier that day and Clem Wilson will already have heard. You see, he hears everything, he knows everything, he's like the East German government of the 1960s and 70s, he has people everywhere.

But Clem Wilson won't give a toss about the result of my trial, or whether justice was done or not. In fact, it wouldn't matter to him if I lost every case I ever did. No, all Clem Wilson cares about is keeping the solicitors happy.

I suppose it's about time that I explained the relationship between a solicitor and a barrister. After the 'how do you defend someone who's guilty' question, this is the second most popular question we're asked: 'What's the difference between a barrister and a solicitor?'

Well, though the answer is no longer as straightforward as it once was, I suppose a good way of looking at it is this: solicitors are akin to GPs – if you are ill, they are the first port of call to give you the once-over, prescribe a bit of medicine if it's not too serious, and listen to your tales of woe. Barristers are a bit like consultants – the ones in the operating theatre wielding the scalpel. And just as in medicine, if anything is seriously wrong when you go to a GP you're referred to a consultant, so it is in law. If the solicitor can't sort out your problem then you'll be referred to a barrister who will be the person who represents you in the Crown Court or similar Civil and Family Courts.

These days, however, things have changed. Now solicitors are also allowed to wield the scalpel, so to speak. It used to be that barristers were easy to spot, because barristers wore wigs and solicitors didn't – now some solicitors even wear wigs. Where a decade ago it was rare for a solicitor to be seen in the Crown Court as very few had bothered to get the extra qualification needed to appear there – now, it's commonplace, and sadly for us barristers, the result is a reduction in our work.

This is a worry for us and a worry for Clem Wilson, because

he's paid a percentage of all the income from chambers, so the less work into chambers means a potential reduction in *his* wages. And this is why he is keen to keep solicitors happy, because he wants them to continue to instruct his barristers rather than do it themselves, or even worse, instruct other sets of chambers, such as, heaven forbid, Extempar Chambers. And, to a certain degree, that relationship works. Clem keeps the solicitors happy, the solicitors instruct us to do their cases and we all get paid. The situation only breaks down if one of his barristers upsets the solicitors.

'I've been looking at your diary,' he told me.

'Okay.'

'It's not very good, Mr Winnock, is it?'

'Well,' I replied, 'it's hard for all of us at the moment – do you know there were fifteen solicitors in the robing room today, fifteen of them! How can we compete with that?'

Clem Wilson looked unimpressed. 'Well, some seem to be managing it better than others.'

That remark was quite cutting – he's calling me a failure. I shrugged.

'Look,' he said, 'perhaps it's about time you considered something else.'

I felt my eyes widen – 'Something else? Like what? I've only ever known the law, what else could I do?'

He tried to smile in a reassuring way at me, but it came out as a smirk. 'No, I don't mean leave the profession – well, not yet, anyway. I mean another area of law.'

'What, like Chancery or commercial?'

This appealed to me. Chancery and commercial barristers earn massive amounts of money, they are the true fat cats of the Bar. They are the boys – and they are usually male – who drive sports cars and have fancy apartments and expensive suits. The idea of becoming a Chancery barrister was attractive.

Clem Wilson laughed spitefully.

'No, I was thinking family law.'

The image of me in a sports car evaporated, and was replaced by one of me in that most desperately sad of places: the Family Court. The Family Bar is even harder up than the Criminal Bar. The Family Courts are where people go to pore over the ashes of their failed marriages and broken families. The barristers who appear there are usually gentle souls who wear woolly cardigans under their robes, whilst the solicitors are the exact opposite – hard, horrible, trenchant – iron-willed storm troopers who will promise their client that they will take their former partner 'to the cleaners' – and then do everything they can to make good their vow.

I have no interest in the Family Courts. I hadn't been there for over five years, when I had found myself literally banging my head against a wall as my client, a rather stinky woman, refused to agree to allow her child to be picked up from McDonald's at 5.30 every Friday for a contact session with the father, insisting instead that it should be 6pm from Burger King. No, I am a criminal barrister – we are the heavyweight boxers of the legal world, the strutting, posing cocks of the robing room – there is no way I'm going to wear a cardie and help society's failed former lovers sort out who gets the telly and who gets the cat.

Clem Wilson looked at me.

'Yes,' he said, 'I think the Family Courts may be the future for you, Mr Winnock, what with your liberal conscience and that.'

I'm not sure how he's concluded that I have a liberal conscience.

'That's why I have taken a brief for you at the Family Court tomorrow.'

'What? No. Thanks Clem, but it's not for me.'

'It's for Whinstanley and Cooper,' he said, then repeated slowly and with more than a hint of menace, 'Whinstanley and Cooper,' in an attempt to scare me. It worked.

'They are a massive firm, Mr Winnock,' he added, 'they bring in lots of work to chambers, and they need someone to do an injunction hearing tomorrow. You are available.'

I sighed. I considered refusing. I considered digging my heels in. But I knew that any resistance would be futile. A big firm of solicitors wanted to instruct a barrister for a hearing and I was to be that barrister. They were far too important to chambers for Clem Wilson to refuse the work. I sighed, and before I could say another word, my Senior Clerk had placed in my hand a small bundle of papers tied with pink ribbon. On the front were the words West v West.

Silently I left the Senior Clerk's room.

So, what is the difference between a barrister and a solicitor? Well, the answer goes far beyond who wears a wig and who doesn't. Whilst some of the traditional differences are being diminished and done away with, in other ways, the distinction is still there and many of us would argue it is just as important as it has always been. Hopefully it will become clearer as my story continues, and, as it happens, the case of West v West isn't a bad place to start to show the complexity of the solicitor–barrister relationship . . .

West v West

I placed my hateful blue bag of shame on the floor then plonked
the brief of West v West on my desk, making sure that it landed
with a disdainful thud, causing my conscientious roommate Amir
to look up. He was busily reading a rather crusty, yellowing law
book.

'Oh dear, you don't look very happy,' he suggested and I
harrumphed and muttered something about having lost a case
that morning. Amir grinned at me – 'Just get it billed mate, and
think about the cheque,' he said, which is the barrister's equivalent
of being told that there are plenty more fish in the sea, just after
being dumped.

He's right though – just move on to the next case, that is what
we do. I looked down at the papers in West v West.

I unwrapped the pink ribbon and started to read it. Why pink
ribbon? I have no idea, but briefs are wrapped in pink ribbon,
they always have been and they always will be (apart from Court
of Appeal briefs, they are wrapped in white ribbon, yep, beats
me too).

I am instructed to represent Mrs Phi Li West; a Thai woman
who came to the UK eight years ago to marry Mr Graeme West.
Things were great at first (aren't they always?), but don't appear

to be now, because now Mrs West wants an injunction and non-molestation order from the court. This will prevent Mr West from going near her and using any violence or making any threat to harm her.

Okay. So far so good, I have enough of a recollection of this procedure to feel confident that I can obtain the injunction as instructed.

I read Mrs West's statement.

I read that she came over to the UK having met Mr West at a function. Yeah, 'function' – only if 'function' is the Thai word for mail-order-bride website. I stopped myself. I know I'm only being cynical because I'm sulking at the prospect of being in the Family Courts.

Amir looked up from his desk. 'So, where are you tomorrow?'

I mumbled my answer miserably, 'Family Court.'

'What?' he exclaimed. 'I didn't know you did family work?'

'I don't,' I said, trying to retain my pride and dignity, 'I'm just doing it as a favour to Clem and the solicitors, you know how things are.'

He shot me a genuine smile, because he's a genuinely nice guy. 'Best make sure you've got your woolly cardie and sandals out of the back of your wardrobe.'

I smiled. But I didn't mean it. I didn't want to be doing a case about a failed marriage.

The rest of Mrs Phi West's story is a rather sad one. They'd been trying for a child, but hadn't managed to conceive. At which point Mr West had, allegedly, started to become controlling of Mrs West, not allowing her out with her friends, hacking into her phone and email accounts, that kind of thing, until finally, they'd had a fight and he had grabbed her round the neck, causing her abrasions and some swelling.

As it happens, as I write this, I'm single. And, when I read stories like the Wests' I'm quite glad that I'm single. Don't get me wrong, I'm not some kind of cynical old bastard who's been cruelly savaged by a love affair, or some kind of commitment-phobe who goes around trying to bed as many women as he can in an attempt to cover up for inadequacies elsewhere, I just haven't met the right girl yet. Which is actually my mother's phrase, but I'm happy to adopt it.

I suppose Graeme West thought he'd met the right girl. I suppose he thought that he'd create a little family and could live happily and contentedly ever after – well, he got that wrong.

The next day I turned up at the City Family Court Centre, a massive and rather ugly modern building constructed at a time before austerity. I didn't need my blue bag – no wigs and gowns in the Family Court.

The atmosphere inside this court is different. Whereas in a Crown Court there is always an air of excitement and suspense, here there is just despondency and despair. These people aren't bad, they're just unhappy.

I stood in the reception area and watched as a little toddler tentatively meandered away from a girl who looked about nineteen years old and who I assumed was his mother. She sat looking vacantly into the middle distance as he waddled towards a Yucca plant, fell into it and started to cry. The girl went to comfort him, hoisting him onto her hip in that instinctive way that only mothers can. She put a dummy into his mouth and he stopped crying and stared at the offending plant.

A door slammed and a fat man stormed into the reception area. He turned and shouted back towards the door, pointing at it angrily. 'I don't care what you or anyone else says, I don't bloody care.' Then he flung his hands in the air and made a kind of growling noise, interspersed with various swear words.

I sighed and wondered if in ten or twenty years' time, one of the toddler's abiding memories of childhood will be of a Yucca plant and a man shouting at the City Family Court.

I'd been told to expect a trainee solicitor called Kelly. I looked around for her, then back at the growling man who was now being moved away by a court usher, when she made herself known to me.

'Are you Russell Winnock?'

I turned around.

'I am,' I said, 'are you Kelly?'

She didn't smile as she acknowledged me, instead she looked at me with total disinterest. Kelly Backworth was quite stunningly beautiful. She had shoulder-length blonde hair, eyes that wouldn't sit still and full lips. She had colour and youth and hope and expectation that shone out amongst the grey despondency of the waiting room. I wondered what she looked like when she smiled. I wished she had smiled at me.

'I've put Mrs West in a conference room around there,' she told me and I beamed back at her.

She then led me into a small conference room where Mrs Phi West was waiting.

Christ, Mrs West was stunningly beautiful as well. She had a long slick of black hair that made its way down the side of her unfeasibly perfect face and onto her chest. She didn't smile at me either.

Kelly Backworth sat down next to Phi West and they both looked at me with grim disinterest, which was confusing – surely, they both need me for what was about to happen.

'Right,' I said, 'Mrs West. Can I call you Phi?' I pronounced her name Fee, as in fee-fi-fo-fum.

'It pronounced "pie",' she replied in a surprisingly grating, heavily accented voice, 'but no call me Porky Pie.' She looked venomously at me as she said this. 'He call me Porky Pie. No call me Porky Pie.'

'Of course,' I stuttered, 'I wouldn't dream of it.'

I introduced myself, as Kelly started making notes and Phi, not Porky Phi, stared at me.

'Right,' I said, 'today's hearing should be fairly straightforward.'

I then tried to describe the procedure I think the court will follow. Although, to be honest, it'd been that long since I'd done a Family Court injunction, I could be kidding all of us, so I'm glad when I'm interrupted by a knock on the door. It's my opponent, Vicky Smith. Vicky is from my chambers. She is friendly, a few years senior to me, and a very good family barrister.

She smiled at me. 'Can I have a word?' she asked, and I mumbled something to Porky Phi and Kelly and made my way out of the room – I have to admit it's a big relief.

'Russ,' she said, 'Clem told me that you were doing this – what's that all about?'

'Just doing the solicitors a favour,' I proffered unconvincingly.

'Okay,' she said, 'well you're going to love this.' She added, 'Follow me.'

I followed Vicky into another small conference room further up the corridor. In it sat a nervous-looking man with strawberry-blonde hair. He is Mr Graeme West. He didn't look at all like I imagined. He looked respectable and normal, handsome too, to be fair, in an outdoors type of way. I find it difficult to picture him leafing through his wife's iPhone or grabbing her around the neck.

'Mr West,' said Vicky, 'this is Mr Winnock, he is representing your wife today. Will you please show him what you showed me earlier.'

Mr West unbuttoned his shirt and revealed a perfect and newly scabbed burn mark in the shape of a large sausage branded into his chest. Ouch.

'I don't suppose your client's mentioned this to you, has she?' asked Vicky.

I shook my head.

'Let's go outside.' I followed Vicky outside and she immediately adopted a quiet, informal tone – 'Russ,' she said, 'that's where she attacked him with a pair of curling tongs just the other day after a row about a new car she wanted.'

'What?' I said. 'Surely not.' I wasn't sure if I could quite picture Porky Phi carrying out such a venomous act of violence.

'He's absolutely terrified of her,' Vicky continued. 'I'll be straight with you – as soon as a Judge sees that, there's no way on God's green earth that he's going to give you your injunction.'

'I don't know,' I said, which I realised straight away was rubbish – Vicky was absolutely right.

'Look,' Vicky continued, 'he just wants out. He thinks next time she'll kill him in his sleep. He tells me that if you drop the injunction, he'll accept cross-undertakings not to see or hurt each other – and he'll bung in the house.'

I considered this quickly before I responded.

'The house?'

'Yes, and it's mortgage free. He tells me that as far as he's concerned, she can have it all. It's a really great offer for her; it'll mean that when the marriage ends, they won't have to go through a prolonged process of ancillary relief.'

I nodded, trying to remember what a prolonged process of ancillary relief was.

'So, let me get this right,' I said carefully, 'no injunction, he agrees not to hurt her, she agrees not to hurt him, and he gives her the house.'

'Precisely.'

I wondered if there was a catch in this, if I was being done up like a kipper by a more experienced hand. But Vicky wasn't like that, and she was right, any Judge worth his salt was not going to be impressed by the fact that the supposed victim attacked her assailant with a hairdressing appliance.

'I'll take instructions.'

I made my way back to the conference room, where Porky Phi and the incredibly aloof Kelly were still sat.

'Hi,' I said with forced positivity. 'Good news, I think.'

Porky's eyes narrowed suspiciously as she awaited my 'good news'.

'Mr West's barrister has told me that if you drop your injunction and the two of you make what's known as cross-undertakings, which are a promise that you make before a Judge, not to use violence against each other, he'll give you the house.'

'The house?' said Phi.

'Yes,' I nodded. 'That's pretty good, isn't it?'

'I have to promise not to use any violence?'

I nodded again as Phi contemplated this, biting her bottom lip as she did.

'I want the car as well,' she said.

'The car?'

'Yes,' said Phi, 'the shiny silver one with no roof.'

I looked at her, then looked at Kelly for some kind of reaction – there was none. 'Okay,' I said, 'the shiny silver car. Leave it with me.'

I went back to speak to Vicky. 'She wants the silver car with no roof,' I said.

Vicky's face formed itself into an expression of exasperation. 'Bitch,' she said, 'I've half a mind to tell her to sling her hook and advise my lad to take her on before a Judge.'

I shrugged. 'Those are my instructions.'

'Right,' said Vicky, 'stay here.'

Five minutes later, Vicky returned to tell me, grudgingly, that

37

Phi can have the silver convertible, which actually turns out to be a pretty nifty Audi TT.

Half an hour after that, we were before a District Judge, a rather kindly fella called Pertwie, who nodded with indifference as we told him that both parties had agreed not to use or threaten violence against each other, and Mr West had agreed to give his wife a five hundred thousand pound mortgage-free house and a fancy German sports car.

I left court feeling fairly happy with my day's work. As I did, Mrs West smiled and shook my hand. 'Thank you, Mr Winnock,' she said.

'Oh, it's nothing,' I said, modestly, 'just doing my job.'

She smiled again. I turned to Kelly, hoping for an equally gushing response from her, but I didn't get one.

I walked back to chambers with a spring in my step. I wondered if I'd get any more work from Whinstanleys, I wondered what I'd have to do to make the lovely Kelly Backworth smile at me. I quickly forgot about Mr West and his burnt chest.

NIHWTLBOE

After rewarding myself with lunch of beef and ale pie and a pint of bitter, I returned to chambers, walking in through the old front door and checking my pigeonhole, where I found a cheque for 55 pounds, payment for a bail application I did six months ago, and a note telling me to go immediately to the Senior Clerk's room.

I assumed that I was going to be praised. I assumed that I was going to be thanked for doing a sterling job securing my client a car and a house worth nearly half a million quid. In my mind I was about to have a conversation with Clem, in which he begged me to do more Family Court work and I told him that I'd think about it.

I was wrong. I was so wrong.

As I entered his office, I could see that Clem was accompanied by two women. One was the surly Kelly Backworth, who was sat looking sheepishly at her feet, and next to her was a rather butch-looking woman whose facial expression reminded me of a volcano that had been grumbling for a few months and had now forced the evacuation of a nearby town. Clem was sat at his desk. As I walked in, smiling, he and Butch woman looked up at me.

It was at this point I realised that I was not about to be praised.

'Please close the door, Mr Winnock,' said Clem. He shot me one of his looks inviting me to guess what was about to happen.

'This is Mrs Murdoch from Whinstanley and Cooper,' he told me. He ignored Kelly Backworth.

'To cut to the chase,' he continued, 'she's not very happy with the way you conducted the case of Mrs West this morning.'

'That I am not, Mr Wilson,' she said, turning from Clem to me.

I felt my face drop. In fact I felt my whole being drop, my soul, my consciousness, the very essence of my existence, all hit the floor as I realised that not only was I about to be bollocked by the volcanic Mrs Murdoch, but that she had actually left her office and made her way across town to deliver the bollocking in person. This was unprecedented.

'Mr Winnock,' continued the volcanic Mrs Murdoch, 'when I instruct someone to go to court and get an injunction, that is what I expect them to do.'

I was truly gobsmacked. Porky Phi left court with a house, a car and a big grin on her chops.

'I don't understand,' I muttered.

'It's quite straightforward,' said Clem, 'you've got yourself confused, haven't you?'

'No,' I said, 'no, I haven't.'

I looked at Kelly, hoping for some support, but she continued to look at her shoes. Mrs Murdoch wasn't buying the confused line either. 'My instructions couldn't have been more simple,' she growled, 'this was a woman who needed the protection of the court, that is why we sought an injunction, and when we instruct Counsel we expect those instructions to be followed.'

'But,' I stammered, 'Mrs West left court with a car and a house.'

'Those were undertakings, Mr Winnock, they don't count for anything. If Mr West changes his mind then they're not worth the paper they're written on.'

Mrs Murdoch had a point, but she hadn't been there, she hadn't seen the fear in the eyes of Mr West, she hadn't seen the way he had capitulated so readily to his wife's demands. Bloody hell, she hadn't seen the perfect sausage-shaped burn mark on his chest. There was no way Mr West was going to change his mind, all he wanted was to get out of his marriage and as far away from his lunatic curling-tong-wielding wife as he could.

'Have you spoken to Mrs West?' I asked.

'Her thoughts are irrelevant,' Mrs Murdoch barked back at me, 'but when her husband next has his hands around her throat, I'm sure she'll want to know why her barrister didn't bother to obtain an injunction to prevent that from happening.'

'It won't happen,' I said. But I didn't sound sure. I didn't sound confident at all.

I knew that Ronnie Sherman would have told her where to go and remind her that he knew best, but I couldn't do it. I wasn't confident enough to say that. I wasn't experienced enough. I didn't have a red bag.

Instead I just shrugged and muttered an apology.

Clem tried his best to appease her. 'Is there anything else that we can do to remedy this?' he said.

'No,' said Mrs Murdoch forcefully, 'you've done quite enough already.' She turned to me. 'Mr Winnock,' she said, 'I can assure you that you will never receive another brief from Whinstanley Cooper.' And, with that, she got up and left, her nose in the air. Kelly followed her, but as she went she shot me a look, a slight movement of her head – did it denote sympathy? Or perhaps pity?

'You muppet,' said Clem.

'Look, Clem,' I said, 'my client had branded her husband with a hair-curling device. Even if I had carried out my instructions, there's not a Judge in the world that I could have persuaded that she was in need of any protection. And besides, she got the house and the car.'

'Yes, and Whinstanley's are denied the drawn out and lucrative divorce case that would have happened if you hadn't sorted it out for them in half an hour this morning. They've lost out on thousands of pounds of legal fees because of you.'

The penny dropped.

He gave me a cold look. 'You do realise, Mr Winnock, that when it comes to Whinstanley's, you are now NIHWTLBOE.'

He spat out each of the letters.

'NI what?' I asked.

'It stands for "Not If He Was The Last Barrister On Earth". Every firm of solicitors has its NIHWTLBOE list.' He now pronounced it newt-ill-bow. 'You lost them money, you won't work for them again, and you've just got to hope that Mrs Murdoch doesn't tell her friends about this the next time the Law Society has one of its shindigs.'

I started to mumble a tentative defence – I started to tell him how my instinct told me that I was doing the right thing – but he had already lost interest, he had already turned away from me and was looking at a computer screen. He completely ignored my protestations of innocence.

'You'd better check in later to see what you're doing tomorrow, Mr Winnock. At the moment you're free.'

I nodded. I had always thought that these were the most damning words that a junior barrister could possibly hear: '*You are free tomorrow.*' They meant that tomorrow no one wants to employ you, no one wants you to represent them, you will be out of court, unemployed, earning absolutely zilch.

I now knew that these were not the most damning words a barrister could hear, I now knew that the most damning words were, 'Not If He Was The Last Barrister On Earth.'

Instinct and the case of Harvey Mannerley

Back in my room at chambers, my three roommates Amir, Jenny and Angus were crouched over Amir's desk looking at some photographs of a pavement.

As I walked in, Amir shouted across at me, 'What do you think, Russ,' he said, 'we're having a debate as to whether this paving stone is a hazard or not. Angus thinks that it is, Jenny thinks that it isn't.'

'Course it bloody isn't,' interjected Jenny, 'only if you were completely pissed and wearing high heels, and then it's your own fault, frankly.'

'Was the complainant wearing high-heeled shoes and pissed?' I asked.

'No,' said Amir, 'he was a pensioner.'

'Well they're always falling over,' said Jenny.

'They need to be protected,' said Angus, 'the duty of care is totally with the council on this.'

'What do *you* think, Ammie?' I asked.

He looked back at the pavement – 'My instinct says that this will settle,' he told me.

And there it is, that word: instinct. It's absolutely fundamental to our line of work. The ability to sniff the air and guess correctly what's being blown towards you; the ability, learned from experience, to accurately predict what will happen in a given case.

Instinct is vital because, as barristers, we are often in a state of ignorance. Think about it: I am not allowed to converse with a jury, I have to guess what they will make of evidence, what they will understand and what they will not. Similarly, I have to second-guess the position of a Judge. I have to instinctively know what will annoy him or her, and what will soothe. And finally, I occasionally have to reach into the mind of a criminal or a client, work out what they are thinking and what advice will be best for them in their particular circumstances.

I'm not saying that I always get it right, what I am saying is that instinct is important and it's not something that can be taught in a book or in a lecture theatre, it is something that is acquired over years of practice, it is something that is honed by getting things wrong, by irritating Judges, by watching others.

It is one of the reasons why barristers get so cross when successive governments have tried to undermine our profession by reducing our rates of pay and allowing others who are not as qualified, not as experienced, who don't possess the instinct, to do our job.

In the case of Porky Pie West my instinct told me that she would not get the injunction she wanted, my instinct also told me that the deal that was being offered was a good one, and that she should take it.

Okay, it *was* a quick decision. It could turn out to be the wrong decision. As Mrs Murdoch said, I'll only know if Mr West comes back and throttles his wife. But, somehow, I don't think that that will happen – somehow, my instinct tells me that out of Porky and her branded husband, the most likely person to see the inside of a courtroom again will be her.

As my colleagues discuss pavements, my mind goes back to the case of Harvey Mannerley.

It was one of my first cases, and it showed me just how important instinct was going to be in my career as a barrister.

Harvey Mannerley was a rather pathetic individual in his mid-twenties. He was accused of harassing an eighteen-year-old girl he had met whilst they were both working in a supermarket warehouse. The girl was called India Williams. She was about to go off to university and found herself, as part of a summer job, working alongside Harvey – well, I say alongside, the reality is that India didn't really take much notice of Harvey.

Where she was young and beautiful with a radiant, gleamingly effervescent smile that was just about to be unleashed onto the world in a million exciting ways, Harvey was a sad man with pallid grey skin and black hair that sat on his head as a greasy after-thought. He was thin and gaunt and had the look of someone who spent hours in his own bedroom, wanking.

He convinced himself that India was smiling for him and he embarked upon a campaign of letter writing. He would send her long, sinister anonymous letters in which he would tell her in fairly unsubtle detail what he wanted to do to her. In short, he was a stalker.

The evidence was overwhelming – his fingerprints were found on some of the envelopes and a handwriting expert had stated that there was extremely strong evidence to suggest that the handwriting on the letters belonged to Harvey Mannerley.

The case took place in small town Magistrates Court. I was young, barely 24, fresh out of Bar School – with very little experience and very little instinct. I was told that I wouldn't have a solicitor with me – you rarely do in the Magistrates Court – and my instructions simply invited me to do my best in the face of very strong evidence.

I met Harvey in the reception area and took him down to a small, airless, windowless conference room in the basement. He wouldn't look me in the eye; something that now, with a few years under my belt, I know is a bad sign. Back then, I knew nothing.

I sat him down and after introducing myself decided to tell him how grave the evidence was. 'I've got be honest with you, Mr Mannerley,' I said, 'I think you've got a few problems today.'

At this he looked up at me, seething. 'I'm not going guilty,' he spat, 'there's no way I'm going guilty.'

'No one's trying to make you plead to anything,' I said.

I paused. The pause was a mistake, a sign of my weakness, my inexperience and lack of confidence, a sign that I wasn't in control. I now continued in a rather stuttering way. 'I respect and appreciate that, that's fine, but, Mr Mannerley—'

Before I could say anything more, he interjected again, 'I ain't pleading guilty. No way. I ain't done nothing.'

'Okay,' I said, 'then can you tell me why your fingerprints are on those envelopes?'

He shrugged. 'Whoever was sending them must have got them from the supermarket where I was working – I used to handle hundreds of envelopes – it doesn't prove anything.'

I sucked my lips in and nodded as enthusiastically as I could.

'Okay, that's fine.' I paused again. It allowed Mannerley to look at me and work out that I wasn't quite as experienced as I was trying to make out.

'How long have you been doing this for?' he asked.

'That doesn't matter,' I said.

'It bloody does to me,' said Mannerley, 'you fucking come in here, telling me to plead guilty.'

'Look, Mr Mannerley, I haven't told you to plead anything. I'm simply pointing out that the evidence is strong.'

'No it's not, it's shit, they can't prove anything. No one has seen me do anything.'

'Well,' I said, 'not only are there the fingerprints, but there's also a handwriting expert who says that your handwriting is the same as that in the letters.'

'That's just his opinion.'

'Well, he is an expert. He spends his life having opinions about people's handwriting. And,' I continued, 'the girl herself is convinced it's you – because of some of the things that you'd said to her.'

He snorted contemptuously at this, then put his hands over his ears and shouted at me – 'I am not fucking pleading guilty. Do. You. Understand?'

At this point, I was actually quite nervous. I realised that I was sitting in a room with a man who may have been capable of anything. I decided that the best thing to do was to simply go into court. 'Come on then, Mr Mannerley,' I said and we made our way into the courtroom where I would mount the defence of 'it wasn't me, Guv,' despite the overwhelming evidence to the contrary.

The Magistrates sat looking at us: the usual three upstanding pillars of the community who are plucked from their day jobs to pass judgement over petty criminals, speeding motorists and those who pose a nuisance to their communities. In this case, the Chairman of the Bench was a tall angular man called The Doctor, because, well, he was a doctor. To the right of him was a man who looked a bit like a frog, and to his left was a woman who looked like she should have been at the Conservative Party Conference lamenting the passing of Margaret Thatcher.

Harvey Mannerley sat on a chair behind a desk to my left. Further along sat the prosecutor. The prosecutor was a Crown Prosecution Service (CPS) advocate by the name of Joe Hunter. I'd only ever been against him once before when he spent most of the time telling the Clerk of the Court how much he was looking forward to his retirement. He was grey and bored and clearly under-prepared. He stuttered as he told the Magistrates what the case was all about – then he called his first witness: Miss India Williams.

India made her way, nervously, into the courtroom and towards the witness box. She was attractive, dignified and harmless – everything that Harvey Mannerley was not. I looked over to my client and saw that he was staring intently at her; he seemed to rise slightly in his chair, as though trying to get a better look. It was creepy.

The prosecutor, Hunter, started to question the witness, inviting her to tell the court her version of events. At first everything was normal. She told of how she was working at Shopsmart Warehouse as a stock clerk and receptionist in the summer before she was due to go to university (the bench love the reference to university, they always do – in their eyes, it instantly makes her a more compelling and credible witness). She told them that Mannerley had also worked there and that she had been friendly to him, but not in a special way.

Then things got a bit weird. Hunter, inexplicably, handed her the letters and asked her to read them out. Miss Williams, clearly uncomfortable, dutifully started to read out the first letter. The contents were extreme, a childish attempt to describe pornographic desires. It was filth. Pages and pages of what he wanted to do to her in the toilets and in the staff room and round the back of the frozen food section. I squirmed uncomfortably in my seat as this young girl was made to read out the words of this horrible, delusional pervert.

And I knew they were Mannerley's words. I just knew it. I know I've already said that we don't ponder for too long about our clients' guilt or innocence, and I know I've said that it is no business of ours if the court convicts or acquits – but, in this case, it was overwhelmingly clear that the words being so innocently read out by this girl had been written by my client.

Even worse, though, was the reaction of Harvey Mannerley. I looked over to him – he was entranced – this was his fantasy brought to life. The trial was no longer a test of his innocence or guilt, but had become an extension of his crime.

I looked over to Joe Hunter, who was stood, disinterested, probably counting the days until he was on his boat or in his French retirement home; I looked at the bench, at the Doctor and the Frog and the Thatcher woman, who were just sitting there impassive.

Then I looked back at Harvey Mannerley – who was now rubbing his thighs in barely contained excitement.

This had to stop. My instinct told me that I had to do something. Even though Mannerley was my client, there was no way I could allow this to go on so I stood up.

'Sir,' I said, addressing the Doctor. I wasn't sure what to say next – you are not taught in Bar School what to do when your client is actually getting off on his own words being read out by his victim.

'Yes, Mr Winnock?'

'Er, can I have a brief adjournment please?' Mannerley shot me the type of look that a toddler might give to his parent when being pulled out of a toyshop. 'I need to take some instructions from my client.'

The Doctor conferred with his colleagues and nodded at me.

I turned to Mannerley. 'Come on,' I said to him – and we went back to the small, airless conference room we were in before.

'Sit down,' I said. I had no idea how I should deal with this, so I decided to lie. 'This is terrible,' I said.

'Why?'

'Because,' I told him, 'this girl is giving evidence in a way that means that this Magistrates Court are going to send you to prison for four years.'

'What?'

'Four years,' I repeated, slowly, even though I knew full well that the maximum sentence that they could impose for this offence in this court was six months.

'Imagine that. Four years in prison, four years of no TV, no computer, no nothing. You, and all manner of psychos and perverts. Do you want that, Mr Mannerley? Because that is what is going to happen if you continue with this.'

At this point Mannerley got up to his feet and started to slowly circle the room, his head in his hands. He was mumbling something – and he was becoming increasingly loud and more and more agitated. I could hear him behind me. I braced myself, expecting him to hit me.

Thud.

I flinched. But he hadn't hit me, I turned around to see Mannerley standing in the corner, banging his head against the wall – 'You all think I'm guilty, you all think I'm guilty.'

'I don't,' I said, which was another lie, 'I just don't want you to spend more time in prison than you have to.'

He turned to me, seething. His fists clenched. His teeth gritted in vicious hatred of me, and, just as likely, of himself. I stood there, looking him in the eye, bracing myself for the violence that I was sure was about to follow.

Instead, though, he turned away from me and ran out of the conference room and out of the court building.

My heart pounding, I went back into court.

'I am sorry,' I said to the bench, 'I'm afraid that Mr Mannerley has just run away.'

The Doctor looked at me – 'Mr Winnock,' he said witheringly, 'we realise that it's not your fault that Mr Mannerley has decided to abscond, but we do question whether it was right for you to ask for a break whilst Miss Williams was in the middle of her evidence.'

I nodded and apologised, because that is what you are supposed to do, but I wasn't sorry that I'd brought the ordeal to an end. Not for one second. The Doctor then granted what's known as a bench warrant for the arrest of Harvey Mannerley, which would mean that the police could arrest him as soon as he was discovered.

As I left court I spotted India Williams standing with her, clearly, very nice parents – they were talking in hushed tones. I went to walk past them, then stopped and turned around.

'Look,' I said, 'I'm not supposed to say this, but if they ever arrest Harvey Mannerley, and if there is another trial, for god's sake, tell the prosecutor that you won't read out any of those letters. You don't need to. The prosecutor can either hand them up, or read them himself without you being in the room.'

I smiled politely and left.

For the record, Harvey Mannerley was arrested four months later. Thankfully I didn't have to represent him again. As it happened, on that occasion, he pleaded guilty and was made subject to a Community Order.

Did I do the right thing? My instinct tells me that I did, but you'll make up your own minds.

The ten greatest trials of all time

If there's one thing that certain types of men like nothing more than doing – it's compiling lists. Me and my university mates would do it all the time – ten greatest FA Cup goals, ten greatest Rock and Roll deaths, ten best albums of all time; you know the type of thing – and, yes, some of the lists that we would compile were law based. I thought I'd share a few of them with you over the course of this book. First up, in no particular order, is The Ten Greatest Trials of All Time.

1. **The Trial of Oscar Wilde (1895)** – this had it all: sex, celebrity, wit and scandal – all in front of a packed Old Bailey as Wilde defended his honour by bringing a charge of criminal libel against the father of his young lover, the Earl of Queensberry. Not surprisingly, given that Queensberry could call a room full of men who had had 'sexual encounters' with Wilde, even Thomas Clarke, the leading Silk representing him, was unable to bring home the case. The cross-examination of Wilde by Queensberry's Silk, the future Irish politician Edward Carson, is legendary.

2. **Donoghue v Stevenson (1932)** – you might not have heard of this case, but you will certainly have felt its implications. This

case established the international concept of negligence, and introduced the legal principle that in some circumstances we owe others a duty of care. Mrs Donoghue bought a bottle of ginger beer, drank it, fell ill, then discovered that there was a dead snail inside the bottle. She sued the drinks manufacturer, one Stevenson, and eventually won on appeal to the House of Lords, with the court declaring by a majority that the drinks manufacturer owed a 'duty of care' to the ultimate consumer – a judgement that has kept hundreds of lawyers in work ever since.

3. **The Trial of OJ Simpson (1995)** – another one involving celebs and sex. Former American football star and film actor OJ Simpson was accused of shooting dead his wife and her lover. The evidence appeared overwhelming, but ace attorney Johnnie Cochrane managed to convince the jury after a year and a half long trial that there was reasonable doubt.

4. **The Trial of Jeremy Thorpe (1978)** – back to the Old Bailey, and the trial that made the name and reputation of George Carman QC. Jeremy Thorpe, the leader of the Liberal Party at the time, stood accused of conspiring to murder his 'gay lover', Norman Scott, after Scott's dog was shot in rather suspicious circumstances. Carman (with a bit of help from the trial Judge) managed to persuade the jury that there was nothing in it.

5. **Roe v Wade (1973)** – a landmark American Supreme Court trial that established that a woman has the right to control over her own body, including the right to abort a foetus. Even four decades later, this one still causes ructions amongst the American people as the right-wing and liberal politicians continue to argue about its merits.

6. **Brown v The Board of Education (1954)** – staying with the American Supreme Court, this time a landmark civil rights ruling that it was unconstitutional for children to be segregated according to their racial background after the parents of black schoolchildren in Topeka, Kansas, challenged the racist policy that allowed discrimination amongst schoolchildren. (And quite bloody right too!)

7. **The Trial of Thomas More (1535)** – there are quite a few grisly trials to choose from around the time of the Reformation, but my personal favourite is the trial of Sir Thomas More. More, former Lord Chancellor and a formidable scholar and philosopher, was accused and tried for High Treason. During the trial he was cross-examined by no less than six of the country's most esteemed legal and constitutional minds as they tried to get him to vow allegiance to the King – he didn't budge, and despite more than holding his own against the onslaught of questions, they convicted him and chopped off his head.

8. **The Trial of Oscar Pistorius (2014)** – Pistorius, the double amputee superstar of South African sport, shot his beautiful model girlfriend, Reeva Steenkamp, in the middle of the night on Valentine's Day 2013. Oscar's defence was that he 'Thought she was an intruder.' Perhaps surprisingly, you might think, the Judge agreed and he was found not guilty of murder, but guilty of 'culpable homicide'. So according to the Judge it was all just a horrible accident.

9. **The Nuremberg Trials (1946)** – described as 'the greatest trial in history', 21 senior Nazis in the dock, charged with various war crimes committed during the Second World War, ranging from the execution of prisoners of war to genocide. Hartley Shawcross and Robert Jackson prosecuting, and an indictment as long as an

airport paperback. One year and one month later, twelve were sentenced to death, three were acquitted and the rest – the ones who hadn't committed suicide, that is – were given various prison sentences.

10. **The Trial of Jesus Christ (approx. 33AD)** – a bit lacking in the niceties of courtroom procedure, but a significant trial nonetheless. According to the New Testament, Christ is charged with blasphemy by the Sanhedrin (an assembly consisting of at least 23 of the cleverest men who would determine the application of Jewish law) in Jerusalem. To this charge, he doesn't appear to mount much of a defence. Indeed, by asserting that he was 'the Son of God', he probably made things a bit worse. After being convicted, as we all know too well, Jesus was taken to Pontius Pilate, the Roman Governor, who upheld the demands for crucifixion. I sometimes wonder how things would have panned out if the trial had taken place in one of our Magistrates Courts, with Jesus being represented by the duty solicitor – 'Your Worships, my client, Mr Christ, intends to plead not guilty to the charge. His defence? Er, he'll be running the "I am the rightful Messiah Son of God" defence. What do you mean that's not a defence in law?'

Dinners, beers and 'what would you do if you weren't a barrister?'

Most Friday nights after court I meet up with Ed and Johnny, two old university mates, at the Erskine Pub near chambers. After a few pints and the stress of the week waned, we reminisce about our happy student days. We all studied law at Leeds – oh how wonderful it was to be a student: Thursday nights at the Students' Union Bar dancing to Oasis and Blur and trying to tap off with girls, failing, then watching the fights break out at the kebab shop and trying desperately hard not to look like a student, because the students usually got their heads kicked in. Days missing lectures, and trying to understand contract law and dreaming about our futures as brilliant barristers.

Most of the students on our course wanted to be solicitors, so we were drawn together as aspiring barristers. In our final year we came down to our Inn in London together to do our dinners. Dinners, or dining and the Inns, are another little secret of the strange world of the Bar. It works like this: once you have completed your law degree and decided you want to become a barrister, you have to join an Inn. There are four Inns: Middle Temple, Inner Temple, Gray's Inn and Lincoln's Inn.

Once you have joined your Inn you have to do 'dining'. That is, you have to go to your Inn and have a meal in the company of other barristers and student barristers. It doesn't matter how brilliant you are, it doesn't matter if you are Plutarch, Petrocelli or Perry bleeding Mason, if you haven't done the dinners, you won't get called to the Bar and you won't be able to practise as a barrister. And it's not just one dinner, oh no, there are twelve dinners. So there you have it, a pre-requisite to becoming a barrister is eating food.

Ed, Johnny and I decided to join Gray's Inn. I can't remember why now, I think the dinners were probably the cheapest. Once we had joined the Inn, every couple of weeks we put on our best clobber and went down to London. I have to say that at first it was exciting to go down to the Great Hall of Gray's Inn. You got to wear a robe and, occasionally, sit next to a proper Queen's Counsel or High Court Judge, who were, on the whole, quite kind and encouraging. One even offered me snuff (which caused a bit of confusion as I thought he was offering me marijuana, which probably isn't a mistake I'd make now).

The three of us were state-school boys; my parents were old-fashioned socialists. I wasn't used to this kind of pomp and ceremony, so wearing your best suit, listening to Latin prayers, drinking too much wine and port and then going on for a few beers at a London club with girls called Prunella, Jemima and Beatrice was new and fun.

But, some time around dinner number six, things started to become a bit tiresome. There are only so many times you can listen to some crusty old Silk tell you how difficult it is for young barristers; or even worse, some chinless, limp-coiffed, posh boy called Giles tell you he has got six different offers of pupilage and he's not quite sure which one to take, when you've been turned down by every set you've applied to.

Still, it was a rite of passage and afterwards the three of us moved to London together and shared a flat in Catford. It was great. We were all in different chambers with different people but we came back each night and sat around drinking, eating takeaway curries and talking about our days, our cases and our clients. We felt we'd done well. We'd worked hard, we'd passed our exams and we felt we'd achieved. Getting to the Bar. Becoming a professional. Mixing with the privileged and the clever and those who were clearly destined for great things. It felt like we had a covenant with the state and society. We'd done the work and now we hoped that we'd be rewarded for our efforts.

For the three of us, it was all so easy, so straightforward; our dreams were being fulfilled, our expectations achieved, we would become the barristers that we had aspired to be.

After a couple of years Johnny moved out to live with Fiona, so we replaced him with this weird guy called Vikram, which didn't really work, as he was a nurse who kept some odd hours. And then Ed met Joanne and he moved out, then Vikram moved out – and me, well, I moved into my own flat.

On my own.

Which, actually, I don't mind at all.

I think.

Anyway, Johnny is at the Criminal Bar in a set similar to mine, and Ed works at a specialist Chancery set.

As I've already alluded to, the Chancery Bar is very different from the Criminal Bar. It is full of particularly clever, academic types who rarely talk to one another and make a load of money. They all seem to be called Rupert or Henry. I'm not sure that Ed fits in. He tells us he works for oil companies and multinationals, but I'm never really quite sure what he actually does. Unlike criminal barristers or family barristers, he doesn't tell you about his cases, in fact the only time he did, we had to tell him to stop because it was just too boring.

Johnny, on the other hand, doesn't stop telling you about his cases. He has a natural and infectious enthusiasm – if he were a dog he would have a constantly wagging tail.

On this particular Friday night, they were already there when I arrived, standing by the bar.

They greeted me with the universal hand gesture for 'what do you want to drink?' and I replied that I'd have a glass of stout.

'Well, gents,' said Johnny, pausing only to take a large glug of beer from his glass, 'I've got some news.'

I assumed that he was going to announce that he and Fiona were having a baby. They'd been married for a year (or is it two?) so it seemed kind of logical that they were going to start a family. But I was completely wrong.

Johnny took a deep breath. 'I'm leaving the Bar,' he said.

We both looked at him.

'What?' said Ed.

'Yes,' he continued, 'I've had my fill. I owe a ton of money, I'm being paid bugger all for working every hour, there's no chance of career advancement – so I've decided: I'm getting out while I'm still young enough.'

At this point a rather strange concoction of emotions filled my mind – first, there was an evil streak of pleasure, Johnny leaving meant one less criminal barrister to compete with; then there was jealousy, at his luck at having something else to go to; then there was respect that he had the balls to get up and do something else; finally, there was sadness, the old team was being broken up.

'What are you going to do?' asked Ed.

Johnny took another big intake of breath. 'I've got a job as a croupier in a hotel in Dubai.'

We both exclaimed, 'What?!'

'Yes. I start next month. The salary is ace. More money per month than I can earn prosecuting burglars and bottom pinchers, I can tell you.'

Now my main emotion was jealousy – a croupier in a hotel, for a ruck of money, it's genius, why didn't I think of it?

'What does Fiona think?' I asked.

'She's mad for it. She's got a job in the same hotel.'

Ed shook his head. 'I can't believe it, you must be bonkers.'

'Look,' argued Johnny forcefully, 'what's the point; we're both lower-middle-class kids who went to university because we were told it was for the best. We got good jobs, in good professions, because we were told that was what we had to do, and we got riddled with debt for the privilege. Now, we can't afford a mortgage, can't afford a pension, can't afford to start a family. It's a joke.'

Johnny had clearly rehearsed this argument before. I imagined him putting it to his parents and in-laws. Leaving the Bar will have made no sense to them, but it made perfect sense to me.

'A croupier,' said Ed with unconcealed contempt, 'come on, you're having a laugh.'

'It's okay for you, Ed,' I said, 'but Johnny's right, for us it feels like we're banging our heads against brick walls. We've not had a pay rise for years, in fact it just gets harder and harder to make a living.'

'Yep,' continued Johnny, 'you boys at the Chancery Bar have got no idea, I was talking to Shanna earlier, you know, from my chambers?'

We both nod and Johnny continued, 'She's about five years call, and this week she went to the Magistrates Court for a firm of solicitors to do a trial in the Youth Court, and do you know how much they paid her? Her bus fare, that's what. They knew she'd do it because she wanted to impress them, in the hope of getting more work. I tell you, fellas, it's a joke, and I've had enough.'

Ed looked at us both, his lips thinned. He knew there was something in what we were saying, and what Johnny was doing.

After a while he turned to me. 'What are you going to do then, Russ? You're not thinking of leaving, are you?'

I shrugged. 'I don't know. Perhaps I'll get a job as an exotic dancer in John's hotel.'

'Seriously,' said Ed, 'what would you do if you weren't a barrister? What would you do if you could do something else?'

And that was the thing. I didn't really want to do anything else. Okay, I am pissed off about the fact that our work was being farmed out to others, and that our pay was being cut, and that we were seen, wrongly, as immoral money-grabbing bastards who would sell our grandmothers for a brief, an acquittal and a bag of cash. I am pissed off with all of this, but – and call me a soft-centred lily-livered old whoopsie if you want – I still see it as a privilege to get up in court and represent people in their time of need. I want to be a barrister, just as I had when I'd sat down with my parents and watched, enthralled, some TV drama where a wonderfully erudite and maverick QC was winning the case against all the odds. That was still what I aspired to be.

'Come on then,' said Ed, repeating his question as if he was cross-examining a witness. 'If you could do something else, what would you do?'

I took in some breath, chewed my bottom lip a bit, shrugged mournfully, then answered, 'I dunno, maybe write, I'm not sure.'

'Well,' said Johnny, thankfully ignoring my suggestion of an alternative career, 'I'm sure I can put a good word in for you at the hotel.'

I thanked Johnny for his offer of assistance, and suggested that it was my round.

Then I saw her.

Kelly Backworth.

The unsmiling, unfriendly Judas who had failed to defend me in any way to her boss when the issue of my conduct in the Porky

Phi case was being discussed and had sat there, with a face as unfeeling as a wardrobe, as Mrs Murdoch and my clerk had declared me a barrister persona non grata – NIHWTLBOE.

I looked over at her. She was with a friend. *And* she was smiling. Oh yes, she was smiling now, great big, happy, unicorn-frolicking rainbow smiles. That was what she was doing now, away from court, away from me.

And what a smile it was – lovely glistening teeth, sparkling behind full lips that were now freed from the shackles of the Family Court and glossed by a shimmering lipstick.

I felt something shout at me from within my consciousness.

Then I walked over to the other side of the bar to where she and her friend were sitting. I wasn't sure what I was going to say. As I approached, she spotted me and, in an instant, the rainbow smile disappeared behind a cloud, the unicorns went back into their shed and the slate-grey misery that she had shown in court returned.

'Hi,' I said.

'Hi,' she repeated, then turned to her friend (who *was* smiling at me with a weird interest), 'this is Russell Winnock,' said Kelly, 'he's a barrister from Gray's Buildings.' I smiled at the friend, and shook her hand. 'I'm Beverley,' she said.

'So,' I said, and turned to the miserably beautiful Kelly Backworth. 'Kelly, what happened? I thought we'd done a good job for Mrs West. Then, whoosh, I'm getting both barrels from your boss.'

Kelly looked down for a second. 'Yes,' she said, quietly, 'I'm sorry about that – she can be a bit of a cow.'

'A bit of a cow,' I exclaimed, 'that's an understatement. I don't know who would come off worse in a fight, your Mrs Murdoch or Phi, the psychopath we were representing.'

A small, barely noticeable smile flickered across Kelly's mouth. Not rainbows, not frolicking mythical beasts, not teeth – but the hint of a smile nonetheless.

'Seriously though,' I continued, 'Mrs West got a great deal, there's every chance that if we hadn't settled things, she'd have left court with nothing at all.'

'But you were instructed to get an injunction,' she said to me, her voice strong, yet friendly. And at this point, I confess, I really, really fancied Kelly Backworth.

'We wouldn't have got one though,' I said. 'You should have seen the burn mark Porky Phi had branded into Mr West's chest.'

'That's the thing, Mr Winnock,' said Kelly, 'I didn't see it. If you'd have shown me, I would have been able to defend you to Mrs Murdoch.'

She was right. Bloody hell. Kelly was completely right. In my enthusiasm, in my desire to sort out the case, I'd forgotten to include my instructing solicitors in the process. And that, more than anything, was why I'd been given such a roasting. I understood it now. I got it. You see it's not all about the barrister, it's not all about the person who stands up in court, the relationship with a solicitor is just as important, and I had neglected it.

I looked at Kelly.

'Please,' I mumbled, 'call me Russ. Mr Winnock makes me sound like the maths teacher everyone hated.'

She smiled again. This time it was a definite smile. There were teeth and everything.

I thought about offering to buy them both a drink, but before the thought could become an offer, Johnny was shouting at me from the other side of the bar, 'Oi, Winnock, are you brewing those beers or what?'

I looked at Kelly. 'I'd better go,' I said, and she nodded.

'And, yes,' I added, 'you're right, sorry, I should have brought you with me to see Mr West's chest.'

'It doesn't matter,' she said, 'we had a phone call from Mrs West today, she thought you were the dog's bollocks.'

Now my face broke into a deep grin. 'Really?'

Kelly smiled again, 'Yes.'

A couple of hours later, I staggered from the pub out into the cold air.

I looked up and contemplated the vastness for a few seconds, then made my way to the bus stop.

I felt sad at the fact that Johnny was leaving the Bar. I remembered us all going to lectures and stressing about assignments and trying to get jobs, and practising our speeches on each other for our mock trials and Bar Finals. I remembered how chuffed we were on the day we were called to the Bar, declared an '*utter barrister*'. Allowed to practise and call ourselves *Learned*, wear a wig and gown. It had all been so exciting. It had meant everything. And now Johnny had given it all up. And that somehow seemed a massive waste. I wouldn't be giving up though – no way. I wouldn't be giving up, because I knew I could do it, succeed, and what's more, Mrs West knew it as well, which is why she'd said I was the dog's bollocks.

The importance of pages

It is rare that a week goes by without me receiving some sort of brief involving drugs – usually involving someone selling them, or stealing people's goods to pay for them. It strikes me that if Parliament made drugs lawful, crime would dry up and I would have to seriously think about an alternative career.

So when I picked up a new set of instructions from my pigeon-hole, I wasn't in the least bit surprised to discover a drugs case involving a man called Simon, who had the misfortune to be stopped by police with ten bags of crack cocaine hidden in his socks.

I looked at the brief and immediately noted from the index that there 49 pages of statements and 27 pages of exhibits – which means the interview, any relevant photographs or other documents. So, in total there were 76 pages of evidence – this is significant.

Why? I hear you ask. You might think that the number of pages is significant because it means that the evidence against my client is strong, or perhaps, conversely, you're thinking that doesn't sound like a lot of pages, or maybe you're feeling sorry for me having to read all those pages.

Well, actually, its significance is far simpler – true the page count can reflect the strength of a case, but not always. In fact sometimes the most damning cases can be contained in a few meagre pages. Nor does the workload really bother us, we'll read all the pages, come what may. No, the number of pages is significant because it is directly linked with how much money each case will be paid.

As I have mentioned, in the main, criminal barristers are self-employed and every barrister doing legal aid work will, at some point, wonder how much they are going to be paid for their endeavours – and the greater the number of pages, the higher the fee.

It works something like this: for the purpose of payment, each case is categorised according to what crime appears on the indictment. Murder, for example, is in the highest category as it is deemed to be the most serious offence, then comes rape, other sexual offences, complicated fraud and so on, all the way down to shoplifting and criminal damage where the cost of repair is under five thousand pounds. There is a flat fee for each of these offences, which is then increased according to the number of pages. For example a burglary with twelve pages of evidence is not going to be worth as much as a burglary with 120 pages of evidence, or a murder with 933 pages.

If the matter goes to trial, then the fee is increased with the payment of a further amount of money for each day of the trial – which are known as refreshers (apart from day two, which, bizarrely, we do for free!).

Now, don't get me wrong, nearly all criminal barristers will take whatever case comes their way, and do their very best, but, because of the way we are paid, a lucrative case would be a rape trial lasting many weeks, with hundreds of pages of evidence, whilst a less financially attractive case would be a theft which goes to trial, lasting two days, with 26 pages of evidence; which is, alas, more common for most jobbing junior barristers.

There is also something called a cracked trial. This is when someone pleads guilty on the day of trial or shortly before, which is worth more than if the person pleads guilty at the earliest opportunity.

The practical implication of all this is that, very often, barristers who are doing the job honestly and professionally will find themselves advising against their own financial self-interest.

Take the following couple of examples.

I was instructed to defend a Polish chap whose family had been involved in a feud with another Polish family. There were over 700 pages on the brief and the trial was listed to last for five weeks – it would have been worth a few bob to say the least.

On the morning of the first day, my client, whose name was Jan Koszlak – a very nice man as it happens, if you put to one side his penchant for attacking people who crossed him with a Samurai sword – came to me and asked if he should plead guilty to the charge. As he said it my heart groaned, or rather, my bank balance groaned. I knew that a plea on day one of the trial would cost me a few thousand quid. I also knew that it was a trial that we *could* win, but that would by no means be guaranteed.

If I was thinking in a selfish way, I would have said, no, you should definitely run a trial. But I couldn't do that, it wouldn't have been right. So instead I said to Jan, 'Well, if you plead now, you'll get a little bit of credit, not much, but it will still be a lesser sentence than if you run a trial and lose. It is,' I said, 'up to you.'

Jan weighed this up, looked at me carefully, and asked, 'What would you do?' A question many defendants ask, and all barristers hate.

'I don't know,' I said, which is the honest response. 'It would be easy for me to say run the trial, but I'm not the one facing the porridge.'

'Will I win?' he asked.

I shrugged. 'I have no idea. As soon as a case goes before a jury, it will have a life of its own.'

'What are the odds?' he asked (another question which all barristers hate), and I answered the way I always do, which is the only safe way to answer: 'About 50-50.'

He nodded to himself, and then said slowly, 'Okay, I'll plead guilty. I can't take the risk of longer time in jail.'

I smiled and told him he was probably doing the wisest thing, but inside I was screaming, 'You've just cost me thousands of bloody pounds!'

Another time, I was sent to represent a man who was accused of grooming teenage girls for the purposes of sex. My client, Ron, was a 42-year-old welder living with his mother, who had been posing on Facebook, and various other social media websites, as Kyle, a sixteen-year-old school boy with Boy Band hair and a detailed understanding of teenager-speak (WTF, OMG, LMFAO etc., you know the stuff).

Kyle was rumbled when he made the mistake of trying to chat up Cindy, who wasn't, as she claimed, a fourteen-year-old, slightly experienced little minx, with a keen interest in One Direction, push-up bras and lads with tattoos, but actually Detective Constable Steve Parker, a 36-year-old father of two who played blind-side flanker for Redbridge RFC Second team and listened to Radio 2. DC Parker was part of Operation Cinderella, a 'honey-trap' police operation. For two weeks he had coquettishly responded to all of 'Kyle's', or should I say Ron's, questions about what underwear she was wearing and if she liked to 'swallow', before enough evidence was amassed to arrest and charge him.

It wasn't actually my case; I had been asked to cover it for another member of chambers. The hearing was simply to fix a new date for a trial. I hadn't read all the papers – just enough to give me a flavour of the charge, and see that there were hundreds of pages of exhibits to cover all the conversations that had gone on – it was, without doubt, a lucrative brief.

When I arrived, Ron was in tears. 'I just want to plead guilty,' he told me. 'I can't take any more.'

'Okay,' I said carefully, 'do you accept what you are accused of doing?'

He wouldn't give me a straight answer, he just wailed and wrung his hands, muttering something that sounded like a guilty man trying to wriggle his way out of what he had done.

I now had a decision to make. If I allowed him to plead, then I would make all the money on the brief – a fee which would have amounted to a few thousand pounds – because it would have been me who cracked the trial. But, if I advised him to wait until he'd spoken to the barrister who was supposed to represent him, I would make 36 quid – the standard appearance fee for what is known as a mention hearing.

Some of you might think that it is an easy decision, a no-brainer, to use that awful phrase. After all, he was telling me he wanted to plead guilty, I wasn't putting any pressure on him. But my instinct (there's that word again) told me that here was a man who needed some advice from someone who actually knew the case inside out and, alas, that wasn't me.

I told Ron that he should arrange to see his proper barrister that week and go over everything in detail with him, rather than make a hasty decision now.

Ron wiped his eyes and thanked me and we rearranged the trial date.

Two weeks later he pleaded guilty to all the charges.

Did I feel annoyed? Yes, of course I did. Did I do the right thing by Ron? Yes, and I don't know many barristers who would have done any different.

Which is another one of the reasons we get so depressed by

the way successive governments have done every little thing they can to reduce our fees. Take photographs: photographs used to be part of the page count – which, if you had a couple of hundred photos taken from a crime scene, would add a couple of hundred quid onto your fee. Now, most photographs are served on a DVD, which counts as one page, even if there are thousands of photos on the disc. It still takes us the same amount of time to look at them, but we are paid as if there was only one.

Then there is something called the 'early guilty plea scheme' which means that if the CPS think that someone is likely to plead guilty, they put them in for a special hearing before they've even served all the papers on the defence – which means we can't bill for the pages that we would have received in the old days.

Is the Criminal Justice System better served by this austerity? I don't know. You'll have your own opinions.

Anyway, the case of Simon the drug dealer had 76 pages, which would not allow me to holiday that summer in the Seychelles or buy a Maserati, but that didn't matter, I would have defended Simon come what may – because that is my job, that is what I do. And, for the sake of completeness, and because I know you're interested, Simon entered a guilty plea to all the charges and was sentenced to three years imprisonment.

A tale of three Judges

If I could give one piece of advice to any aspiring barrister it would be: never annoy your clerks. Because if you do they will punish you, in a particularly snide way in which only they can. One Sunday evening not long after I was declared NIHWTLBOE, I traipsed into chambers to get my briefs, held the wad of ribbon-bound papers in my hand and cursed.

The bastard clerks.

I cursed their very existence. I cursed their families. I cursed the very air they breathed. They were clearly annoyed with me and had their revenge by giving me three cases in three different courtrooms in front of three different Judges. It's called cross-courting.

This would teach me. They had known that.

I felt my innards groan, picked up my work for the night and trudged back home.

This is, though, a good opportunity to tell you about Judges. Because the next piece of advice I would give a young barrister is: never annoy Judges either. For they play a huge part in your life, sitting there, God-like on their bench, a gigantic and omnipotent presence in the court. From your first day as a barrister, Judges take a disproportionately significant role in your conscious thinking. As a baby barrister, one of the first questions you ask whenever you get anywhere near a court is, 'What's the Judge like?' Your heart will leap if you are told that he's 'nice'; but, if the answer is that 'he's a bit of a bastard', you feel your stress increase as a dark cloud of doubt manoeuvres itself above your very existence and you fear that most awful of things – a humiliating public bollocking.

As I made my way home that evening, I knew that with three different cases in three different courts, there was every chance that the next day, I wasn't going to annoy not just one Judge, but three. Great.

Part 1 – His Honour Judge Percy and the case of Tommy Nutall

The problem with cross-courting is that each Judge expects you to be in his court ready and able to start at 10.30am, which is the start of the court day, so being in three different cases, and not being able to produce clones of yourself, means that there is every chance that two of the Judges will be mightily hacked off when they glance towards the Bar and see an empty space where a barrister is supposed to be.

And one of the first rules of how to make a Judge happy is physically being in their court when your case is called on.

My first case that day involved a burglar, Tommy Nutall, who was due to be sentenced in front of His Honour Judge Timothy Percy.

Judge Percy held no fear for me. He was a fairly new appointment, which was good for me, and good for Tommy Nutall. You see it used to be that Judges were appointed with a 'tap on the shoulder' once they had reached a certain level of seniority at the bar. It was a 'jobs for the boys' arrangement, and meant that on occasions some absolute dinosaurs found themselves on the bench – real lunatics who oozed prejudice and spite and would bully anyone who got in their way. Now, thankfully, the rules have changed and judicial appointments are subject to open competition, with interviews and assessments – and the system is much better for it.

I went to see Tommy in the cells and discussed his case with him. Like so many others, Tommy's problem lay in his addiction to Class A drugs. He was not intrinsically a bad person, he was a junkie – and in his desperation to pay for heroin and crack cocaine he stole people's stuff. Now, don't get me wrong, theft is a crime and he should be punished. But there is a distinction between those sad, pathetic individuals who commit crimes to get the drugs they crave, and the seriously bad people who sell them the drugs and make vast profits.

And like so many others addicted to drugs, prison was just part of Tommy's life. He was only 27, but had been convicted of over 80 offences. He had been in prison on remand for over two months for burgling a garage and stealing a push-bike, a chainsaw, a bag full of washing and a small fridge. He was caught riding the push-bike unsteadily down the road, with the fridge and washing balanced precariously on the back. He told me that he regretted it, that he had been desperate, and that he is now drug-free and healthy. He showed me some certificates that he had obtained in literacy and numeracy and that his partner was pregnant.

'That's all good, Tommy,' I told him. 'I'm going to tell the Judge a little bit about your background, a little bit about what happened, and a little bit about your plans for the future, is that okay?'

He nodded and I smiled back.

'And I'm going to tell him that you're sorry, but I can only tell him that if it's true.'

'I am sorry,' he answered quickly, 'what was I thinking – I was off my tits – who steals a bag of laundry?'

I took that as remorse, of sorts, and moved on.

'Your pre-sentence report suggests that you might be eligible for a drug rehabilitation order, what do you think about that?'

He gushed at this news, 'I'll do anything, Mr Winnock, absolutely anything, I just need a chance, I'll do a curfew, a tag, anything.'

'Good,' I said, 'because you're nearly 30, Tommy, you could do with getting off the gear, mate.'

'I'll do anything,' he repeated.

The pre-sentence report is a report given to the Judge that has been compiled by the Probation Service. It tells him about the offender's background, his attitude towards his offending and it makes a recommendation as to sentence – for the old school, tap on the shoulder Judges, the PSR doesn't always help, but for the new ones, it can do – though, of course, ultimately it is the Judge's decision whether to send someone to prison and for how long.

We went up to the courtroom and Judge Percy looked benignly at the assembled throng. I was confident that both Tommy and I would get a fair hearing. I sat down on Counsel's row and listened to the prosecutor. He gave a rather wordy account of Tommy Nutall's crimes and I started to become conscious of the time – 10.35. I could hear my name being called over the tannoy: 'Russell Winnock is required in courtroom four.' I felt my stress level increase, but for now I had to concentrate on persuading Judge Percy not to send Tommy Nutall to prison.

Speeches in mitigation are tricky. If you get it wrong, you could end up making it worse for your client, whereas a good one may secure a good sentence and make your client and your solicitors happy.

The art, I think, is to try to make the job as easy as you can for the Judge, to guide them gently towards the answer. I started by telling the Judge that any burglary is really serious. This is a bog-standard mitigation point – if you try to give the Judge a wink and nod and tell him that stealing from someone's garage really isn't all that bad, you are liable to make things worse for your client and yourself.

I then told him that my client was desperately sorry for what he had done and fully expected to go to prison today. Now the Judge knows that the condemned man is sufficiently sorry and realistic enough to bow to the power of the court.

Then I went into my sob story – 'Tommy had a difficult upbringing,' I told the court – which is true, he was put into care at the age of seven. 'Tragically, it's all too familiar,' I continued, 'for young men with little in the way of a positive male role model, and none of the stability that most of us take for granted, to lapse into a world of drugs and public disobedience.'

I noted a movement of the Judge's head, which I took as encouragement.

'What Tommy Nutall needs, Your Honour, is help.'

At this point Judge Percy looked up at me. 'Has he ever been made the subject of a drug rehabilitation order, Mr Winnock?'

Bingo. I've led the Judge to my way of thinking. 'Only once,' I told him, 'but that was sadly a failure, but he was younger then. Perhaps if the court was thinking along those lines, it would impose a curfew as well, perhaps as part of a suspended sentence.'

The Judge thinned his lips as he contemplated this. 'What are his personal circumstances at the moment?'

At this point I have to decide whether to tell the Judge that Tommy has knocked up his Mrs. This can go one of two ways: some Judges will see it as good motivation for someone like Tommy to change his ways, but others may see it as an act of feckless irresponsibility.

I took a punt and decided to tell the Judge about my client's impending fatherhood.

'Well, Your Honour,' I began earnestly and brightly, trying to convey a happy event with the tone of my voice, 'Mr Nutall will go and live with his partner who is expecting their first child.'

But I've got it wrong. Judge Percy's mouth droops rather dramatically. 'Oh,' he said, 'was that the wisest thing in the circumstances, Mr Winnock? I mean, wasn't it a bit reckless of Mr Nutall to start a family with all the problems he has?'

Crap. I'd hoped that Percy would have been more positive. I now needed to salvage things. 'Well Your Honour is, of course, right, but perhaps the onset of fatherhood could provide the incentive that this young man needs to finally rid himself of drugs.'

The Judge looked at me doubtfully, considered his papers again, picked up his pen and then started to chew his lips, thoughtfully.

I need to tie things up.

'Your Honour,' I declared, 'Mr Nutall knows, indeed expects, to go to prison today. He knows that burgling people's garages and stealing their possessions, their intimate possessions at that, won't be tolerated – but, Your Honour, perhaps, on this occasion, just this once, the court can consider dealing with him in a way that will help him overcome his addiction. Because, Your Honour, if this man was clean of drugs, then this court can be absolutely confident that he would be free from crime, and a drug rehabilitation order, rather than just prison, may help him achieve that.'

I was now giving it the full puppy-dog eyes and droopy, fat bottom lip.

'Hmm,' said Percy. He made me work for it, I had to persuade him of Tommy's living arrangements, his certificates, his motivation to work, and then I had to go through the blessed sentencing guidelines, before we all discussed whether the offence is aggravated by the fact that he stole a bag full of dirty washing, as the contents may be of sentimental value.

It was all done very pleasantly, but it took ages. By the time the merciful Judge Percy had given my client a twelve-month sentence of imprisonment, suspended for two years, it is five past eleven. I was now 35 minutes late for two other Judges.

I turned to see my smiling client disappearing from the dock and rushed out into the corridor – just in time to hear the tannoy again – 'Could Mr Russell Winnock of Counsel go to court four immediately please.'

There was an urgent tone to the voice and I felt my stress level go up another notch.

Part 2 – His Honour Judge Marmaduke and the case of Peter Hilton

I ran to court four.

I rushed in, my gown flowing behind me, my wig sliding down my sweaty, glistening forehead and ending up at a jaunty angle.

He was already sitting there – His Honour Judge Marmaduke. Bugger. If Judge Percy is friendly and objective, then Marmaduke is hostile and prejudiced.

'Your Honour,' I began breathlessly, 'can I apologise if I've kept the court waiting.'

'It's not just me you should be apologising to,' he said viciously. 'It's the ushers, it's your opponent, Miss Finnigan, it's the dock officer and the defendant, Peter Hilton.'

Yeah, right, like Marmaduke cares about the defendant.

I turned to the defendant, Peter Hilton, who seemed slightly amused, and then to my opponent, Jenny Finnigan, who is a solicitor advocate with a reputation for being difficult. She smiled at me in a sickly sweet way that made me think of a snake.

In the case of Peter Hilton I am for the Crown, I am the prosecutor. The case is to be mentioned before the Judge because the CPS have failed to obtain some key forensic evidence from a bottle that was, allegedly, used by Peter Hilton in a fight in Spectacles nightclub. I know that the CPS have still not managed to get this done, despite an order from a Judge telling them to do so, and I know that this will cause the Judge deep consternation.

I also know that it's not in any shape or form my fault – it's not even my case, I am covering it for a colleague – which is something we all do from time to time – but even so, as I'm the one standing up to represent the Crown, I'm the one in the firing line, so I will have to take the hit. Again, it's something that we all do from time to time.

'Now, Mr Winnock, in your unexplained absence, Miss Finnigan was telling me that the CPS have still not disclosed to the defence the forensic evidence that was promised six weeks ago.'

Yep, just as I expected, judicial displeasure.

'That's right, Your Honour.'

I knew immediately that my answer was not a good one. I had not made the Judge happy, I had not reduced *his* stress, I had not assisted him at all. And, that is what Judges want.

Although someone like Marmaduke will profess not to care very much, and does everything he can to give the impression that he doesn't care very much, the reality is that he, like almost all Judges – even the old ones, the prejudiced ones and the horrible ones – does care. And when they get stressed as a result of the pressure of their job, that is when they get cross, that is when they shout.

And Marmaduke was now shouting.

At me.

'Well, Mr Winnock, what are you going to do about it?'

'I'm sorry, Your Honour,' I continued, 'but I'm afraid that there is very little that the Crown can do other than ask for more time.'

Again, it's not a helpful suggestion, again, I've not assisted the Judge. He explodes as if I've just asked him to give me the kidney of his firstborn grandchild.

'More time, Mr Winnock?'

'Yes.'

'Why? You've already had six weeks to obtain this evidence,

you haven't done it, this man is waiting for his trial – why on earth should I give you more time?'

I know the truthful response to his question; the truth is that the CPS have no money, and no resources, and that the poor sod who should have been doing this task has also been forced to do umpteen other tasks. He knows this, I know this; we both know that as a result of cuts to their budget, the CPS have had to make lawyers and caseworkers redundant. They now run a vastly reduced staff, and the result is that things get forgotten, things get overlooked. Evidence which would once have been chased up and secured, isn't, and as a result some cases are not prosecuted, or when they are prosecuted are done so in a half-cock way that makes it much more likely that the defendant will walk free.

In this particular case, the victim of the attack received 60 stitches to wounds in his face and neck – he will forever bear the scars of his night out. He wants justice. And I can understand that.

The evidence against Peter Hilton consists of some grainy CCTV footage, which doesn't really show the actual fight, and the witness statements of a couple of drunk people who were present. Peter Hilton says that they've got the wrong man. He may be right, I don't know. But I do know that any forensic evidence will be absolutely crucial. It may well prove beyond doubt that at some point Hilton held the bottle that was used in the assault. It may mean the difference between justice being done or not. And if a guilty man goes free, that will not be the fault of any lawyer, it will not be the fault of the system – it will be the fault of the state, who can't pay for the investigation to be carried out properly.

I realised that Judge Marmaduke was now considering making an order that the Crown be prevented from relying upon any further evidence – this would significantly undermine the chances of the Crown getting a conviction. Jenny Finnigan realised it as well – she sniffed an opportunity, and got to her feet.

'Your Honour,' she began with a greasy confidence, 'the Crown have had the bottle since this offence was committed, that's more than enough time to have it tested for DNA or fingerprints. It is surely about time for the Crown to either drop this weak case against him, or go to trial with what they've got.'

Marmaduke harrumphed and moved in his chair, then screwed his eyes up and focused on me.

'Well, Mr Winnock, what do you say to that?'

It was now time to think on my feet, to remind Marmaduke, who is normally such a pro-prosecution Judge he would probably bring back trial by fire if he could, about the implications of doing this.

'Well, Your Honour,' I said, 'of course I sympathise with Miss Finnigan and the plight of her client.'

'He doesn't want your sympathy, Mr Winnock,' bellowed Marmaduke.

'No,' I said quietly, 'but we must also remember the plight of Mr Steven Brown in all of this.'

'Who's he?' shouted the Judge.

'He, Your Honour, is the unfortunate victim – perhaps I can invite Your Honour's attention to the photographs of Mr Brown taken the morning after he was bottled.'

Marmaduke declined my invitation, but I'd done enough. He has remembered that even though the CPS have messed up, even though the state has messed up, even though he hates me – he hates Mr Hilton a whole lot more.

'Well,' he said, his face contorting, 'the CPS can have three more weeks.' He now pointed at me: 'That is the final order of the court, Mr Winnock, if they have not obtained the evidence by then – tough. Do you understand me, Mr Winnock?'

'Yes, Your Honour.'

I nodded again then cast a glance towards the clock. It was now 11.30 – one more case to go. One more Judge to placate.

Part 3 – Judge Mariner QC and the case of Yusuf Salam

Judge Mariner QC was a different type of Judge again.

He is not a shouter like Judge Marmaduke, nor a liberal like Percy, he is an intellectual, a proper lawyer, a former commercial Silk, who enjoys coming into the Crown Court from time to time to show everyone just how clever he is.

And he is clever.

I reckon that if his brain was taken out of his cranium and set free, it would unravel to the size of Croydon.

But for Judge Mariner QC, having a brain the size of a London suburb has one drawback, it means that he is quite slow; constantly proving how clever he is takes time. But on this particular morning, that suited me, as it meant that by the time I had rushed into his court, he still hadn't got round to doing my case. I felt relieved. At least I wouldn't be getting a telling-off for being late.

The atmosphere in Judge Mariner's court was heavy, with a confused air about it, like the astro-physics section of a university library. I sat down at the back of court and saw that my friend, a young barrister called Danny Utaka, was on his feet. He was looking at Judge Mariner QC with the facial expression of a man who has no idea what the other is talking about.

'So,' said Judge Mariner, 'I suppose the case you'll really want me to consider is the recent Court of Appeal decision in R v Clarke?'

I knew straight away that Danny Utaka had no idea what the case of Clarke is about. In fact I'd have put a lot of money on Danny having never even heard of the case. And I knew that he now had a split second to make up his mind about whether to try to bullshit and claim to know about the case, or come clean and admit that he hasn't the foggiest what the Judge is going on about.

I felt for Danny. He was about five years call. He was young and eager and appeared mainly in the Magistrates Court. He was still at the stage when he thought that he had to know every answer to every question posed by a Judge. He hadn't learnt that it's actually alright not to know everything. It is a process every barrister goes through. But, until we know that it is actually sometimes okay to be less than 'learned', the trap of pretending to know something is one we all fall into. And poor Danny was falling headlong, arse over tit into it.

'Yes,' he said earnestly, 'the case of Clarke . . .'

The Judge leant towards him, imploring him to continue, he looked deep into Danny's eyes, testing him. Don't get me wrong – he wasn't doing it in a vindictive way, Judge Mariner, bless him, believes that most people should be as brainy and well informed as he is. He didn't realise that poor Danny had no idea about the case of Clarke and was trying desperately to sound clever and informed because he has yet to learn how to be stupid and clueless in a confident way.

Danny squirmed – he started to leaf through his copy of Archbold, the 3000 page, criminal law bible that all criminal barristers use. He was desperate. I knew the signs, I knew that he would be manically trying to find something in the massive book that would help him, but the more he looked, the smaller the words would appear and the more confused he would become. I knew that he would now be certain that every lawyer in the whole world was looking at him and smirking.

I knew it, because I've been there. I've felt the shame. I've felt the confusion.

'I'm sorry, Your Honour,' he said, 'if you could bear with me one second, whilst I find the reference.'

Judge Mariner QC sighed, then put Danny out of his misery. 'Don't worry, Mr Utaka,' he grumbled. 'Clarke simply states the position in relation to consecutive sentences for those who have breached suspended sentences.'

'Ah, yes.'

They muddled through it. Danny left the court sweating and will almost certainly go home and question whether he is cut out for the Criminal Bar (he is); Judge Mariner QC will feel a frisson of disappointment that another barrister is not as well informed as he is, coupled with the sly joy of knowing that another barrister is not as well informed as he is.

I gave Danny a look of solidarity as he walked past, but I don't think he saw me.

I was up next.

I was defending Yusuf Salam. He was charged with Possessing 160 ecstasy tablets with the intent to supply them at a music festival in Kent. Today was his chance to plead guilty or not guilty to the charge.

He entered a plea of not guilty.

'What is his defence, Mr Winnock?' asked Judge Mariner QC.

'He accepts having the tablets, Your Honour, but he denies intending to supply them.'

'160 ecstasy tablets?'

'Yes, Your Honour.'

'What was he intending to do with them?'

'Take them, Your Honour.'

'That's an awful of tablets for one man, Mr Winnock.'

'He's a very committed dancer, Your Honour.'

Judge Mariner looked carefully at me. 'Are you familiar with the recent case of Rosenthal, Mr Winnock?'

Ha, there's no way I'm falling for that one.

'No, Your Honour. I've never heard of it.'

Twenty minutes later, I left the courtroom, tired, slightly sweaty but relieved – I'd survived.

The kangaroo court of Lincoln Prison

It was a wet, miserable three-hour drive to Lincoln Prison. Three hours watching my windscreen wipers scrape the globules of grey winter spit off the windscreen, to take part in the travesty masquerading as justice that is a Prison Adjudication – and all for next to no money. I arrived there in a bad temper and I knew things weren't going to get much better.

It is an austere old prison, Lincoln. It dates back to a time when we really knew how to treat our prisoners with absolute and utter brutality. It was built for hanging, not for rehabilitation, though I suppose that the thought of it must have deterred all but the stupidest or most hardened of criminals from committing their misdeeds.

Do I think prison works?

Yes, for some, no, for others. Call me an old tree-hugging softie, but in my experience there has to be a rehabilitative element, because making sure that someone doesn't commit the crime again is surely just as important as punishing them.

On arrival I had to provide my credentials and undergo a search, which includes an X-ray followed by a thorough examination of my crotch from the snout of an eager Springer Spaniel called Keith, which seemed to amuse the guards. Then, once Keith had finished with me, I had to undergo a frisking from a burly bloke with halitosis.

I was then escorted across some rather dour yards, through about twenty locked gates and heavy doors and onto 'C' wing where I would meet my first client.

Stanley Ojo is charged with having a fight with another prisoner in the canteen. That was all I knew about his case, yet I was supposed to defend him at a Prison Adjudication in front of a District Judge, where, if he was found guilty of the charge, there was a chance that he would receive an extra 45 days of prison.

The prison guard led me to a waiting area and instructed me to stay there, telling me that the case of Ojo is first on in about five minutes.

'Hold on,' I said, 'I'll need to speak to Mr Ojo before his hearing.'

He looked at me suspiciously, then trotted off to speak to someone else. A few minutes later, he returned. 'Follow me,' he said. And I did.

He led me to a cell which was about eight foot by ten foot. Inside, there were five men – two sat on the bottom bunk and three on the top – judging by their uniform of blue sweatshirts and tracksuit bottoms they were all inmates.

I was confused.

'Who's Stanley Ojo?'

'I am,' said a large black man with a rather scary collection of scars across his forehead and nose. He jumped down from the top bunk.

I shook his hand. 'I'm Russell Winnock,' I said, 'I've come to represent you in the adjudication.'

He looked pleasantly surprised and there were murmurs of approval from the other men.

'Right, Mr Ojo,' I said, 'why don't you tell me in your own

words what this is all about.' Which is barrister speak for, I haven't got any papers or read any papers and I haven't got the first clue what you're supposed to have done.

'Well,' said Mr Ojo in a deep, booming, yet surprisingly jolly voice, 'I supposedly punched Scotty O'Neil in the dinner queue. But I never.'

The rest of the lads still sitting on the bunks murmured their agreement, 'No, he never.'

'Okay,' I said, 'is there a statement from Mr O'Neil?'

'No,' said Ojo, 'he doesn't want to say anything.'

'Right, is there a statement from anyone?'

'Only a screw, Marsden.'

'Twat,' echoed the lads from the bunk-bed.

'What does he say?' I asked.

'He says I punched him, but I never.'

'No, he never,' came the refrain.

'Okay,' I said, 'in that case, you're not guilty. Now, who are you guys?' I immediately regret using the term 'guys', which makes me sound a bit too middle-class, a bit too much like a politician posing for a photo opportunity with a bunch of boys on a Youth Training Scheme.

Stanley Ojo introduced them in turn.

'This is Jimbo, Ian, Hawksy and The Moth.'

I nodded, 'Okay, now, did any of you witness anything?'

'We were all there,' said Jimbo.

'Great,' I replied, 'and what happened?'

At this point I started to appreciate that taking a proof of evidence from four potential witnesses in the presence of the accused isn't ideal, but, alas, this is the best I can do. In any event, as soon as I ask what happened, all four of them pulled out pieces of paper.

Stanley Ojo looked pleased. 'I've taken statements from all of them already, Mr Winnock,' he told me, and with that they all handed me their piece of paper, upon which was written, in exactly the same handwriting, a brief account of how Stanley Ojo and Scotty O'Neil had a brief but friendly disagreement over a phone card in the canteen, which culminated in Mr O'Neil and Mr Ojo slapping each other on the shoulder and agreeing to disagree on the subject.

'Hmm,' I said, 'and what does this officer Marsden say?'

'He says that I punched him repeatedly, but I never.'

'No, he never.'

'Okay, and where was he standing when he says he saw this happen?'

'Behind some doors on the corridor.'

I was starting to feel the beginnings of a defence coming on.

'And what injuries did Mr O'Neil suffer?'

At this point, the men looked downwards and shuffled in a slightly uncomfortable way.

The Moth answered, 'He was already injured on account of getting beaten up the day before.' The Moth is quite terrifying, with jet-black hair, pale skin and two dark eyes that peered at me.

'Was that anything to do with you, Mr Ojo?'

Stanley Ojo didn't like this question. 'No.' His answer was emphatic.

At this point, the door opened and the same guard who led me in earlier told me that District Judge Meyer was ready to start. I protested and told him that I wasn't ready, but he just shrugged and told me that I'll have to take that up with the Judge.

We were then marched to another room, where Judge Meyer sat looking decidedly bored at the top of the table.

'Good morning, sir,' I proffered, and he made a sort of wheezy sound in response.

Sitting next to him was a prison guard who opened the proceedings by telling him that the first case concerned Stanley Ojo. As he introduced the case, I noted, to my horror, that according to his security badge, the prosecuting prison guard was called Marsden – surely, I thought, the prosecutor can't also be the main witness.

I started to protest. 'Before we start, sir,' I said, 'I am a little concerned that I haven't been furnished with any statements and that the prosecutor is a witness in the case.'

Judge Meyer's top lip curled upward. 'You're not in the Crown Court now, Mr Winnock, this is an adjudication, an inquisitorial hearing – I'll weigh up the evidence and assess the credibility of all sides.'

'But, I would still like to see the evidence, sir.'

He sighed, then looked at the prison guard. 'Do you have a spare copy of the statement?'

'His solicitors were sent one, sir,' replied Mr Marsden.

And the Judge looked at me with an expression that said 'tough'.

What happened next will stay with me forever. Mr Marsden gave his evidence to the 'adjudication' in about three minutes – saying that he saw Stanley Ojo repeatedly punch then kick one Scott O'Neil.

I then cross-examined Mr Marsden and, if I say so myself, I gave him a hiding. I had him admitting that he was behind a door, 60 metres away and that his view was obscured by a number of large prisoners who were in the dinner queue. I then asked him why he didn't take any action whilst this beating was supposedly going on – and Mr Marsden had no answer.

I felt good – this may be a dodgy court, I told myself, but my brilliant advocacy will win the day – justice will be served.

I confidently called my witnesses – Stanley Ojo gave a good account, and the others, Jimbo, Ian, Hawksy and The Moth all stuck stoically to their script.

I then looked Judge Meyer in the eye. 'I invite this court to find my client not guilty of this charge,' I said confidently, 'there is no statement from the alleged victim, the only witness had an obscured view and the court has heard accounts from four independent witnesses, none of whom describe any violence.'

District Judge Meyer looked quizzically into the distance and sucked the tip of a ballpoint pen. Finally he turned to Officer Marsden. 'Are the witnesses who have given evidence today known acquaintances of the accused?'

'Yes sir,' said Marsden.

'Thank you,' said the Judge. 'Mr Ojo,' he continued, 'I find the case against you proven – you will be sentenced to spend an extra 28 days in custody at the end of your sentence.'

At this point I found my face contorting into a scowl and the word 'What?' was released involuntarily from my lips.

'Twenty-eight days, Mr Winnock. Please return to your wing, Mr Ojo.'

I felt like banging my fist against the table. I felt like shouting and bawling against the injustice, but I didn't. I got up, nodded and asked if I could be excused because I needed time with my next client.

Judge Meyer nodded back and I stomped out of the room to prepare for my next Prison Adjudication, my next battle.

Escape from Lincoln Prison

My next client was a Scouser called Ryan Neallie. He had been accused of failing a drug test.

I was led to his cell, he was alone. He started to talk at me from the moment the cell door was opened:

'Are you my brief?' he asked, his eyes wide and protruding against his gaunt angular cheekbones. He stared at me, but I'm too angry to go into my usual spiel about who I am and how I'll do my best to represent him, instead, I nodded and asked him what he'd been accused of.

'I've failed a piss test,' he told me.

'Okay,' I said, 'well, I'll tell you now, with this Judge, if you've been taking drugs in prison, he's going to throw the book at you.'

Neallie's face dropped when I told him this.

Drugs are rife in prison. So are mobile telephones, alcohol (often brewed using porridge oats and orange juice, which you would think would cure even the thirstiest of alcoholics), pornography, tobacco and protection rackets.

In some ways, the presence of drugs is the most pernicious of all. The nightmare of drugs is often what has got the prisoner incarcerated in the first place. The sentence should be a chance to get off drugs, not end up even closer to them. All too often drug addicts come out of prison just as addicted as when they went in.

Ryan Neallie turned to me and pointed a shaky finger in my direction. 'That can't happen,' he said, 'I'm due out next Friday, that's my release date, I'm out of here then.'

'Not if you're convicted of this,' I told him.

Neallie started to pace up and down the cell – his face creased up as he considered his fate, it is clear that he has been counting the days, the hours, the minutes, until his release date, he has probably planned every second of what he'll do when he gets out – where he'll go, the people he will see, the fruits of freedom he will enjoy once again.

'I've been in here 27 months,' he told me, 'I've got to go home next Friday.'

'Well,' I said, 'what's the evidence of the test?'

He handed me a document that outlined how Prisoner Ryan Neallie had provided a specimen of urine for testing and the test had proved positive for opiates.

Suddenly he stopped pacing.

'Can you get this hearing adjourned?' he asked.

'I'm not sure, on what grounds?'

'I don't know, you're the brief, you think of something.'

Now it was my turn to pace the cell as he stood by his bed.

'There's no statement from the officer who took the sample,' I suggested.

And Neallie's face broke into a smile. I could see now that he had blackened front teeth, the result of methadone use. 'There should be one, shouldn't there?' he said.

I shrugged. 'I can ask the Judge to adjourn so that a statement can be taken. But I can't guarantee he'll go for that.'

'How long would an adjournment be?' asked Neallie.

'I can ask for three weeks.'

'By which time, I'll be released,' said Neallie, 'and the adjudication can't interfere with me release date.'

'No,' I said, 'no it can't.'

Neallie smiled now, a full, gurning, happy, black-toothed grin, and I smiled back – I wasn't at all convinced that what I was about to do was morally and ethically within the code of conduct for barristers. In fact I was pretty sure it wasn't. But, by now, I was enthused by a potent mix of wanting to do the best for my client, and wanting to get one over on District Judge Meyer.

When I appeared before District Judge Meyer for the second time that morning I knew that my plan was a risky one – I doubted very much that it would work.

Once again Officer Marsden opened the court – 'This is Ryan Neallie, sir, he has provided a drug test that has proved positive for opiates. It is his third positive test in the last six months.'

Judge Meyer frowned, then started to write something on a form. 'Anything to say, Mr Winnock?'

'Yes,' I said assertively, 'Mr Neallie is entirely innocent of this offence.'

'Why?' said Meyer, without looking up. 'What's his defence?'

'We say that the positive sample couldn't possibly have been his, and that there must have been a mix-up in the test procedure. I respectfully request an adjournment so that a proper statement can be taken from the officer who conducted the test.'

Meyer looked up at me, his eyes narrowing as he turned to Officer Marsden. 'Is there such a statement, Mr Marsden?'

Marsden looked flustered. 'There isn't, sir.'

Meyer's lips thinned. 'How long will it take to obtain one?'

Marsden started to root through a bundle of papers. 'Er,' he stammered, 'about three weeks, the officer who took the statement is on leave.'

'Very well,' said Judge Meyer, 'we'll adjourn this case for a period of three weeks.'

I held my breath. I waited for Officer Marsden to tell the District Judge that this date will be beyond Neallie's release date, and that in three weeks' time, Neallie will not be here to face the court.

But Marsden remained silent.

I too remained silent. I felt my heart beating. Should I say something? I don't know. I don't bloody know. But before I'd had the chance to decide, I'd risen to my feet, nodded to the District Judge, and left as quickly as I could before someone worked out the scam.

Ryan Neallie grinned at me as we left. I wish he hadn't – it makes us co-conspirators.

I was escorted out of the prison. I left the wing. I went back through the yards, through the gates and heavy doors, I got to the foyer where Keith the Springer Spaniel lay sleeping next to the guard with the halitosis. I could now see the exit, I could see through the window that it had stopped raining and the sky was blue. I could see liberty. I walked purposefully towards it. I strode out towards my freedom, towards the blue sky – then, suddenly, behind me a phone rang, then a voice cried out – 'Hold on, mate.'

I took another step. Then stopped.

'Are you Mr Winnock?'

'Yes,' I said.

'Were you just doing the adjudications?'

'Yes,' I repeated.

'You're wanted by Judge Meyer.'

I turned and was escorted backwards, back into the darkness of the prison, back through the gates which are locked and the doors which are bolted. I was escorted away from the blue sky, away from freedom, back onto the wing and back into the room where the adjudications were held.

District Judge Meyer sat at his desk. Scowling.

Bugger.

'In that last case,' he bellowed, 'you engineered an adjournment to a date beyond the prisoner's release date.'

'Yes,' I replied, with a quiet defiance.

'You knew this?' he asked.

'Yes,' I nodded.

'That's preposterous.'

I shrugged my shoulders. 'It's not up to me,' I said, 'I'm not allowed to act against the interests of my client.'

'But you're not allowed to mislead the court either.'

'I didn't mislead anyone,' I said. 'I was never asked – if someone had asked me when Neallie's release date was, I'd have told them. I assumed that Officer Marsden would have been aware of it.'

Judge Meyer was now snorting with rage. 'That's bullshit and you know it.'

The word 'bullshit' made my eyes involuntarily widen, Judges never say 'bullshit', never – 'Sorry,' I said. But my apology was hollow. He knows it and I wanted him to know it.

'I've a good mind to report you to the Bar Council, or to your Head of Chambers.'

I nodded, I feel quietly confident that my Head of Chambers would support me on this one – I was less sure about the Bar Council.

'I'm sorry,' I said again, 'but I was never asked the question.'

District Judge Meyer chewed his lips, glared at me, then dismissed me.

I made my escape as quickly as I could. Breathing a great glug of air as I eventually emerged from the prison.

Had I acted properly? Well, probably not by the book. Should I have volunteered the information about Neallie's release date? Possibly, I don't know.

Nor do I know if District Judge Meyer ever contacted the authorities about the case of Ryan Neallie. Perhaps he did. Perhaps the incident was logged in the 'big black book' that some barristers are convinced is kept by the Lord Chancellor's Office, in which is written all the things that each of us has done wrong, to be held in reckoning and considered again on that fateful day when someone, somewhere, is considering whether or not you should become a Judge. Perhaps, one day, a few crusty old High Court Judges, or whoever it is has access to such things, will open the big black book, blow away the dust, then run a hoary old finger down to the alphabetically listed names, until they reach Russell Winnock, upon which one of them will read through pince-nez spectacles: 'Ah, yes, here we are, Winnock: he once failed to tell a District Judge about the release date of a prisoner *and* made him utter the phrase – bullshit.'

Hmm, unlikely, but who knows.

A chambers meeting

We don't have many chambers meetings, thank god – they are almost always gloomy affairs. The meetings are arranged at short notice, and we are all instructed to attend. The agenda is usually dominated by some terrible event that, yet again, spells doom for us all.

So, when I got an email telling me that I had to attend a chambers meeting to discuss our response to the '*Government's proposed changes in the fee structures*', my heart sank.

And, judging by the funereal procession of barristers who traipsed into the chambers library two days later, I wasn't alone in my pessimism about the hour or so that would follow.

My spirits weren't lifted by the presence of all four of chambers' Criminal Silks: Thomas Sadwell QC, Richard 'Dicky' Brindle QC, Yussef Lachmi QC and Timothy Belton QC.

QC, QC, QC and QC.

They were already perched in the library like four massive silverbacks, ready to pounce into action at the merest hint of an argument or discussion – because that is what QCs do best – they pontificate, argue, discuss and talk – a lot, and often about themselves. They have been awarded the title Queen's Counsel because they do these things in a way that is intellectually superior to everyone else in the room, or their effortless confidence at least gives that impression.

QCs, and in particular Criminal QCs, are without doubt the masters of all they survey, they are the heavyweight boxers of the robing room, they strut and posture in court like muscle-bound sprinters before a 100m final. And if they're the sprinters, then us juniors are the ones who dutifully hold the little box into which they place their discarded tracksuits as they strip down to their vests.

If all four of the Criminal Silks have turned up for a meeting then even by the standards of chambers meetings, things must be bad.

Thomas Sadwell, head of our chambers, opened the meeting.

'Thank you for coming,' he said to the sea of unimpressed faces. 'I wanted to gauge people's reaction to the proposals by the Ministry for Justice to the change in our fees.'

'It's all bollocks,' said Dicky Brindle, who is probably the biggest silverback of them all, and even managed to sound clever when uttering a response as crude as that.

'Yes, thank you, Dicky,' said Sadwell and continued, 'The proposals are set out in the document that was emailed to each of you, which I hope you all received and read.'

There was a faint murmuring of assent at this, and I murmured along, though I have no idea if I received the email – and certainly haven't read it.

'In short, they're proposing massive reductions to graduated fees and even greater reductions to Very High Cost Cases.'

'What do you mean by "massive"?' asked Lachmi.

'About seventeen per cent,' replied Head of Chambers, and there is a gasp.

See: gloom and despair. We knew it was coming, we knew that there would be further reductions to the criminal legal aid budget, we knew that it would be massive. What we don't know is how to respond to these proposals. You see, barristers, who are trained to argue on people's behalf, are absolutely rubbish at arguing in defence of themselves.

If we were teachers or nurses or railwaymen, the response to a seventeen per cent cut in our wages would be immediate – we would down tools, put on donkey jackets and man the pickets. But for us it's a bit trickier. The older fellas, including the four Silks in the room, know that once upon a time the Bar did very well out of the legal aid scheme. There was a time when they could claim huge fees for not doing very much – and there is a certain amount of guilt knocking around about that; whilst the younger ones, such as myself, have only known these leaner times. We are the ones who entered the profession after the party had finished, who know nothing other than cuts to our fees and a diminishing amount of work – our mindset is that we are just pleased to be doing the job and that any money we get for it is a bonus.

I'm not trying to make you feel sorry for me, for us, that is simply the way it is.

The mood of the meeting turned from despair to anger – my roommate, Jenny Catrell-Jones, was in uproar – 'I'm not having it,' she bellowed. 'Why should we have our fees cut for doing a good job when bankers up the road in the City do a shit job, cripple the economy and get a huge bonus for their efforts? I spent ten hours preparing for a rape case last week – will I be paid for it? Will I hell. If a banker had to work for ten minutes for nothing he'd be bitching about buggering off to Frankfurt or Hong Kong.'

Jenny had now opened up the floodgates – the meeting descended into an exchange about how much work each of us has done for no money. As is often the case with barristers, it started to get competitive: with each story about how much work someone has done for no pay, someone else has to chip in with an even more impressive one – I half expect someone in a minute to suggest that they worked without sleep for an entire week and had to actually pay the Legal Aid Board for the privilege, which would probably prompt someone else to chip in with 'That's nothing, I gave a kidney last month – didn't get a penny.'

But we are right to be angry – our ancient and revered profession is being slowly killed off by cuts to fees and changes to the ways in which we are able to conduct our work.

The uproar was brought to some semblance of order by another of our Silks, Tim Belton. 'Okay, Tommy,' he said to our Head of Chambers, 'what is it proposed we do in response to these proposals?'

'Well,' said Thomas Sadwell, 'the Criminal Bar Association is going to ballot all members over a proposed strike.'

'Strike?' exclaimed Belton.

'Yes,' said Sadwell, 'a day of action.'

There was a silence as we all contemplated this – we knew that striking is not easy, that we were all bound by a code of conduct that says that we must appear in court and represent our clients' best interests. We all knew that barristers had never taken industrial action, and that if we did, the right-wing press would have a field day calling us 'fat cats', and accusing us of feathering our nests as rapists and murderers went free. It wouldn't be pretty, and it almost certainly wouldn't succeed.

'We can't sit back and do nothing,' said Jenny Catrell-Jones, 'I propose that we as a chambers should support any action.'

'I'm not sure that we can do that,' said Lachmi, and the meeting now descended into an argument about the legality of collective action, which is another problem with assembling a room full of barristers – at some point they will all have an argument. Usually over some small legal technicality, which is wholly peripheral to the issue.

Twenty minutes later it was agreed that Gray's Buildings Chambers were opposed to any further cuts to legal aid, and that individual barristers would come to individual decisions about whether to strike or not.

We traipsed out of the library. Around me, I picked up different desperate conversations from various learned colleagues – some were genuinely disturbed, talking about having to re-mortgage their houses or leave the Bar altogether, but for others, the problem was somewhat less acute, one moaned about his kids' school fees, another wondered aloud about whether he could pay for a week skiing in Chamonix. I thanked all of our collective lucky stars that these conversations wouldn't be overheard by a journalist from the *Daily Mail.*

My roommate, Angus Tollman, sidled up to me. 'Will you go on strike then, Russ?' he asked.

I shrugged. 'Yes, I suppose I will. After all, we've got to do something, haven't we?'

And I'm right about that. I know I am. Most people don't ever want to have anything to do with the courts and the legal justice system – but, when they do, they want to be confident that the people representing them will be experienced, professional and skilled. Sadly, the way things are going, we will end up with a system where only those who can afford it will get experienced, professional and skilled barristers, whilst everyone else will have to take what they're given and that could mean a kid just out of law school or someone who, sadly, just isn't up to the job.

I hated the idea of striking, but, alas, as I plodded despondently out of the library and up to my desk, I realised my colleagues were right, we can't just roll over and die, something had to be done, we have to try to save our profession.

R v Kenny McCloud

Clem Wilson called me into his room. I immediately felt a little frisson of nerves; especially when I saw that he was smiling at me – 'I've just had Hayes, Finkelstein, Brewer on the phone,' he said, referring to a firm of solicitors who'd recently given me a couple of briefs.

'Okay,' I said, nervously.

'They're very pleased with the cases you've done for them,' he continued, and picked up a substantial bundle of papers wrapped in pink ribbon. 'So they've sent you this.'

I took the brief from him as though accepting a birthday present. 'Wow.' I said, 'thanks.'

'One thing though.'

'Sure, what?' I sounded eager, because I was eager.

'You have to have a conference with the client tomorrow morning, first thing at Pentonville Prison.'

'Sure, no problem.'

I looked at the front cover, it said, R v Kenny McCloud.

Kenny McCloud. My first reading of that name.

It would be a significant case.

There is something great about getting a brand new, untouched brief. A brief with your name on. A brief that someone has looked at and decided you are just the right person to defend their client, look after his interests, perhaps win the case for him.

It felt great arriving home and putting the papers in the case of R v Kenny McCloud on my kitchen table. I looked at them for a few seconds, untouched and smooth, then decided to save them, like a child leaving his favourite sweet, until I'd had some tea. So I made dinner, then put on some music.

I often listen to music when I'm reading my briefs – and it can't be any kind of music either, I mean Neil Young is god, but distorted guitar and anthemic folk rock isn't conducive to concentration. I find anything from trance and trip-hop to Gregorian monks and sixteenth-century choral music best. I put on some Thomas Tallis and opened the brief of Kenny McCloud.

I started with the indictment, or charge sheet. Immediately I saw that this was by far the most serious case I had ever been given – there were sixteen counts, or charges. I read the first one: Rape. It told me that Kenny McCloud, on a date between the 16th October 1975 and the 15th October 1976, raped his daughter, Jessica McCloud, a girl aged six, by placing his penis inside her vagina, knowing or believing that she did not consent. It was the description of statutory rape of a child, chilling in its cold, clinical legal language.

The count of rape was followed by another nine similar counts against Jessica McCloud. Then there were another eight counts – this time the girl was called Karen McCloud, his other, older daughter, then aged eight.

They are what are called specimen counts, which means that they are just an example of what was going on regularly and for years.

I started to read the transcript of Jessica McCloud's account:

'I remember being six years old. I remember I was six because for my sixth birthday I had a puppy called Ralph and Ralph would be with us when my Dad did what he did.'

I looked at the indictment again, 1976. I pictured *Top of the Pops*, hairy men and girls with bell-bottom trousers and floral blouses. It seems cold in 1976. Cold and grey.

I continued to read. I was no longer just pleased to have received such a significant case, it is no longer about me and my career and my life as a barrister, it's about the destruction of lives, it's about tragedy and horror.

'I first remember my Dad taking me and my sister for a walk, we used to go to a disused timber works that was near to the heath where we lived. It is not there anymore, it is where B&Q is now.

My Dad tied up my dog outside the works and made me and my sister go inside; I can't remember what he said to make us go in, but we just followed him. We were in some kind of disused workshop, I remember there was glass on the floor and piles of old paper and sheets of wood. I then remember him grabbing me first and trying to kiss me. It wasn't like a normal kiss, it wasn't like a Dad kiss. I remember that his breath smelled. I didn't know what to do. I was wearing a summer dress. He pulled it up and tried to get me to touch him, down below.

At this point my sister tried to hit him and he got angry. He took a metal dog chain and tied her up against a pole. He then tied me against another pole. He then . . .'

Here, there was a pause in the transcript and the interviewing police officer had to prompt Jessica McCloud, now a woman in her forties, by telling her in a gentle way that she was doing really well, and that it would soon be over. Jessica then carried on describing the worst kind of abuse you could imagine – a campaign of violence and sexual assault. She described how her mother was an alcoholic and that she would ignore her and her sister when they told her that they didn't want to go out on walks with Dad and how every time it would be the same, her and her sister, crying, sobbing, tied to a pole, hit with a dog chain and raped.

Her sister's account was similar – she also recalled the smell of her father's breath and the feel of the metal dog lead on her bare legs, already red with the cold of the outdoors. Karen seemed stronger. There were fewer pauses, less need for encouragement from the officer, her voice did not falter.

I read it all. I read the notes from the school teachers who remembered the girls complaining that they had welts on their back and how often they would come to school dirty. And the social workers who said that the records from that period had been destroyed, though one retired social worker could remember going to see the girls because they were worried that their mother was unable to cope, but concluded that no action needed to be taken. I read the report of Jessica McCloud's psychiatrist who told of her depression and her inability to cope, which had led to a period of alcohol abuse.

I then read Kenny McCloud's interview.

This was important, this was the first chance I had of discovering what my client said about these allegations. I wondered if he would accept his guilt. I doubted it; sex offenders rarely do. I was right – he denied everything. He claimed that he hadn't seen either girl for twenty years and that they were probably after his money. 'They're probably just like their mother,' he said, 'drunken whores.'

It was after midnight by the time I finished reading every page of the brief. Every statement, every document, every word of Kenny McCloud's stinking interview. I had devoured each page and found myself in a strange dark place. I am his barrister. I am *his* barrister. I had to prepare for the prospect of confronting his daughters with their 'lies' and putting forward my client's case, when I knew that the accounts given by the women were absolutely and impeccably truthful. I knew that they had suffered.

I put the brief down. I put the pink ribbon back around it. I *was* pleased and exhilarated to be entrusted with such a big case, but I knew full well that I had now entered a dark world.

Suddenly, I felt lonely in my flat. I wished I had a flatmate or a girlfriend, someone to talk to, someone to remind me of my own humanity. Instead, I put on late-night TV – there are some reruns of *Friends* – and fell asleep.

The ten greatest fictional lawyers

Some lawyers will deny watching a courtroom drama on the telly or in the cinema – funny, they deny it, but they all seem to know the plots. Me, I don't mind admitting that I love them, even when they're awful and I find myself screaming, *'You'd never do that in a real court, the Judge would kill you,'* at the TV, I still enjoy them, perhaps that's *why* I enjoy them.

So, here's my list of the Ten Greatest Fictional Lawyers; again in no particular order:

1. **Jaggers from *Great Expectations*** – this is the lawyer who helps Pip reclaim his fortune from Magwitch. Dickens knew all about lawyers, having once been a Clerk. Although Jaggers is not Dickens' best known lawyer, what always resonated with me was his constant need to wash his hands as though he was trying to expunge the dirt of his clients – I really get that.

2. **Perry Mason** – the original courtroom-drama superhero, Mason was a star of books, radio and film. He doesn't appear to have ever lost a trial and had an amazing ability to shoehorn a confession from the real 'murderer'. I doubt that Mason ever got a bollocking for being late to court.

3. **Kavanagh QC** – as I've confessed earlier, Kavanagh QC was my boyhood hero. A gruff Northern Silk brilliantly portrayed by John Thaw, Kavanagh QC was exactly how I expected every great lawyer to be – and to be fair, one or two have lived up to that fictional expectation.

4. **Fred Gailey** – he's the attorney who represents 'Father Christmas' in *Miracle on 34th Street* – and manages to persuade the Judge that Father Christmas exists – fair play, a good result in what must have been a tricky brief.

5. **Tony Petrocelli** – classic maverick US attorney, Tony Petrocelli, appeared on our TV screens in the 1970s and, like Perry Mason, also seemed to never lose a case. Living in a camper van, Petrocelli also had something that every advocate would die for, a catch-phrase: he would look coolly at the jury, run his hand through his hair and say, 'Let's go back to the scene of the crime.' Marvellous.

6. **Martha Costello QC** – wonderfully portrayed by the amazing Maxine Peake in the TV drama *Silk*, Martha is another Northern working-class barrister who becomes the champion of lost causes because she cares so much about her clients.

7. **Atticus Finch** – from Harper Lee's *To Kill a Mockingbird*, the lawyer every lawyer wants to be – a man of integrity, intelligence and moral superiority. Immortalised on the silver screen by the peerless Gregory Peck – I mean what jury or judge would disagree with Gregory Peck – the answer is none!

8. **Saul Goodman** – most of my clients would give their right arm to be represented by *Breaking Bad*'s Saul Goodman. Goodman will, literally, do anything to protect the interests of his clients. His

brash, gaudy demeanour is perfect, allowing him to be under-estimated by his adversaries as he focuses on the job in hand. So popular he's now got his own TV show.

9. **Tom Hagan** – Standing Counsel to the Corleone family – wow, what a brief that is! All Hagan has to do is keep The Godfather, Vito, out of the clink, and the family's business out of the courts. Robert Duvall plays him with a ruthless, understated cunning in Coppola's seminal film.

10. **Lawrence Hammill QC** – if Kavanagh was my boyhood hero, then Lawrence Hammill is the lawyer that I'd now love to become. Hammill is the retired Silk in the wonderful Australian film *The Castle*, who comes to the rescue of the blue-collar, fair dinkum Aussie family, the Kerrigans, when they try to oppose the state's attempt to compulsory purchase their house. In a rousing closing speech, Hammill, who is acting *pro bono* (for free), tells the Australian Supreme Court that the love and memories that come with a house cannot be compensated for in law. Genius – definitely worth a watch if you haven't seen it.

Meeting Kenny McCloud

I met Harry Ashton at the gates of Pentonville Prison. Harry Ashton is a former Metropolitan police officer who is employed by the solicitors, Hayes, Finkelstein, Brewer, as an outdoor clerk or legal executive, or some similar title. I am told that there was a time when most criminal solicitors firms had a former copper who would oversee police station interviews and take statements from clients and witnesses and act as a backup to the barrister – a bit like the proverbial gamekeeper turned poacher. Now few firms can afford to employ them – they're a luxury, no longer covered by legal aid. And that's a shame, because the experience and skill these men brought was invaluable to everyone who had anything to do with the process of justice.

I'd not met Harry Ashton before but I'd seen him and knew his reputation – fierce and uncompromising.

We shook hands. I smiled. He didn't.

'This is one of the worst I've ever read in my forty years,' said Harry. I'm not sure how to react to this.

We entered the prison and were ushered to a room where Kenny McCloud sat waiting for us. He was old, in his late sixties now. He had thick glasses and long dirty hair. His breath smelt of tobacco and I noted yellow stains around his fingers and unshaven mouth. He had a slight tremor.

I introduced myself. 'I'm Russell Winnock,' I said, 'I'm the barrister who's going to look after you.'

He turned to Harry Ashton with a strange smirk.

'Why've you sent me a boy? How's he going to look after me?'

His accent was hard, guttural, working-class Glaswegian. His tone was mocking.

Harry's expression didn't change.

'Mr Winnock is one of the best young criminal barristers around,' he said, 'you're lucky to have him. So you just listen to what he's got to say.'

The old copper's words lifted me. Even though I realised that he would have said this regardless of who he was with, I felt at once stronger, more confident.

I told McCloud about the procedure. I told him about the credit he'll get if he pleads guilty and the massive sentence he'll get if he's convicted by a jury at a trial. I told him that I'd do everything I could to defend him, but that no one can deliver miracles and that if the jury didn't like him, then he'd be convicted.

He looked at me impassively, his eyes never leaving mine, never blinking, the only movement the slight involuntary shake of his hands and forehead.

'So,' he said, after I've finished, 'is the evidence strong?' A smile played across his face as he asked me this question. I tried not to be scared of this man. I tried not to hate him. Neither emotion is the least bit helpful to me. I knew that I had to keep focused, I couldn't let myself be distracted by emotion, because as soon as I started to feel sympathy for the complainants or revulsion towards my client, I wouldn't be able to represent him – and that is all I'm here to do, represent him, calmly, professionally and dispassionately – for right or wrong.

'Your problem is that there are two complainants,' I told him, 'and that makes it much more difficult – I mean, a jury might believe that one of the women is lying, but they're going to find it much more difficult to believe that both of them are.'

He contemplated this. 'What about any other evidence?'

'Not much, really,' I told him, 'no forensic evidence, and no real corroborating witnesses. Just your word against that of your daughters.'

'Well, they're lying,' he snarled.

'Okay,' I said, 'then you should have a trial, Mr McCloud – and a jury will decide.'

He stared at me as he considered this. I could see that Kenny McCloud was the type of man who has taken and given beatings all his life; able to control people by fear, he probably thought that he could somehow do the same with a jury, bully them into acquitting him.

I went through his daughters' statements with him. I asked him about dog leads and timber yards and dresses and boozy breath and he replied with a simple and terse: 'Didn't happen', to each proposition.

'What about the dog?' I asked him. 'Do you remember a dog called Ralph?'

'I don't remember any bloody dog,' he said. Somehow I find that particularly poignant – why did he have to lie about it? Surely everyone remembers their pets?

Eventually, we parted, shaking hands. Always shake hands with your client. That's what I'd been taught – regardless of what you thought about them.

Outside, I turned to Harry Ashton – 'What do you think?' I asked him.

'A proper bastard,' said Ashton.

'Yeah, but he was very clear that none of this happened, wasn't he?' I said naively.

'Well he could hardly admit it, could he?'

'No, I suppose not,' I murmured.

I was glad to leave Pentonville Prison, though I knew that I'd be back with Kenny McCloud soon enough.

Cross-examination and the case of Shandra Whithurst

On the face of it, Shandra Whithurst's case was pretty straight-forward. She was a large, jolly woman in her late forties who had been charged with shoplifting. She had gone into a supermarket, wandered around the fruit and veg aisle for a bit before walking purposefully over to the make-up section where she appeared to place four packets of 'Luscious Lips Lip Liner' inside her bra. Her problem was that all of this was captured on CCTV, which showed her in fairly clear HD quality, wandering from the cosmetics over towards the exit, making no attempt to pay, and being apprehended by a couple of massive security guards who manhandled her into a display of Czech lager as she protested her innocence. Interestingly, though, when the police searched her, there was no sign of the lip liner.

Shandra had elected to be tried by a jury rather than in a Magistrates Court. In her case, this was probably quite a good shout – you see, her defence depends upon a jury being confused by the fact that, even though CCTV footage clearly showed her putting items inside her clothing, the absence of any actual goods when she was searched might cast doubt on that. I knew that a bench of hardened Magistrates who had heard it and seen it all before wouldn't be the slightest bit concerned about the absence of the stolen goods, but a jury just might. I also knew that a jury would be more likely to be appalled by the sight of a couple of burly security guards laying into a nice middle-aged Afro-Caribbean woman – especially if I got the cross-examination right.

I met Shandra in a conference room at court. She was lovely. We watched the CCTV together. We watched the clear images of her movements as she wandered from fruit and veg to the cosmetics – where she clearly tucked something into her bra – then towards the exit.

'Is that you?' I asked her.

'Of course it's me,' she said.

I smiled, then tutted appropriately as we saw the security guard grab her, causing her to fall backwards into the stack of canned beer. When the video had finished I asked her if she wanted to see it again. 'No,' she said, 'I know what I did and didn't do.'

'Good,' I said, and at this point, I took off my wig, scratched my head and asked the question that I had to ask.

'Miss Whithurst,' I said, 'look, I've got to ask you this.'

She smiled nicely at me as I paused. 'What on earth are you doing over by the make-up aisles with your hands down your top?'

She leant in towards me, and whispered, 'I was itchy.'

'Itchy?'

'Yes.'

'You weren't stealing anything?'

'No.' She is emphatic in her denial.

'And the four missing Luscious Lips Lip Liners have got nothing to do with you?'

'Absolutely not. Young man, what would I do with luscious lips, I've already got luscious lips.' With this she laughed throatily. I smiled. She would be a perfect witness in her own defence.

'Okay then,' I stood up, 'let's go into court.'

Inside the courtroom, His Honour Judge Smithson was looking decidedly bored. Smithson had a reputation for being lazy and doing anything he could to avoid the trials that kept him from the golf course. As he spied me, he sat up. 'Ah Mr Winnock,' he said, 'are you defending Miss Whithurst?'

'Yes, Your Honour.'

'Is this *really* going to be a trial?'

'Yes, Your Honour.'

'What about the CCTV footage – pretty damning isn't it?'

'Not in the absence of any actual stolen goods,' I replied.

The Judge contemplated this for a few seconds, his lips turned inadvertently into his mouth, before he turned to my opponent, Sam Wilkins. 'Mr Wilkins,' he said, 'in the absence of any actual goods, how are you going to prove theft? A bit thin isn't it?'

The prosecutor was equally robust. 'The CCTV footage clearly shows appropriation, Your Honour.'

The Judge sighed wearily. 'Very well then, gentlemen, let's get on with it.'

The jury piled in. The usual suspects: middle-aged men in sports jackets; old ladies with newly done hair; youths just thankful that they are in the jury box and not the dock, and the single attractive female.

They looked disappointed when they were told that they were about to try a case involving the theft of 25 quid's worth of make-up. They were probably hoping for something involving a bit of death and mutilation. Still, this was what they had and I was determined that they would end up seeing things my way.

Sam Wilkins opened the case for the Crown, then called his first witness – one Eddie Horton.

Eddie is the first of the two massive security guards who would be giving evidence. Wilkins gets to question him first. Wilkins is a sure-footed if unspectacular prosecutor. He took Horton through his examination-in-chief, which allowed Horton to describe in his own words how he spotted a large lady of African appearance 'clearly conceal items of make-up within her clothes'.

'Don't be shy,' said Wilkins, 'where exactly?'

'Her bra, Your Honour,' said Horton coyly.

After Wilkins had finished, it was my turn to cross-examine the witness.

Some barristers swear that there is an art to cross-examination, a particular way to best put forward your case and take down a witness. Some barristers write down all their questions with meticulous care; some do it effortlessly off the top of their head because they are that good; and some, let's face it, find the whole process a challenge. Me, well, I have no set way. Maybe I will once I've got a few more years under my belt, but at the moment, when I get to my feet to cross-examine, I'm never entirely sure what I'm going to do until I've started.

You see, to me, being on your feet questioning a witness in a Crown Court is, and I don't want to sound excessively dramatic or self-important about this, an intensely human experience.

For me, when I deal with a witness, I am embarking upon a series of rather intimate relationships: first, with the witness, who I am questioning; second, with the Judge, who I am having to ensure doesn't stop me for asking irrelevant or unlawful questions; third, with my opponent, who wants to beat me; fourth, with my client, who wants me to ask the right questions and put their case forward effectively; and fifth, perhaps most significantly, with the jury, who you want to draw towards you.

In this case, I would be attempting to get this jury to dislike Mr Horton, but I wouldn't bully him or shout at him, ridicule him, or patronise him, because there is a good chance that they would end up disliking me if I did that. If I can possibly help it, I won't call him a liar, either, because if I suggest that, and the jury don't agree with me, then me, my case and my client are doomed.

Instead, I would attempt to get him to agree with me as much as I could, because that will make it easier for the jury to agree with me in due course.

I would of course try to trip him up, but I would do so in the nicest possible way.

And, in accordance with one of the first and most important rules of advocacy, I would try to avoid asking him questions to which I didn't know the answer – because if I looked silly, I'd lose the confidence of the jury, which would be disastrous.

I got to my feet, trying to look confident. Trying to look like I knew everything there was to know, trying to give the impression that I was a massive and glorious bull elephant and that the courtroom belonged to me. Of course I have no idea if I achieve this because no one ever tells you.

'Mr Horton,' I said. And all eyes fell on me.

It began.

It is theatre, and that's why I love it.

I started by asking a few easy questions – stuff he couldn't possibly disagree with.

'You're a big man, Mr Horton?'

'Some might think so.'

This is the best response he could have given me. It's evasive and told me straight away that he was going to be defensive. Most juries don't like defensive, evasive witnesses. What he should have said, the correct, easy answer that would have posed me more difficulties would have been, 'Yes, I am, massive.' But Horton wanted to be clever, so he doesn't give me a straightforward answer, and in the process of trying to look clever, he made himself look shifty.

I questioned him about the supermarket and the procedure and his training.

'How are you trained to deal with people who may have been shoplifting?' I asked him.

This is an open question, by that I mean that I haven't put it to him as an assertion which requires only a yes or no response, as in 'You're trained to be polite and helpful aren't you?' which is the way we normally ask questions when we want to control the witness. I've asked him an open question as I've got a good idea what he'll say, and the answer will have more force coming as a result of this type of question.

'We all undergo very specialised training in dealing firmly, yet fairly, with those who are suspected of theft.'

'So you'd never assault anyone?'

'No, certainly not.'

'You'd never attempt to injure anyone?'

'No.'

He had now cottoned on to where I was going with this line of questioning. So have some of the jury. As I said, it's theatre and they're desperate for more, they want to know what will happen next, they want to get as close to the action as they can.

'I'd like you to look at this then please.'

I pushed the button on the video remote control and the images of Shandra Whithurst being approached by Mr Horton and his mate appeared. I stopped the tape. 'That's you there, isn't it?' I said.

'Yes, it could be.' There he was again – evasive – of course it's bloody him!

'*Could be*, Mr Horton? Well it is, isn't it?'

'Yes, I think so.'

At this point Judge Smithson got involved. 'What do you mean, you think so? Is it or is it not you?'

'It is, yes.'

I gave the jury a quick look of exasperation. Just a little one, nothing too much, but enough to let them know that I shared their irritation at the witness's wriggling – a look to suggest to them that we were in this together.

'Thank you, Mr Horton.' I spoke clearly, as polite as a Boy Scout.

I now played the next bit of the video, the bit that showed Miss Whithurst put her hands in the air, then move away from the security guards as they tried to grab her.

'Was Miss Whithurst trying to avoid you at this point, Mr Horton?'

'Yes, I believe she was,' he said.

'Or perhaps she was just telling you that she was innocent?'

'Well . . .'

'That's what she was doing, wasn't she, protesting her innocence?'

'Yes, but we'd seen her on CCTV stealing something.'

'I'll come on to that, Mr Horton, but first . . .' I played more of the video. The two men grab Shandra and she topples over.

'Were you taught to assault customers as part of your training, Mr Horton?'

'She fell,' he answered.

'You pushed her, Mr Horton, look, you can see it again if you like. You and your colleague push this lady into the display of beer, don't you?'

At this point the court was enraptured – in fairness to Mr Horton, he probably was trying to apprehend her, but it didn't look good on the CCTV, and the fact that he now didn't seem to give a toss just made it worse for him. It was an exercise in getting the jury to sympathise with my client.

I moved on. 'Now, Mr Horton, you've told us that Miss Whithurst was a thief.'

'Yes.'

'What makes you say that?'

This was a bit of a dumb question by me, I've given him a free kick, a chance to simply regurgitate what can be seen on the earlier part of the CCTV footage. I cursed myself as soon as the stupid words left my stupid mouth.

'Because of what we saw on the CCTV.'

But he slipped up. I'd been saved. My heart leapt. This was an unexpected opening.

'Who saw it on the CCTV?'

'Well, control saw it, and they relayed a description of the offender to me.'

'So you didn't see it yourself?'

'Not exactly, no.'

'Well did you or didn't you?'

'No.'

'So why in your police statement did you say *you'd* seen the CCTV footage showing Miss Whithurst steal some goods?'

'Well . . . it was a slip-up.'

'No, Mr Horton, you were misleading the police and this jury.' I turned emphatically towards the jury, beseeching them with my eyes and the expression on my face: look at this liar who is trying to mislead all of us.

'So what else have you got wrong, Mr Horton?'

'Nothing,' he said.

'You're sure?'

'Yes.'

'So *you* never saw Miss Whithurst do anything wrong?'

'Not me personally, no.'

'And so you just went up to a woman who, for all you knew, was entirely innocent and pushed her over.'

'Well . . .'

'I bet they didn't teach you that on your course, did they, Mr Horton?'

I sat down, I felt ace. I felt like Perry bleeding Mason.

It took the jury twenty minutes to acquit Shandra Whithurst. She gave me a massive hug as she left.

'Thank you, Mr Winnock,' she said, and I looked coy and bashful, 'you are the best barrister in the whole world.'

'Oh,' I said, and did a little limp-wristed 'give over' gesture with my hand.

'From now on, whenever any of my friends get caught by the police they'll be coming to you.'

I wanted her to stop now. Even I was getting embarrassed.

But, funnily enough, as you'll soon see, she was as good as her word.

The City Magistrates Court

I've already mentioned the Magistrates Court a few times, so I'll explain a bit more about it with a case I did a while back. Now, don't get me wrong, the institution of lay magistrates trying their peers, or supposed peers, on less serious matters is a commendable aspect of our system – one which I would fight to retain (or at least write a strongly worded letter to retain). But, for any criminal barrister with an ounce of ambition, the Magistrates Court is a place to cut your teeth, a place where lessons are learned before you move on to the more serious cases in the Crown Court. The fact that I was still doing work in the Magistrates Court a few years into my career was a source of annoyance to me.

The City Magistrates Court is a terrible place; like a holding pen for the people who have been left behind by society. On arrival, you are immediately hit by the smell of despair that oozes from the pores of the petty thieves, junkies, pissed-up fighters, blokes who hit the Mrs on a Saturday night, kids with ASBOs, disgruntled drivers who were 'never going that fast', and parents who want the ground to open up and take them back to a time when their errant kid was still sweet and innocent.

That morning, I entered through the wooden double doors and sighed to myself.

The atmosphere here is different from that in the Crown Court; the Crown Court still holds fear for those who are summonsed to appear in it, the foyer and waiting areas are still cloistered with a hush of respect, whereas a trip to the Magistrates Court is more of an inconvenience. Those who are here don't treat this place with any kind of reverence and the result is a simmering anarchy.

I made my way to court six. The court was in session and a ridiculously young-looking advocate was stuttering his way through a prosecution opening. In the back row was my mate Johnny. I was pleasantly surprised by the sight of him sitting looking quite interested in the case, even though he was not in it.

I sidled up to him. 'Hello,' I whispered. He didn't turn to me, instead he whispered back, 'You should hear this, mate.' He said, 'The bloke in the dock is up for bigamy, he's had three wives on the go for the last five years.'

'Christ,' I said, 'what's he doing here, hasn't the poor man suffered enough?'

'At one point,' continued Johnny, 'to stop one of them from finding out, he completely re-wired the telephone junction box for the whole of his area.'

'Crikey.' I looked at the tired, pasty-faced, ordinary-looking man in the dock – our eyes met and he looked away, ashamed. He's another person for whom a chain of wrong decisions had led to him finding himself at the wrong end of the criminal law.

We were interrupted by the usher, an ancient portly man, who leant over towards me. 'Are you representing Danny Hooper, Mr Winnock?'

I nodded.

'Well he's slumped by the back door.'

I groaned and took myself off to the back door of the court building to find my client Danny Hooper passed out by the door. I leant over him. 'Danny,' I said, gently at first, then louder,

'Danny!' I contemplated giving him a bit of a shake, but thought better of it – Danny was filthy, diseased and occasionally violent.

'Danny!' I shouted this time and he opened his eyes, for a second he frowned, clearly thinking, 'Who the hell are you?' then appeared to recognise me, and got to his feet with surprising agility.

'Alright,' he said.

'Remember me, Danny?' I said. 'I'm Russell, Russell Winnock, remember, the barrister who's looking after you.'

'Alright,' he repeated, then added quickly, 'I haven't done nothing, Mr Winnock.'

'No, you have,' I told him, 'you threw a kebab at a copper.'

'What copper?'

'The one who was trying to move you on because you were swearing at the tourists.'

He looked vacantly at me. 'I don't remember no copper,' he said quietly, 'or any tourists.'

'Well, you're going to have to plead guilty to it, Danny. There are five coppers and about 25 Japanese tourists who were all there, and *they* weren't off their tits on sherry.'

At this he opened his mouth and revealed a single black tooth and gave me a phlegmy laugh.

'Alright,' he said, 'what's going to happen? Am I going down?'

'Not for a kebab. If you'd thrown a grenade at him, it might have been different.'

He laughed again. 'Comedian you are, ain't you.'

I smiled and shrugged, then a wave of alcohol fumes from his breath hit me. I decided to lay off the gags.

'Come on,' I said, 'we'd better get into court.'

With that, Danny picked up the bottle of sherry that was sitting half consumed by the wall.

'You can't bring that into court,' I told him.

'I'm not leaving it here,' he said.

And I considered reassuring him that unless a group of wandering vicars happened upon it, his sherry was probably safe – but I didn't. Sherry, you see, was important to Danny. As a former methadone addict, due to the devastating effects that methadone has on the taste buds, it was now just about the only thing that he could taste. Heroin took away most of his youth and his health, the methadone that they put him on to take away his heroin cravings took away his teeth and his senses, and the two bottles of sherry he drank a day in place of the heroin had taken away his mind.

There was no way he was going to let anyone take away his sherry.

I watched as he placed the sherry bottle inside his coat and then put his hands inside his pockets to secure the bottle. We made our way to the courtroom.

The usher placed Hooper in the centre of the courtroom, right in front of the bench of Magistrates.

He stood there, his hands in his pockets and his head slightly swaying as the waves of twenty-odd years of substance abuse crashed around in his cranium.

'Are you Daniel Mark Hooper?' asked the Clerk.

'I am,' said Hooper, somewhat more confidently and coherently than I had expected.

'Just a second,' interrupted the Chairman of the bench. 'Mr Hooper, you are in a court of law, please take your hands out of your pockets.'

I cringed at this – I knew that Hooper was using his hands to hold the bottle of sherry concealed inside his coat. I knew that Hooper knew that removing his hands would dislodge the bottle. For a second he stood there with his hands still inside his coat pockets as he contemplated what to do.

I watched him, enthralled. Everyone else watched him, confused.

Then, slowly … gingerly … he started to move: first he plunged his hands far down into his pockets, bending his knees as he did to get extra depth, then he started to rummage around the waistband region of his tracksuit bottoms as he clearly attempted to transport the bottle into his underpants. All the time, he stared at the bench and they stared in wonderment back at him. Eventually, after what seemed an age, like a magician pulling a rabbit out of a hat, he pulled his hands out of his pockets, a big grin forming on his face. I half expected him to add a triumphant 'Ta-Dah!' But thankfully he didn't.

I gave the bench my usual speech about how his life had been blighted by drugs and drink and how he now had Hepatitis A, B and C and how there were the first glimmers of hope because he did actually turn up for one of his probation meetings, which was progress, as previously he'd been too pissed.

The Magistrates sat through this, impassively, then retired, leaving me wishing I was in the Crown Court doing a big case, as Danny Hooper snored gently on a seat in the corner.

Johnny came up to me again. 'You've got to get away from this, Russ, while you still can.'

I smiled and shrugged. 'You could be right.'

'You only have to say the word, and I can try to get you a job in our hotel, they're desperate for people like us out there.'

I shook my head. 'I can't do it,' I said, 'it's still important to me. And anyway things will get better. Eventually, someone will realise that we actually do a good job, an important job.'

'They won't, Russ. Who wants to come to somewhere like this? Who cares what happens to people like him?' He motioned towards the sleeping Hooper. 'Most people just think they should throw away the key to his cell.'

I shrugged again. 'Maybe you're right.'

The Magistrates came back and sentenced Danny Hooper to a further period of supervision.

He slithered out of the court. I left as fast as I could.

A couple of weeks later I saw him again by the bus stop, he came bounding up to me. 'Mr Winnock,' he said, a bottle of Cockburns Extra Dry in his hand, 'I was in court the other week.'

'Yes,' I replied, 'I know.'

'No,' he said, 'I had this other barrister, he was great, really knew how to talk to the court he did, real gift of the gab.'

'Yes mate,' I said, 'that was me.'

'No, Mr Winnock, this bloke was ace. Wasn't you. I thought I was going to prison for sure, but he kept me out, supervision.'

I sighed.

The Magistrates Court in the country

Not all Magistrates Courts are like the inner-city hell that is City Mags. As a baby barrister barely out of Bar School, I was sent to the middle of nowhere (well, a small town about forty minutes from Ipswich to be precise), to prosecute the Magistrates Court list.

I arrived at the small town Magistrates Court eager, with a clutch of files, each of which I had read and prepared thoroughly.

I parked my Ford Fiesta in a space that was reserved for 'Attorneys At Law', which made me feel fantastic, then made my way to the old slate-grey building. The foyer to small town Country Court was very different from the big city Magistrates Court. Sure, there were the same drug addicts hanging around, but they were addicts without the desperate grime of inner-city urban junkies. And yes, there were dishonest people as well, and nasty, violent people who had reasserted the masculine hierarchy of the village just after chucking-out time. But, even though many of the crimes were just as serious and the criminals just as hopeless, the feeling of desperation that is present in the urban courts was absent.

The foyer was quiet. As I opened the door, I could hear a pin drop. I looked at the nervous faces of those summonsed to appear, then looked for an usher.

'I'm the prosecutor,' I said. 'I've come up from London.'

'Oh,' she exclaimed, her voice reaching a high pitch of excitement, before looking me up and down like an aunt might look at a nephew she hasn't seen for a while, 'come up from London,' she repeated, 'come this way.'

I was led into a small courtroom that was dominated by a massive square wooden table and a roaring fire. The usher motioned towards the roaring fire. 'Don't tell the Lord Chancellor's Department,' she said, 'they tried to ban it,' then she winked at me.

'Where do I sit?' I asked.

'You sit there,' she said, motioning to a space just in front of the fire, 'the Magistrates sit there, the defence solicitor, who is usually Mr Mulhearn, sits there, the Clerk sits there and the Colonel sits there.' She gestured to various seats around the large table.

'The Colonel?' I asked.

'Oh yes,' she said, 'the Colonel.'

I was too perplexed to enquire further.

I sat down and a little while later the various protagonists filed in. The Clerk was a middle-aged man with a beard, the Magistrates were two middle-aged men and one middle-aged woman wearing a striking green hat; and Mr Mulhearn was an ancient and massive man, who grinned at me as he sat down. At this stage there was no sign of the Colonel.

'Up from London, are you?' asked Mr Mulhearn.

'Yes,' I answered.

Mulhearn turned to the Magistrates and repeated to them, 'Up from London, he is,' motioning towards me with his thumb.

'Very nice,' said the lady in the hat and the Clerk may have said, 'Bless him.'

Still no Colonel.

I stood up and the proceedings began.

The first set of cases concerned road traffic offences – which are always dull. We had about 50 speeders who'd been caught by a particularly cunningly placed camera off the Thetford bypass. My opening for each case was exactly the same, it went something like this: 'This matter involves a Mr Harold X, he was driving his Ford Y, on the 25th May, when the Police static camera, 7892VK, photographed him driving at a speed of 37mph in a zone which is governed by a speed limit of 30mph.'

And, for the first 50 or so, the Magistrates simply fined the person £60 and gave them three points to go on their licence. Then, suddenly they got a bit fractious. Without warning, after I'd told them that a Vera Watson had been doing 35mph, the previously disinterested female Magistrate in the hat turned to her two colleagues and said, 'That's a bit unlucky, I mean, isn't there a margin of whatsit?'

'Yes, a margin of error,' said the Chair as the other chap on the bench nodded in agreement. 'Yes, there's a margin of error.'

'I mean, I know that stretch of road,' hat lady continued, 'it's easy to forget that it's a 30.'

For a few seconds I just sat there and listened, I had no idea where their conversation was going. If they suddenly let off Mrs Vera Watson, then they'd have to let off every other driver as well, and in any event, Mrs Watson had pleaded guilty.

At this point, the door opened and in walked a florid-looking gentleman wearing a heavy tweed coat.

The Colonel had arrived.

'Ah, Colonel,' said the Chair, 'you'll know the Thetford Bypass.'

'Indeed I do,' replied the Colonel, 'it's a terrible stretch of road, got one of those damn awful speed cameras on it.'

I now felt as though events were taking on a life of their own. I had spent three years in university and one year at Bar School studying law, and I had no idea whatsoever what role a Colonel could play in events, or indeed whether he was lawfully allowed to play any part at all. Nor was I entirely satisfied that the Magistrates Court had the power to pardon people who had been 'unluckily' caught speeding. And to top matters off, I was also now burning hot from the open fire that was rampaging a few feet behind me, threatening to singe the backside of my best Marks and Spencer suit.

I looked to the Clerk for guidance but he seemed happy to let them all get on with it.

Sweaty and confused, I decided to say something.

'Your Worships,' I ventured gingerly, 'I think that the law about speeding is what we call strict liability – I mean, being a bit unlucky isn't a defence, you've either driven over the speed limit or you haven't.'

The Clerk turned away from me and muttered something to the bench as the Colonel stared at me with his eyes screwed up and his front teeth bared.

'Yes, very well, Mr Winnock,' he said reluctantly, 'we'll accept that. Please carry on.'

I did carry on, Mrs Vera Watson was fined £60 and given three points to put on her licence – she will never know how close she came to being let off.

By mid-afternoon the open fire had rendered the courtroom a furnace. I was sweating profusely and my face had turned a dark shade of red, whilst the Colonel and at least one of the Magistrates were snoozing happily as I read out the facts of one crime after another.

We'd moved away from the road traffic offences and were on to a series of plea hearings. I, as the prosecutor, opened the facts of various incidents of petty crime, and Mr Mulhearn, who represented every single defendant, told the Magistrates Court what they should do. Fair play to him, he was right on every single occasion. He knew about the people, he knew about the circumstances and he knew what the appropriate sentence should be.

Then we came to a case involving a young backpacker, called Jamie Smith, who had stolen a gemstone from a local girl he had gone home with after a night in the Horse and Feathers Pub. He'd been caught at the bus stop the next morning with the gemstone in his rucksack, trying to get a coach to Norwich.

He appeared before the court a rather contrite and pathetic young man who didn't seem able to explain why he'd stolen the stone. Mr Mulhearn clearly had little sympathy for him and rushed his mitigation.

The Chair of the bench looked at me. 'How much was the stone worth, Mr Winnock?' he asked, which, in fact, was a very fair question, but one to which I didn't know the answer.

'I'm not sure,' I said, as I started to leaf through my papers, looking for something that would tell me.

'Well, shouldn't we know?'

'Yes, sir,' I stuttered, as sweat gathered at the small of my back and I started to worry that my nylon suit trousers were about to go up in flames at any moment. 'Yes, ah, here we are. The stone is described as being a small lump of green Beryl. I'm afraid that it doesn't say the value.'

'Oh,' said the Chair, then he looked to the two somnolent Justices of the Peace either side of him and muttered sotto voce, 'Do either of you know the price of Beryl?'

At this point, the Colonel roused himself. 'Beryl, you say?'

'Yes,' we all said.

'Depends on the quality. If it was one carat then just over a hundred pounds, if it was 30 carats, then closer to a hundred and eighty.'

No one questioned the Colonel, no one questioned his right to give expert evidence. I certainly didn't and nor did Mr Mulhearn.

'What do you have to say?' said the Chair to Jamie Smith.

'I'm sorry,' he said, 'I don't know why I did it, I just saw it there and took it. I didn't know it was worth that much.'

The Chair sentenced him to do fifty hours community service. 'If you come to our towns and steal, you'll do some work as punishment,' he said, and we all nodded. It seemed like a proper punishment.

I left that day, hot and sticky from the sweat that had dried on my shirt, and got into my car to drive back down south.

I never went back to that court, they've closed it down now. Like many of the other small town courts and small town firms of solicitors, the perceived wisdom is that they are too expensive to be trusted with the job of ensuring justice. But with each one that disappears, justice takes a step further into the shadows. You see, justice shouldn't be about finance or economics, and in some respects it's not even about the law. It's about the interaction of people, and the communities that they live in and the way they respond to each other and live side by side. If you remove that link between the law and the people, then you make justice a little bit more remote.

Now everything is heard at a massive Law Centre in Ipswich, where no doubt the Colonel isn't even allowed through the door. Are the people better served? Is justice done in a better way? I doubt it. What do you think?

The fall of Kenny McCloud

I was eating an apple when I picked up the slim bundle of papers from my pigeonhole. I looked, without thinking too much, at the top sheet, and could see that it was a letter from my instructing solicitors in McCloud's case. It said simply, *'Counsel will note the content of the Notice of Additional Evidence sent to us by the Crown!'*

The exclamation mark should have told me that something significant was contained in the new evidence. Solicitors don't usually use exclamation marks.

I opened it and started to read as I made my way up to my room. It was a statement from a DC Simons. My first thought was that it was what we call continuity evidence – when a police officer makes a bland and usually uncontroversial statement saying that he oversaw the placing of tapes or evidence in a safe place, so that no one can suggest that something has been tampered with – but this statement was much, much more significant. In the case of Kenny McCloud, it was absolute dynamite.

I telephoned my solicitor straight away and asked them to arrange a conference with McCloud for the next day. Then I put my head on my desk and tried to chase away the images that were forming in my head of the vile timber yard and the most evil man

I had ever met whipping his two little daughters with a dog chain, before tying them up and raping them.

The next day, I met Harry Ashton outside Pentonville for the second time. He looked grim-faced at me. 'You've seen the new evidence then?'

'Yes,' I said.

He nodded. 'Not great for Kenny is it?'

'No,' I said, 'nor his daughters.'

'No,' said Harry, and his already grim face became even grimmer.

We entered Pentonville and made our way through the security and the endless heavy locked doors until we reached the room where Kenny McCloud sat waiting for us.

He seemed more alert than last time, but in every other respect was the same crumbling, decaying human wreck as before.

'Good morning, Kenny,' I said, deliberately using his Christian name. He nodded in response, then exchanged a look with Harry Ashton. He knew that he might be able to kid me, but he wouldn't get anything past the old copper.

I sat down opposite him and looked him firmly in the eye, and took a breath. 'Look,' I said, 'Mr McCloud, the last time we met you told me that you were innocent of these allegations.'

'Aye,' he said, his head trembling just a little as he fixed his eyes on mine.

'And I respect that,' I continued, 'I respect your right to have a trial. And if we have a trial in this matter, then I can assure you that I'll do everything I can to put your case before the jury in the best way I can.'

'If,' he said, his eyes narrowing as he stared at me, 'you said *if* we have a trial.'

I nodded slowly at him, then pushed the Notice of Additional Evidence across the table towards him.

'We received this yesterday,' I said, 'it's a new statement from the leading Detective in this case.'

He glanced down at it, then back at me.

'Would you like me to read it out to you?' I asked.

'No,' he said, 'you can just tell me what it says.'

I began, 'The Detective has acquired your medical records and the medical records of your daughters going back to the 1970s.'

His eyes narrowed further as he considered this.

'It appears that in 1976, you suffered from genital warts and also venereal disease, syphilis.'

He nodded.

'Is that true?' I asked.

He shrugged. 'I can't remember.'

'Well,' I said, 'I've been through the records and it is clear that someone with your name, date of birth and address, was treated for both of these conditions from May 1976.'

He gritted his teeth and began breathing heavily out through his nose.

'It also appears that both your daughters were also treated for genital warts and syphilis at the same time.'

I watched now as his eyes screwed shut, his breathing becoming heavier. I glanced at Harry Ashton, who sat with his mouth slightly open staring at the sight of Kenny McCloud drowning under the weight of what he was being presented with.

'Look,' I continued as gently as I could, more gently than the situation deserved, more gently than this man who had poisoned his own daughters with his inhuman lust deserved.

'You do realise what this means don't you?'

Without opening his eyes, without altering his heavy bull-like breathing, he nodded.

'It means that it is going to be almost impossible for you to win your trial. Medical evidence in a case like this is absolutely damning.'

He continued to nod and I noticed now that tears were pushing themselves through his screwed-up eyes.

'I will do what you tell me, Mr McCloud,' I said. 'If you still want to put this matter before a jury, then I will respect your right to do that, but . . .' I paused, and Harry Ashton finished my sentence for me '. . . but you'd be mad to do so.'

At this point something strange happened, something unexpected, something that you could never be taught about in any textbook or university seminar. McCloud reached his hand across the table and placed it on top of mine. It felt cold and clammy. I wanted to move it, I wanted to move away from the table and run as far away from this monster as I could and scrub my hands with hot soapy water. I had never experienced a situation like this, I had never been this close to someone who had so brutalised the lives of two children: *my* childhood contained nothing like this, *my* childhood was about bikes and fun and games and being told off for not going to sleep and not doing my homework and then kissed on the forehead before bedtime. My childhood was about being dropped off at school and having sweets on a Friday night and moaning about going to the supermarket with my mum. There was none of this darkness in my childhood, there was no timber yard, no dog lead, no waiting with dread to be told by my stinking father that I had to go for a 'walk' with him.

Yet here I was with this man, in his story, the story of him and his weakness and his daughters who had their one and only chance of a happy childhood destroyed by the man who was now holding my hand.

We sat like that for a minute or so, until I had to ask the question, 'Do you want to plead guilty now, Mr McCloud?'

He nodded, all the while never opening his eyes, all the while keeping his hand on mine.

'Okay,' I said, 'look, I've got to ask you this as well – you don't have to answer, but it may help both of us if you do.'

He opened his eyes now and looked at me, finally moving his hand away from mine liberating me from his icy grip, to wipe the tears from his face and smear the lens of his glasses.

'Are your daughters telling the truth about what happened to them?'

He took a deep breath then averted his eyes from mine to the desk, then shook his head slowly. 'I won't answer that, Mr Winnock.'

'Alright,' I said, 'but you realise that I can't really say much on your behalf when you're sentenced if you don't tell me much now.'

He nodded. 'Aye,' he said, 'that's fine.'

I got him to endorse my brief with his instructions that he intended to enter a guilty plea of his own free will, then I shook his hand, feeling once again its clammy stickiness and wishing that I could plunge my own hand in a tub of ice-cold water.

A week later, Kenneth Ernest McCloud was sentenced to sixteen years imprisonment for the rape and indecent assault of his two daughters.

They were both present in court when he was sentenced. They sobbed as the facts of that dark time and that dark place were opened to the court. I turned towards them at one point: two shaking, terrified, middle-aged women, now desperate to grasp what they had left of life, what he had left them to live with.

In mitigation, I simply asked the Judge to give him credit for pleading guilty. There was nothing else I could properly do or say – my job was done.

STRIKE!

On the night before the strike, my dad telephoned me. This was odd. If you asked me how many times my father had picked up a telephone to call me in my adult life, I would have struggled to think of any single occasion. Yet here he was, just before the ten o'clock news, a voice at the end of the line:

'Hi Russ, it's Dad.'

My father comes from a time when dads were understated and quietly masculine; men who neither failed nor succeeded but simply existed to add cement to the structure of the family unit. I don't remember him playing with me, but I'm sure he did; I don't remember him taking me to places, but I know that's not true; I don't remember him teaching me or instilling in me any words of great import, but I know I'm doing him a disservice – because he is responsible for so much that I believe in and hold dear.

He was an English teacher and had retired the year before after forty years in the classroom. Forty years at the same school. They presented him with an original first edition of George Orwell's *1984* at his retirement do and he had struggled to make a speech, his voice breaking and his eyes watering as he tried to thank everyone.

'Were you upset, Dad?' I asked him later. 'No lad,' he said, 'I was overcome by a huge sense of relief that I'd done everything properly.'

That was my father – if a job was worth doing and all that.

He had been the first Winnock ever to go to university in the late 1960s. His dad had been a draper and his grandfather, my great-grandfather, a farm hand. Slowly the Winnocks had moved socially upwards – labourer, artisan, teacher, lawyer. If things continued in this vein, my son would be, what? Member of Parliament? Permanent Private Secretary to the Ministry of Defence? Third member on the left in a Boy Band?

'I was just reading about the barristers' strike, Russ, and I wanted to check that you were alright.'

I was surprised by this. 'Yes, of course, why wouldn't I be?'

'Well,' he said, 'it must be difficult. It says in the paper that barristers have never been on strike before.'

'Technically, we're not on strike,' I told him, 'we're not allowed to strike – technically, we're not going to court because we're all in a meeting.'

'Oh,' said my dad, 'what kind of a meeting?'

'A meeting to talk about what a bunch of bastards the government are for cutting our money.'

He chortled, which made me happy. 'Will you get into trouble?' he asked. 'It says in the *Guardian* that the Bar Council might have to punish anyone who doesn't show up for court.' I now realised that he was concerned about me, about my career, he was worried that I might throw it all away – he was being a dad.

'No,' I said, 'don't worry about that, I'm lucky that I've managed to square it with my clerks and the court, I'll be fine.'

'That's good,' he said, then repeated thoughtfully, 'that's good.' Then there was a pause. Unless we were talking about Huddersfield Town or politics, there were often pauses when we spoke. Eventually he continued, 'Because we support you, you know, me and your mother – I mean, everyone has the right to withdraw their labour if the conditions and the pay aren't fair.'

'Thanks Dad.'

'Sometimes you've got to make a stand.'

'Thanks.'

There was another pause, before he added quietly, 'Just as long as you're going to be alright.'

Then he handed me over to my mother, who asked me the three questions she always asked: did I have a girlfriend yet; was I eating properly; and was I involving myself with any gangsters – her three favourite topics, the answer to each of which was a resounding no.

And so the next day we went on 'strike'. We marched to the Royal Courts of Justice in our wigs and gowns. The juniors from Extempar Chambers had made a massive cartoon replica of the Minister for Justice out of papier mâché. Bloody show-offs.

We stood and chanted rhymes about saving legal aid and justice for all. The Chairman of the Criminal Bar Association and some friendly and worthy politicians made friendly and worthy speeches telling us how important we all were and how it was a fight to the death to save the system of fair and honest justice for all in our country.

I listened and chanted and clapped, and yes, I felt the exhilaration of being part of a crowd. But I felt sad too, that some of the people I was with, good people, honest people, were being forced to make papier mâché effigies and shout about building bonfires and putting the Minister for Justice in the bonfire, which, strictly speaking, is a threat of violence and probably against the code of conduct.

I also felt a touch of embarrassment that I was standing by Jenny Catrell-Jones, who was wearing an Armani suit and carrying a Louis Vuitton handbag and had to leave after a bit to have her nails and hair done – which is hardly akin to the miners in 1984 or the Dockers strike in Liverpool. Because it is true, many of my learned friends *are* from privileged backgrounds and talk about lack of money and dire financial straits in a way that they have only experienced in the abstract.

Not that I begrudged us our right to protest against the cuts in our pay, not at all, because the fight to save the Criminal Bar and legal aid goes far beyond the financial needs of a few young lawyers. I mean, think about it, there you are, an honest, hard-working normal person going about your business, when one day, out of the blue, you have a knock on the door and are confronted by a policeman telling you that someone you love has committed a crime, or worse, that you have been accused of a crime – and you know you haven't done it, or, perhaps you have done it, but it isn't nearly as bad as it's been made out. In those circumstances you would want someone who has a genuine and professional talent to represent you, and the reality is that if the cuts continue then many of the best and brightest will leave the criminal bar and go and do something else.

But, sadly, many in the media don't seem to understand this, and predictably, on the day after our strike, the right-wing press had a field day, ignoring the issues that were being raised and focusing instead on the expensive handbags and suits of those who were on strike. 'Fat Cat Barristers Man the Picket Lines,' said one headline, whilst another asked, 'Is This the Most Privileged Picket Line Ever?'

Eventually, as the applause for the last speaker subsided and the reluctant strikers traipsed away to prepare for the next day in court, I retired to the pub with a few of my new comrades. I felt like getting pissed and thirstily quaffed my first pint before spotting my roommate, Angus Tollman, by the bar. He was with

James Conroy, an experienced old hack from another chambers. I went to join them; Conroy was already in mid rant. 'Ten years ago no barrister worth his salt would admit to having financial difficulties, to say you were skint was the same as saying you were crap. But now, I don't mind admitting it, I owe the Revenue a fortune, and it's not because I can't do my job, it's because they don't bother paying me. If I'm not made bankrupt this year, I'll eat my wig.'

'What did you think of the demonstration then?' I asked them.

Conroy gave a weary shrug, before adding dismissively, 'For all the good it will do us. We're Pandas, boys, and the bamboo is fast running out. If I were your age, I'd go and do something else.' He sighed and downed his pint, before adding sarcastically, 'And what did those idiots from Extempar Chambers think they looked like with that massive bloody cartoon thing! I suppose it'll get them on the telly.'

I grinned. 'Yes, any more legal aid cuts and they'll have to sell their espresso machine.' I turned to Angus Tollman. 'What about you, Angus? What did you think?'

He averted his eyes for a second, looking uncomfortable. 'I wasn't there.'

'Oh,' I said. I was shocked by this, I felt my hackles go up, I was now expecting a bit of a row. I found myself poised to tell him that he had let us all down by breaking the strike, and that it was alright for him with his wealthy background – but saving legal aid was important for those without his family's wealth. Instead I just asked him why, as abrasively as I could.

'Well,' he answered, 'I've been defending in a sexual assault trial this week.'

I nodded, I'd heard him talk about it.

'We asked the Judge if the court wouldn't sit today to allow us to join the action, but she wouldn't let us. She said that if we didn't turn up, she would be . . .' he paused and did the air quotes gesture with his fingers, '. . . "disappointed".'

'Which Judge?' I asked.

'Palfryman,' he said, which surprised me, Her Honour Judge Palfryman always gave the impression of being as helpful as she could to the Bar. 'We were halfway through the evidence of a young kid, you see,' he continued, 'there was no way that the court wouldn't sit, we couldn't make the kid wait another two days before finishing his evidence. I can understand that, the kid was only nine years old.'

I understood too. The Judge was right. Angus was right. I wouldn't be taking him to task, he would be spared my revolutionary zeal. He had done what all of us would have done – no case involving a child giving evidence about a sexual assault could be adjourned, and no decent barrister would have allowed that to happen. I just wished that the *Daily-bloody-Mail* and all the others who called us fat cats and accused us of being out to save our own pay packets could understand this.

Football, violence, and the case
of Archie Finch

I arrived at City Crown Court to represent Archie Finch in a matter of violent disorder full of confidence. In case you're wondering, Archie Finch isn't his real name, he's the son of a footballer, obviously not called Finch, who played for Arsenal and Chelsea about thirty years ago.

The thing about Archie was that, although just like his dad he adored the beautiful game, he was more interested in the dark side of football: the violence, and everything that went with it – the careful organisation that would see the meeting of two rival gangs, the culture, the camaraderie, the fashion, the pursuit of the weak, the flight from helmeted police on horseback, counting the casualties and reliving it all down the pub afterwards.

Archie had been at it for years. He was an elder statesman in one of the long-established Chelsea crews – organised football hooliganism at its most brutal.

He and about 50 of his mates had ambushed a load of lads from Birmingham, but unfortunately for them, the police had prior knowledge of it and had pursued the Chelsea boys down a dead end and arrested Archie and a few others.

And now, here he was in the Crown Court on charges of violent disorder.

I swung into the robing room with the instructions to represent him clutched firmly in my fist. This was great: a multi-handed case with other barristers with a collegiate atmosphere replacing the usual feeling of being on your own, having to make decisions yourself and taking all the stress on your own shoulders. Jenny Catrell-Jones was for one of the other defendants. She was already haranguing the poor prosecutor, a CPS in-house lawyer called Adam Sinclair, who faced the dreadful prospect of having to fend off a pack of six barristers. For him, it would be the same loneliness and stress, but worse because he was outnumbered by those of us on the defence side.

'No,' he said, trying to avert himself from Jenny's steeliest glare, 'I'm not prepared to let you out of it.'

'Why?' said Jenny. 'My client is a man of impeccable character – he's the manager of a clothes shop on Oxford Street, have a heart will you, Adam, for god's sake.'

'No,' repeated Adam.

'Well where's the evidence?' continued Jenny.

'Jenny, it's all on CCTV.'

'The quality is rubbish.'

'The quality is brilliant.'

Jenny scowled as she turned towards me. 'Bloody CCTV. It's the bane of our lives. You know, Russell, there was a time when a case like this would be a joy – loads of pissed-up witnesses all saying something different, there would be three-week trials, loads of pages, and a nice fat cheque at the end of it all – now, it's all captured on CC-bloody-TV. I mean you can't do anything in public these days without it being captured in High Definition – how's anyone supposed to plead not guilty to anything?'

She paused. 'Anyway, who are you for?'

'Archie Finch,' I said.

'Oh,' she said, 'they gave you Finchey did they? Good luck.'

I wasn't sure what she meant by this – but I was soon to find out.

I met Archie Finch in the foyer. He was a heavily set man, muscular and with an air of menace. He had tattoos up one arm professing his love for Chelsea FC and someone called Keeley. He had small eyes and looked as though he would be ready for an argument at the drop of a hat.

I led him to a small conference room, and gave him my usual cheery speech about it being his case and me doing anything he instructed. He sat there calmly, displaying no emotion whatsoever. Then I told him about the CCTV. 'I've watched it, and I have to say, it doesn't look good, Mr Finch. At one point you are seen throwing a police dog at a horse.'

He nodded, then his body language changed and he leaned towards me. 'This is what's going to happen, Mr Winnock,' he said politely, but somewhat menacingly. 'You're going to go to the prosecutor and tell him that all the boys will plead guilty to an affray.'

'I'm not sure I can do that, Mr Finch,' I said, 'I can only speak for you.'

He nodded again. 'I understand that,' he said, 'but, you can tell their barristers that is what will happen and the rest of the lads will fall into line.'

'Okay. But what makes you think that the prosecutor will accept a plea to the lesser charge?'

'Come on, Mr Winnock,' said Finch, 'you know better than that. What prosecutor would go through the hassle of having a trial on a violent disorder when there's a plea to affray on offer?'

I was now being completely dominated by my client. He was telling me things, rather than the other way round – this wasn't how it was supposed to be.

'But you'll still probably get a prison sentence, even for an affray,' I ventured, trying to reclaim some semblance of control.

'Yes,' he said, 'but we both know that sentence is going to be in months, not the years I'd get for a violent disorder.'

He was right.

He *was* in control.

'Just as long as I don't get a banning order,' he added.

'I'm afraid that's inevitable,' I said.

'No,' he replied, 'it's not.'

'I think it is,' I suggested, rather meekly.

Finch was forceful, yet polite, as he recited, chapter and verse, the correct section of the Football Spectators Act that meant, in law, a Judge didn't have to give him a banning order which would prevent him from attending football matches upon his release.

His small eyes bored into me. He had fought on terraces in the 1980s, he had caused mayhem abroad in various tournaments, he was fearless, completely mad, and knew a great deal more than I did about the law in relation to football banning orders. I was quite petrified of him.

'I'll check that,' I said nervously.

'No need, Mr Winnock – I'm right.'

He was right, of course he was right – and I felt pretty stupid.

As he predicted, the prosecutor happily accepted the affray and he and his five co-defendants all duly pleaded guilty. And as he predicted, the Judge reluctantly accepted that he couldn't ban them from football stadia, so instead he gave them twelve months imprisonment.

Finch smiled as he went down; he knew he'd be out in less than six months, ready to get back to doing the thing he loved most – fighting.

I left court chastened. I didn't feel particularly learned, I had met my match.

The unwilling criminal

Archie Finch knew exactly what he was doing; he knew that he was going to commit a crime the moment he sent out a message to a few of his closest and most trusted lieutenants telling them that the firm from Aston Villa would be waiting on some disused land off the Talgarth Road. He knew when he ran towards them, shouting 'We are Chelsea, super Chelsea,' with a stick in his hand, before going on to pick up a police Alsatian and attempt to throw it at a police horse, that he was committing a crime. He knew it, he craved it, and he took the decision of his own free will. He was now starting his prison sentence and he could have no complaints.

There are many like him, those who make that decision to burgle a house or download indecent images or sell drugs, people who know from the moment that they form that intention to carry out that particular act that they are in danger of going to prison – because they know that society doesn't actually tolerate what they're about to do.

Peter Drake on the other hand hadn't meant to commit any crime. Peter Drake was a vet. A man of 62 years with an unblemished record of good works and good behaviour. He had never been in trouble in his life, he meant no harm to anyone.

159

One evening in October a couple of years ago, Peter Drake went for a pint in his local, The Grasshopper. It wasn't something he did very often, but that evening, he nipped in to meet his practice partner, Graham Laugherty. Graham was late, so Peter Drake had a pint of bitter. Then, when Graham arrived, he bought him a second pint of bitter. They talked for about fifty minutes, during which time, Peter Drake, being a nice kind of fellow, bought Graham a pint back.

And one for himself.

And it was that one for himself that took him over the legal limit for driving. That one last pint as they discussed the possibility of changing the brands of a certain drug that they stocked for worming cats; that last pint as they watched the quiet pub ease into the evening. One more wouldn't do any harm. When they'd finished it, Graham offered to get another round in, and Peter Drake put his hand over the top of his glass and said, 'No thanks, I'd better not, I'm driving.'

He said that because he didn't want to be a criminal, but he became one the moment he sat down behind the wheel of his car and started the engine. Peter Drake thought he'd be fine, it was, after all, only two miles to his home and he'd only had a couple – well, three – pints, but still, what could go wrong?

He drove through the centre of his village. He drove towards the zebra crossing, a crossing that he had stopped at thousands of times. And just before he did, he leant over to get his mobile phone, which had slipped into the footwell of his passenger seat, and he started to send his wife a text message telling her to put the tea on.

And in that second, over the limit and distracted by the act of sending a text message to his wife to tell her he was on his way home, he drove his car into Miss Julie-Anne Botham and her baby daughter Charlotte and killed them both.

He had meant no harm. He had not intended to break the law. He hadn't meant to cause immeasurable and everlasting suffering to the Botham family. He had simply had one pint too many and texted his wife.

I received the papers in the case of The Crown v Peter Drake and cringed. Cases involving Death by Dangerous Driving are always awful – it is difficult to find justice in these cases, no one involved has set out to harm anyone else when they wake up that day. Peter Drake had broken the law by his own stupidity not by his intent. But, saying that, the young woman and her baby had not deserved to die. There would be no winners here.

I met Harry Ashton, the old Met copper and solicitor's outdoor clerk in the robing room at suburbs Crown Court.

'Is he here, Harry?' I asked, and he told me that Peter Drake had been here since they opened the doors an hour ago.

'Bad business this, isn't it?' I said.

And Harry shook his head. 'No sympathy,' he said emphatically.

'Really?' I enquired. 'Come on, we've all chanced our arm after a couple of pints, he was barely over the limit.'

'It's not that,' said Harry, 'three pints and most people drive even better, it's the texting. Any tosser who texts whilst driving and kills a young mum and a baby deserves everything they get.'

We went downstairs to the foyer to meet Peter Drake. He was sat on his own, lonely and nervous, totally out of place amongst the druggies and the wife-beaters, the fraudsters and the wastrels.

'You're going to have to plead guilty,' I told him. 'The police have looked at your phone and found the text that you sent to your wife seconds before the collision.'

He nodded, quietly sighed then asked, 'Will I be sentenced today?'

'Yes,' I told him, 'the Probation Service have written your report, so the Judge will want to sentence you immediately.'

He nodded at me with thin lips and sad eyes.

'I've packed a bag,' he said, 'I didn't know what to bring.'

I looked at the small tweed holdall he had in his hand. The type of thing a middle-aged, middle-class man would take on a golfing weekend away or a business trip. I imagined its contents – a matching zip-up wash bag, neatly folded pyjamas and a nice shaving kit.

'I'm sure it'll be fine,' I said.

The court was packed. The family and friends of the deceased had all turned up, they always do in cases like this – I don't know if it's part of the grieving process or what, but for some reason, there is a desire amongst those close to a deceased person to see the final reckoning of the person who was at the wheel.

Some of them were wearing pink T-shirts with a picture of the dead little girl and her dead mother, to show their solidarity. Peter Drake walked head down into the dock. There were a few murmurings of hissed hate projected towards him. He sat alone, utterly guilty, utterly shamed and utterly scared.

I knew the next forty minutes were going to be difficult. I knew that nothing I said would have any bearing upon the inevitable sentence that was awaiting Peter Drake; I also knew that if I wasn't careful, I could incur the hatred of the pink-T-shirt-wearing family of the two innocent people who had died as a result of my client's folly. They hate him, and I'm the bastard who is representing him, I'm the one who they can project their hatred towards. How can you represent a monster like that? That is the question they all want to ask of me.

The Judge came in – Judge Percy, you remember him – he's a nice Judge, perfect for a case like this. I knew that Judge Percy would ensure that everyone was treated fairly, I knew that he would resist the temptation to treat Peter Drake like the murderer the people in pink thought he was.

The prosecutor, Raj Hasan, told the Judge the awful facts, and they were awful – Peter Drake's Volvo was doing about 35 miles per hour when it hit the mum and the pram, knocking the seven-month-old baby fifteen feet into the air. The mother then died of internal bleeding, her last words were to ask about her little girl.

As Hasan went through the facts, a woman, who I took to be the woman's mother, the baby's nan, was helped, sobbing, from the court.

Inwardly, I groaned. What could I say? How could words ever do justice to the way any of these people were feeling? How could I possibly have conveyed my client's utter wretchedness, how his previously blemish-free life had been torn apart by his own mistake? A single mistake. His life ended that day as well.

I got up to my feet and asked the Judge if he had read the fifteen references that had been written on behalf of Peter Drake.

'Yes, thank you, Mr Winnock,' he said.

They were good references as well – kind words from local councillors and doctors and lawyers and other upstanding members of the community, and one from his wife, who tells of his love for her, their two children and four grandchildren. She wasn't at court because he told her not to be. He knew she had already suffered enough.

'Your Honour,' I said, 'Peter Drake is a man who knows that the family of Julie-Ann and Charlotte will never recover from the terrible way in which their lives were taken from them. Your Honour, he knows that it is no consolation to them. Every waking moment of every day he regrets what he did more deeply and profoundly than I can possibly articulate.'

Judge Percy nodded, it wasn't easy for him either. I continued. I wasn't on my feet for long, only long enough to tell the Judge about Peter Drake's remorse, and how he helped treat the injured woman, and how his life was now devastated. The last point provoked an angry comment from the public gallery of the court, so I didn't labour it. They were right, he may have been devastated, but at least he was still here.

Judge Percy sentenced him to four years imprisonment.

His life as a vet and a pillar of the community was over. He would never again nip down to his local and chat with the landlord in the free and easy way of a man of good character. He would never hold his head up in the same way; for the rest of his days, there would be a voice in the back of his mind that would remind him in whispered tones that he had killed a baby and a young mother – everything he did would come back to that.

The family and friends in pink didn't think the sentence was long enough. How can it be fair, they said, four years, for the lives of a beautiful young woman and her baby? And they're right – it wasn't enough.

But in this case, there was no right, there was no justice – there was just law and process.

I left court as quickly as I could.

Wigs and gowns

You probably won't have done this research yourself – so I'm going to help you. If you search the Internet, you will find websites to satisfy every sexual proclivity known to man and woman, but you won't find anything relating to sexy barristers wearing a wig and gown. It just doesn't exist, because no one finds barristers in wigs and gowns remotely sexy.

No one.

I mean, and trust me on this, there are websites about sexy plumbers, websites about sexy vicars, websites about nuns and monks and teachers (tons about teachers), there are even websites dedicated to sexy librarians – but not a single one that will show people, learned or otherwise, dressed in wigs and gowns and posing in a provocative way.

Why? Because they are just not sexy.

You never get adverts with the hunky barrister in his wig and gown, emerging in slow motion through flames with a puppy in his arms. A horsehair wig and austere black cape just doesn't do it for anyone.

I once had a brief fling with an Irish girl, not long after I'd started at the Bar. One night after a few drinks we were back at mine and she asked me if I would put on my wig and gown. On request, I went into the bedroom, donned my courtroom kit and re-entered the lounge in what I hoped was a provocative way.

She looked at me, her face fell, and she left twenty uncomfortable minutes later.

When she declined my invitation to go for a drink some other time, she told me that it wasn't me it was her, and that she saw me more as a friend. But I knew the truth, it was the sight of me in my barrister's clobber. After that, she could never see me in the same way again. To her I had become devoid of sex.

And that, I suppose, is actually why we still wear them, in your wig and gown you are neutered and anonymous.

Some would get rid of the wig and gown in a flash. My mate, Ed Douglas – you remember him, the brainy guy at the Chancery Bar – he'd get rid of them in a second. He describes them as anachronistic and divisive. 'How can you,' he tells me, 'with your lower-middle-class comprehensive school background, be in favour of something that has its roots in the privileges of the nineteenth century?'

'I do,' I say, 'and long may the wig and gown continue.'

There have, in the last few years, been attempts to do away with them. There was a ballot a couple of years ago, but the overwhelming majority of criminal barristers voted to keep the ancient outfit.

And that's how I voted, in favour of retention, and enthusiastically so, even though my own wig makes me look fat, rather weird and about as sexy as a pot of yoghurt.

So, why?

Well, it's a bit like this: in my wig I am no longer Russell Winnock. I am no longer a man who enjoys the music of Neil Young, supports Huddersfield Town, watches Scandinavian detective TV dramas and once fell madly in love with a girl called Becky. I am merely a functionary of the court, I am 'Learned Mr

Winnock', I am the prosecutor or the defence advocate, I am the person who asks questions of witnesses but doesn't have to answer them.

I am allowed to be all of these things because of the disguise of the wig. It brings anonymity, it turns me from a person into simply another player in the theatre of the court.

There you are, telling a girl that she wasn't really raped, that she was completely consenting to the act of having sex with this random stranger. You know that it's rubbish, your client knows it's rubbish, the jury have already decided that it's rubbish and condemned the defendant, yet you have to go through it as best you can, regardless of the pain you are causing, because that is your job, that is your role in the system.

Some people think that we enjoy that, and perhaps sometimes we do, but not always, and that's why the wig and gown helps. It means that at the end of the day you can take it off and walk away, and that act of transforming yourself from being a barrister back to being a human being – someone who would never in ordinary day-to-day life make such an assertion or ask such a question – completes the metamorphosis back to normality.

Murder

I was in my room with Amir Saddique, who was reading me extracts from an article on a Spurs website, which suggested that they were about to buy a player from an unknown Brazilian team for forty million quid.

'I mean forty million!' exclaimed Amir. 'That's just crazy. What kind of business spends that much money on something as brittle and as untested as a Brazilian midfielder, it's bonkers.'

Before I had time to tell him that at Huddersfield Town the nearest we get to a Brazilian is when one of the girls who serves behind the bar gets her bikini line done, the phone went and I was summoned down to the Senior Clerk's room.

I felt fairly confident that I was not in any trouble, but still, the summons from Clem Wilson is always enough to make your heart beat with a more trepidatious rhythm. That rhythm turned to outright fear, however, when I went through the door and spied Mrs Murdoch and Kelly Backworth of Whinstanley and Cooper Solicitors, who you will remember have said they would not instruct me if I was the last barrister on earth.

I looked from face to face, my eyes finally resting on Clem. I felt sure that they were about to tell me that Porky Phi had been killed by her husband, and that it was all my fault.

Clem talked first and seemed oddly upbeat. 'Look, Mrs Murdoch,' he said, 'young Mr Winnock here is absolutely petrified.'

She looked stony-faced.

Clem now smiled at me in a rather slimy way. 'They've come to give you a brief,' he said.

'Eh?'

'You recently represented someone called Shandra Whithurst,' interrupted Mrs Murdoch.

I nodded.

'Well,' she said, 'it turns out that Miss Whithurst was very happy with the way you represented her.'

'Er, good,' I stammered.

I was now utterly confused as to why Mrs Murdoch and Kelly Backworth were here talking about a shoplifter I managed to get off a few weeks earlier.

'Well,' continued Mrs Murdoch, 'Shandra has a niece, called Tasha Roux.'

'Yes?'

'Who is currently in a police cell having been arrested on suspicion of murdering her partner.'

'Right,' I said, still unsure what this had to do with me.

'She's likely to be charged with murder in the morning, and, despite our best attempts, her aunt, Miss Whithurst, will only accept you as her barrister.'

'Me?'

'Yes.'

I tried to stifle a smile as the penny dropped and cascaded from my brain to my twitching lips. I looked over to Kelly, who seemed to be stifling a smile as well, though I might be wrong.

Clem interjected, 'Yes, Mr Winnock, I've told Mrs Murdoch that you'll be quite happy to be the junior in a murder case, won't you?'

Would I? Too bloody right I would. My first murder. This is

precisely why I came to the Bar in the first place. This was a proper case!

Good old Shandra Whithurst. God bless her. I felt like laughing out loud, but thankfully realised that would be wholly unprofessional.

Mrs Murdoch continued, 'Of course, you'll be applying for a QC to lead you.'

'Of course.'

'Good, and Kelly here will be the fee earner from our place doing the brief. You two can start work on it this afternoon, if that's okay?'

I smiled now. I couldn't help it.

'It'll be a pleasure,' I said, 'but, Mrs Murdoch,' I ventured, 'I thought that you wouldn't instruct me if I was the last barrister on earth. I thought I was NIHWTLBOE?'

The old solicitor scowled. 'For reasons best known to her, Mr Winnock, Miss Shandra Whithurst thinks that you are the *only* barrister on earth.'

I smiled again as Mrs Murdoch bade us all good day and left the room. I looked at Kelly – Christ, she was gorgeous.

'What's it all about then?' I asked her.

'She's killed her boyfriend, probably in self-defence.'

Brilliant. A proper issue in a murder trial. This was exactly what I'd been waiting for ever since I'd sat down with my mum and dad and watched *Kavanagh QC* on the telly all those years ago. This would be my biggest case yet. Thank you, thank you, thank you, Shandra Whithurst.

Facebook

That night, I placed the few skimpy pages concerning Tasha Roux on my kitchen table and looked at them. The facts were these: Tasha Roux was 23 years old and had pushed her partner, a man named Gary Dickinson, over the stairwell of the sixth floor of their block of flats, killing him. In her interview she had claimed she had pushed him in self-defence.

All I had was a few statements from police officers saying that they had arrived to find Tasha crying by the top of the stairwell and Gary Dickinson dead at the bottom. There were also a couple of statements from neighbours saying they'd heard one almighty row, followed by a scream.

I read them, listening initially to my chanting monks – which was too creepy in the circumstances, so I changed and listened to The Cocteau Twins, whose unfathomable lyrics and ethereal guitars worked just fine – then, out of curiosity, I clicked onto Facebook and checked the profile page of my client Tasha Roux.

It isn't the first time I've checked the Facebook page of a client or a witness in a case, and yes, it is true, I confess, that if the witness or client is a woman under 30, I'm slightly more likely to do so than if it is some meathead bloke in his forties.

The Facebook page of Tasha Roux was just as I expected it to be. There were pictures of her with groups of girls of a similar age, smiling and holding drinks, wearing their best frocks, pouting and tilting their heads like all girls seem to do when they're having their photo taken in a nightclub.

And, chillingly, there were pictures of her and the deceased Gary Dickinson, together, by a swimming pool, with blue sky behind them and the clean plastic white of a sun lounger beneath them as they smiled for the camera.

I formed an instant impression of both of them.

She was beautiful, young and slim. She didn't look vulnerable though, in fact quite the opposite. She had a small tattoo on her shoulder and a strong, street-wise texture to her face and lips. She was no fragile beauty, but rather a woman whose looks might see her end up with the wrong kind of man.

As for Dickinson, I probably shouldn't say it, but I instantly had him down as a twat. A hard man, clearly very impressed with his own biceps, who almost certainly had a string of convictions for violence and drugs and petty crime. He had short hair and a menacing closed-mouth smile. His tattoos spelt out the names of children he'd sired and the parents who outlived him.

There were already comments on her Facebook page. Some were supportive, some not. One said, *'Stay strong bby – we luv ya XXX'*, whilst another hoped that she would '*rot in hell*' and called her a skank and a whore.

I sighed. Bloody Facebook.

It's massive, we all know that, but what many won't have considered is the way in which it has become increasingly significant in the courts, and in particular the Criminal and Family Courts. There is rarely a case today in which Facebook doesn't play some kind of role.

Sometimes it is used to help in the identification of witnesses. Increasingly, victims or witnesses will be told the name of the person who allegedly beat them up or mugged them, and, armed with this information, they then go onto Facebook and confirm the identity. And this is a problem, it's fraught with difficulties. It's not a proper identification, particularly if they've made it before they've made a statement to the police. Think about it. Normally, an individual makes a statement to the police in which they describe the individual who they say committed the crime. They tell the police officer that the person has, perhaps, brown hair and blue eyes and is about six foot and as much else as they can remember, and if the issue of identification is important (if the suspect denies it's him), then there will be an identification parade.

But if the person looks at Facebook before talking to the police, the description that they give to the police isn't a description of the person they remember committing the offence, but a description of the person they've seen on Facebook, who they've been told may have committed the offence. And, with the best will in the world, they may have got that wrong. It is, as I say, fraught with danger.

Then there's the temptation for jurors to do what I've done and go onto Facebook and look at the pictures and profile pages of those who are involved in the case. Like me, they'll make instant judgements about someone based on their photos and comments, and yes, like me, the judgements will be unfair and more often than not wrong. Judges now have to warn jurors about going on Facebook. They tell them that in doing so they risk going to prison for contempt of court, and the jurors sit there and nod, but I often wonder how many jurors have a little sneaky look, just to be nosey. After all, as long as they keep quiet about it, no one will know. But it does pervert the process, because that juror will have been party to some information that no one else has seen, which the defendant has no chance whatsoever of rebutting.

But Facebook doesn't just affect witnesses and jurors; the Internet has created new crimes that people commit that they couldn't before. Crimes involving the grooming of underage girls and boys for sex by old perverts who masquerade on Facebook as teenagers.

Or that chap in the North West who, during the riots a few years ago, wrote on his Facebook page that he was going to start a riot in his home town. Even though everyone told him not to be so stupid, no one actually lifted a finger in anger and the bloke himself never actually left his house let alone threw a petrol bomb or looted a branch of Sports Direct, he received a prison sentence of four years for his trouble.

Similarly, I once represented a young woman who had posted the name of a rape victim on her Facebook page – which is a crime. I asked her why she had done it and she told me that she put everything on her Facebook page. That was the way she communicated, everything went on there – every thought, every picture, every night out, every argument, everything. She couldn't understand what she had done wrong. I remember asking her if she thought that was wise, and then immediately regretted asking, because to her it was a way of expressing herself, and who am I to criticise that.

I clicked onto my own Facebook page. Johnny Richardson had sent me a message inviting me to his '*Off to Dubai Leaving Party*'. No doubt once he was gone I'd keep in contact with Johnny through Facebook. He would post pictures of him and his smiling wife on camels, in casinos and on beaches, and I would comment and feel close to him, whereas in reality the relationship wouldn't be the same.

I went to turn my computer off but stopped, paused, and clicked onto another Facebook page. Kelly Backworth's page. I looked at her profile picture as the rest of her pictures were for friends only, and I wasn't, yet, one of those. Her profile picture didn't really do her justice, it was of her standing outside a church, probably at a wedding. I toyed with the idea of asking her to be my friend, but I decided against it. I didn't want her to think that I was touting for work *or* trying to shag her, either way would be totally inappropriate. After all I had a brief in a murder case now. That, surely, made me a serious barrister.

I took one last peek at her profile. Under relationship status it said 'blank'. What did that mean? Did she have a bloke? Was she single? Bloody Facebook telling us everything and nothing of importance.

I turned my computer off. Soon I would actually meet Tasha Roux in person, not a face on a computer. An actual person facing the most damning charge of all: murder.

The case of the sizzling Gypsy sisters

Another question I've been asked over the years, granted, usually by blokes, is whether I've ever fancied one of my clients, or worse, ever been tempted to have, for want of a better expression, a fling with any of them.

The answer to that is a resounding no.

As you will have gathered, most of my criminal clients are male and, even if I was that way inclined, almost always in the clutch of some kind of addiction which usually comes with an associated unpleasant medical condition. As for my female clients, though they are not universally unattractive, the reality is that the places we meet, and the circumstances of our brief relationships, means that romance – or even a bit of harmless rumpy-pumpy – is about as far from our collective minds as it is possible to be. And in any event, one glimpse of me in my wig and cape and even the most committed nymphomaniac would be rendered passionless and indifferent.

Of course the Bar Council would disapprove of any kind of inappropriate behaviour between a client and her or his learned advocate. And quite right too.

However, I must confess, and after all this is a book about confessions, that I did have a brief unprofessional thought during the case of one Maggie Casey.

Ms Casey was a traveller, a proper Gypsy girl complete with model looks, a massive family, an unfathomable Irish accent and a rather reckless attitude to the law of the land, shoplifting in particular.

She had been accused of stealing a water pistol from Woolworths in Basildon.

And I, as a very junior barrister barely out of Bar School, had been sent to represent her.

Her instructions were that her nine-year-old brother Joseph had picked up the pistol and put it in her bag and that she had known nothing of the theft until she was stopped at the doors. This was significant because Joseph, being only nine, was under the age of criminal responsibility and therefore couldn't be prosecuted, but Maggie, being seventeen, could. I got the feeling the Casey family knew this.

When I entered the waiting area of Basildon Mags, I was confronted by what appeared to be a dance troupe: a gaggle of young, beautiful women, all wearing incredibly tight clothes and with immaculate make-up. Frankly, I'd never seen so much fake tan in my life.

As I stood there, they all looked up at me and I felt my throat instantly dry up. 'Er, is anyone here called Margaret Casey?' I asked, and was met with a barrage of giggles.

'I am,' came the answer, and a long-lashed, flaxen-haired lovely in an astonishingly low cut top stood up from one of the seats and walked towards me. Five other girls, similarly dressed, followed behind her.

'And these are my sisters, Mary, Molly, Magda, Shona and Patty,' she paused, 'and that little shite is Joseph,' pointing at a grubby little lad with a crew cut, 'the fecking reason we're here.'

'Right,' I said. 'Okay. I'm your barrister, Russell, Russell Winnock.' I felt my blue polyester M&S tie tighten around my neck as I became conscious of the fact that I was desperately trying not to look at her chest, or come to that, any of her five sisters' chests.

'Shall we go and find a room where we can talk?' I asked.

This suggestion, which I make to all my clients, provoked further giggling.

'Can my sisters come as well?' asked Maggie.

'It's better if we're alone,' I suggested, cue more giggling and a very twinkling smile from Maggie. 'If you say so, Russell,' she said, and she may have winked.

Maggie Casey won her trial. The Magistrates heard little Joseph make a rather rehearsed admission that he had meant no harm and didn't understand that you had to pay for the gun and that his sister had no idea, and, 'as God was above him,' he'd do everything he could to make amends. A confession which he repeated word for word, when he was cross-examined by the prosecutor.

Afterwards I bade the girls goodbye, shook a couple of them by the hand, wallowed in a bit more giggling, and left the court building to make my way towards the car park. After I had gone about 50 yards or so I heard a shout.

'Mr Winnock.'

I turned around and could see that Maggie and her sisters were standing in a row a few metres from the front of the court building.

'Which one of us has got the nicest arse?'

With that, the six girls mooned me.

I grinned all the way back to chambers. I bet that never happened to Lord Denning.

Bail

I walked into the City Magistrates Court with my chin up and my head back. I wasn't there for the poxy motoring list, or some fight outside a kebab shop just after closing time. I wasn't defending some junkie who'd been caught stealing razor blades and legs of lamb from supermarkets (strangely, the items of choice for shoplifting drug addicts), or a kid passing joints around his mates. No, I was there for the first hearing in a murder case. My first ever murder case. And to mark the occasion, and in an attempt to appear as barrister-like as I possibly could, I'd decided to wear my most garish pin-striped suit, one which I usually avoided as it made me look like a bit of a pompous arse.

But today that was precisely the look I was aiming for, because I was counsel on a murder and that, as far as I was concerned, made me the most important barrister in the building – and didn't I bloody know it.

I met Kelly Backworth in the foyer and walked up to the door of court one, where I was accosted by Shandra Whithurst. 'Mr Winnock,' she said, 'thank god that you are here.'

'Hello, Miss Whithurst,' I said, in a voice that I assumed was similar in tone to that used by superheroes when they're being thanked by people they've just saved from burning buildings, 'how lovely to see you again.'

'She's not guilty of this,' said Shandra, 'I swear to you, Mr Winnock, she is not guilty of this. That Dickinson man was a complete thug, he used to beat her and pimp her out and everything.'

I frowned, and glanced at Kelly, who was standing close by, as ever, giving absolutely nothing away.

'I tell you what, Miss Whithurst,' I said, 'I'm going to speak to Tasha, then, at some point, I'd like you and me to have a proper chat about everything. Is that alright?'

She nodded, then thanked me again, then grabbed both of my hands and assured me that Tasha was essentially a good girl.

This was good. This was me as Counsel in a murder case, this was me being confident and clever in my pin-striped suit. I swanned into court and declared loudly that I was there to represent Tasha Roux.

At this, the court went quiet. A group of men of a certain age, build and haircut, who were conferring at the back of court, turned to me and looked me up and down. Clearly this was the murder squad, and standing with them was Josh Benedict-Brown of Extempar Chambers. Josh is a very confident and very able barrister a couple of years senior to me. He is clearly expensively educated and speaks with a plum in his mouth and a whole bag of plums stuck up his arse and, annoyingly, he was wearing an even more garish pin-striped suit than me. Damn. His suit was every inch the alpha suit in the room.

'Hi Russ,' he said, before adding caustically, 'you been sent to do the legwork in the Mags for this Roux case?'

'No,' I smiled, 'this is my brief.'

'Oh, well done,' he said, making no effort to hide his surprise, 'first murder brief?'

This threw me. The truthful answer was 'yes', but I didn't want to let on to anyone, especially the whole bloody murder squad, that I was green in the ways of cases involving dead people.

The words, 'not especially,' came tripping out of my mouth, which confused both Josh and me. He looked at me for a second, then asked me if I would be applying for bail.

'Yes,' I said.

'Well you won't get it will you?'

'We'll see,' I said, though I knew he was probably right.

I turned to the Clerk of the Court and introduced myself. 'Russell Winnock,' I told her, 'here to represent Tasha Roux.' She seemed uninterested. 'We'll get to you in about ten minutes, Mr Winnock, the Judge wants to get you away.'

'Okay,' I said, then started to look around for anyone else who I felt needed to know that I was in the courtroom and that my client was faced with a charge of murder.

'Perhaps we should go and see Tasha now,' said Kelly, who didn't seem particularly impressed with my posturing.

'Oh, yes, right.'

We left the court and made our way past the usual suspects, then down the steps that led to the cells, through the security doors, past disinterested security guards and into the corridor of locked doors. Behind each and every door, I knew, would be a tragic tale, but today I was only interested in one such tale.

Tasha Roux sat quietly in her cell. She looked very different from her Facebook page. In Facebookworld she was confident and sassy, opinionated and outgoing, she went on sunny holidays and drank cocktails. Here, in this dark cell, she was scared – plain and simple.

'Miss Roux?' I asked, and she nodded. 'Hi,' I said gently, 'I'm Russell, I'm here to look after you.'

She nodded again, I could tell that she was sizing me up, I

could tell that she was asking herself the question 'Is this man on my side?'

And I was. As I stood there looking at her in her prison garb, I was most definitely on her side. I vowed that I would do all I could to help this young woman. And that is what I told her.

'I'm going to ensure that you get the very best representation throughout your trial,' I said, 'and, I'm going to try to get you bail,' before adding quickly, 'but, Tasha, don't get your hopes up. The chances are that they won't give you bail because of the seriousness of the charge.'

She nodded, then added with a reed-like voice, 'Will I be found guilty?'

I breathed in, then sighed deeply before answering, 'I don't know,' I said. 'Look, I'll tell you what, I'll come and see you next week wherever you are and we can talk about it properly then. Is that okay? At the moment I don't know much about the evidence, because they haven't served it on us yet, so I don't want to start making you promises I can't keep.'

She looked up at me, her big brown eyes imploring me. 'Will I go home today?' she asked. 'Will you be able to get me bail?'

I sighed again. 'I'll try my best.'

She seemed happy with this.

We went upstairs. I would try my best. I would do battle with Josh bloody Benedict-Brown, I would do everything I could to get this woman bail. I would wave the trusty sword of British justice around the court and remind the District Judge that everyone is presumed innocent and that Tasha Roux has no record of offending or absconding or committing offences on bail and that she was going to fight to clear her name. Judge, I would say, let this young woman prepare for the fight of her life from the comfort of her own community and the bosom of her family.

District Judge Barnes refused bail.

'Mr Winnock,' he said, 'you're not addressing a jury now – bail is refused. I've concluded that the nature of the charge is so serious that there is a real possibility that Miss Roux will be tempted to breach her bail. Take her down please.'

This wasn't good. I turned to Kelly. 'Bollocks,' I said, hoping that Kelly might tell me how good my bail application was, swoon in admiration at my advocacy skills, comment on my wonderful suit, anything. But, instead, she replied in her usual frosty way, 'You were never going to get bail, were you?'

We left court and Josh Benedict-Brown followed me out. 'Russ,' he said, 'the good news is that the CPS have allowed me to have a leader.'

'Oh,' I said. This was good news, because if the prosecution had a Silk, then there was every chance that a Judge would let me have one as well. 'Great.'

'I'm going to be led by Roger Fish.'

'The Fishmeister!' I exclaimed. This news was petrifying. Roger Fish QC, aka the Fishmeister, was one of the best criminal advocates around. He had just successfully defended a senior civil servant accused of selling state secrets to the Chinese – it was a case that no one said he could win, but such were his forensic skills and power with the jury that they acquitted him.

'Who'll you instruct?' asked Benedict-Brown.

'I'm not sure,' I said, 'haven't given it much thought yet.'

Which was a total lie, I had thought about it constantly since I'd got the brief, but now I was going to have to make my mind up for real. Who was going to be my Silk in my first murder case?

Silk

Right, now seems a good time to say a little bit more about Silks: who and what are Silks? And why, for that matter, are they called Silks?

Silks, or Queen's Counsel, to give them their proper title, are the most senior barristers. They tend to have no fear of any Judge, jury, witness or piece of law. They get away with all kinds of little tricks and devices that we more lowly juniors wouldn't dream of doing, and they ultimately have the final say on any big decision in any big case because the chances are that their experience and judgement will be better than yours.

They are called Silks because their gowns are made of silk, simple as that. Whereas mine is made of cotton, well polyester-cotton mix, if I'm going to be honest, and I think you can get them in viscose now as well.

In theory, I could choose any Queen's Counsel in the land to lead me in the case of Tasha Roux. In reality though, I had to be careful. Different Silks had different foibles and were cluttered by different bits of political baggage.

If I got my choice wrong it could turn the thrill of being led in a big case into an arduous experience fraught with stress and ending in epic failure. It was a big decision. I decided to get some advice from Jenny Catrell-Jones.

'It's a tricky one, Russ,' she said. 'My advice is that you don't want to choose a Silk who's too brainy, because, before you know it, he'll have you drafting up schedules and reading up on obscure aspects of law and all sorts.'

I nodded intently, yes, I didn't fancy that.

'Then again,' she continued, 'you don't want some ancient old bastard either, because, remember, as the junior, if he dies or his prostate packs in or similar, then bingo, you're out of the co-pilot's seat and into the limelight.'

I nodded again, there was wisdom in those mixed metaphors. 'And Russ, as you know,' she continued, 'the junior taking over successfully from the leader to win the case only happens on the telly. In real life, only bad things happen once you lose your leader and find yourself going solo.'

She was right. 'So who would you pick?' I asked.

'For your case?'

'Yes.'

'I'd probably go with the Fishmeister.'

'I can't have him, he's bloody prosecuting me,' I whined.

'Ah,' she replied, which was code for 'Hard luck, you're completely stuffed.'

I went back to reading the depositions I'd been sent. Later that morning, I was summoned to Clem Wilson's office.

'Mr Winnock,' he said smiling in a syrupy way at me. Funny how civil he was now I had a decent case.

'You'll be needing a Silk for your murder.'

'Yes,' I said, 'as it happens I was talking about that only this morning.'

'Well,' he said, 'as you know, you can have any QC in the whole known universe if you like.'

'Yes,' I said, then added by way of a lame joke, 'so many Silks, so little time.'

'Any Silk,' he continued, ignoring my attempt at humour, 'just as long as you choose someone from here.'

Here. Okay. I could see the wisdom in this. Choosing a Silk from my own chambers would make me quite popular with the seniors and would be easier from the point of view of work.

I considered my options: Thomas Sadwell QC, Richard 'Dicky' Brindle QC, Yussef Lachmi QC and Timothy Belton QC.

Tommy Sadwell, Head of Chambers, was a decent bloke, but now, alas, probably past his best. Rumour had it that he was considering retirement, having been passed over for a job on the High Court bench. I liked Tommy but I wasn't sure I could work with him. To me he seemed from a different age, it would be like working with your granddad.

Then there was Dicky Brindle, another popular barrister. He was, however, famed for his ultra-laid-back attitude. I remember once being at the Old Bailey and watching the ashen face of his junior, Jimmy Connolly, as it got to 25 past ten on the first morning of a trial before Dicky finally came waltzing through the doors of the robing room, with the untouched pink-ribboned brief in his hand, declaring, 'So, Jim, what's this all about then?'

No, Dicky Brindle was a rollercoaster ride I could do without.

Yussef Lachmi was a different kettle of fish again. A wonderful orator and advocate, a real star performer, but the view on the street was that he tended to ignore his junior altogether as he dominated the show from start to finish.

I pictured Tasha sitting there forlornly. I'd vowed to help look after her, and somehow ceding everything to my leading counsel wasn't attractive.

Which left me with Tim Belton. Christ, he wasn't a particularly appealing choice either. Belton was a stickler, a proper lawyer, who relished nothing more than arguing every point until everyone else would be worn down into submission. As much as I respected Tim, I wasn't sure I could stomach that level of intensity. I imagined long nights, just me and my chanting monks, as I drafted submissions and charts and documents. No, he wouldn't do.

I looked at Clem. 'I'm not sure,' I said, 'I suppose Yussef Lachmi would be great.'

Clem shook his head. 'Yussef is going to be stuck in a case involving a series of dead Belgians buried under a shed in Ealing, it'll take him forever to prepare it. I'm not sure he'll have time to do your case justice.'

'Okay, what about Tim?'

'He's doing the most tedious fraud imaginable in Birmingham, it's going to last for ten months.'

'Dicky Brindle then?'

'No, no, no. You don't want Mr Brindle for your first murder do you?'

'I suppose not.'

I scratched my head: as ever Clem was two steps ahead of me.

'Well, I suppose that only leaves Tommy Sadwell.'

At this Clem got up and walked over to the door and shut it, then he turned to me and started talking in a hushed voice, as though he was about to impart upon me some great secret: 'There is another name,' he whispered.

'Oh,' I whispered back, though I had no idea why I was whispering. 'Who?'

'Charles Parkman.'

'Charles Parkman?' I was now completely confused, Charles Parkman was a Family Silk, I couldn't ever remember him doing crime.

'But, he's a . . .' I stuttered and Clem finished my sentence, 'Yes, a brilliant lawyer and a fantastic advocate.'

'I was going to say Family Silk.'

'Mr Winnock, Charlie Parkman was doing criminal cases in the City Crown Court when you were still working out how to tie your shoelaces.'

I thought of Tasha. When I said that I'd do everything for her, I hadn't envisaged asking a Family barrister to lead me, Silk or not.

'No, I think I'd rather have Tommy, Clem, if it's alright with you.'

Clem Wilson shook his head. 'No, Mr Winnock, Head of Chambers is going to be too busy to do that much court work. What with all this industrial action and political campaigning that's going on. Mr Parkman will be just fine, and he's available. In fact he can't wait to get back into the Crown Court.'

'But they've got Roger Fish,' I whimpered.

Clem Wilson just smiled. 'Don't you worry about that, Mrs Murdoch says that you've got a very good case.'

'Yes, exactly, and she's not going to be too chuffed if we've got a Silk who hasn't done a Criminal trial in fifteen years.'

'Au contraire,' said Wilson confidently, 'Charlie Parkman and Jeanette Murdoch go back years, they were at Oxford in the same college apparently. She's more than relaxed about giving him a brief.'

I sighed. I got it now. It had all been a bit of a set-up. I was going to be led by Charlie Parkman whether I liked it or not. And I knew why, it was as obvious as the nose on Clem Wilson's face. Charlie had been a bit strapped for work, probably had a big tax bill or a school fee to pay, and had turned up in Clem's office asking for a bit of work, any kind of work. And, of course, being a Silk, he couldn't do just any work, it would have to be something that was commensurate to his station, and, as it happened, Tasha Roux's case fitted the bill.

I felt deflated. I was going to be led, but I hadn't expected it to start like this.

I thought I'd better phone Kelly and start telling her what a great Silk Charlie Parkman was.

The ten greatest Crown Courts in the land

Now, before you ask, no, I haven't been to every Crown Court in the land – indeed nowhere near. But I have been to quite a few, which is one of the nice things about the job, getting to travel to different parts of the country. I have now reached a stage in my career where there are certain things that I look for in a Crown Court: helpful ushers, a nice robing room with not too much animosity against 'out of town Counsel', a little bit of ambience and history, and, of course, a good café.

With this in mind, here is a list of my top ten favourite courts.

1. **The Lord Chief Justice's Court, The Royal Courts of Justice** – the Royal Courts of Justice is to a barrister what Wembley Stadium is to a footballer. When you arrive here, the heart beats that bit faster and the beads of sweat form like a reservoir around your wig. You know that you are in a big case and you have no idea how it is going to go. It gets the number one spot for its grandeur and overwhelming sense of majesty.

2. **The Old Bailey** – perhaps the most famous Criminal court in the world. The Show Courts are immaculate, thick with the whispered echoes of hundreds of trials, hundreds of great speeches, hundreds of moments of drama. Again, if you're here, you know you're doing something significant.

3. **Lancaster Crown Court** – Lancaster Crown Court needs to be seen to be believed. Based in an old castle on a hill above the town of Lancaster, the old assizes court is situated in what appears to be some kind of medieval hall, replete with suits of armour and coats of arms of long-dead knights on the walls. The time I appeared there, I felt as though I had been transported back to the time of Camelot.

4. **Sheffield Crown Court** – I like the architecture of this court; it's a kind of post-modern septangle built in the 1960s. The courts are impressive, particularly the ones where the jury boxes are situated on a sort of raised stage, which allows them to see everything that is going on, which is how it should be. Not the friendliest of robing rooms though. Some sod swiped my gown when I was there.

5. **Isleworth Crown Court** – this makes my top ten solely for reasons of nostalgia, as I did one of my first Crown Court trials here, defending a young woman on drugs charges. The court itself is an old hospital and has none of the allure or historical resonance of some of the others on this list, but it will always have a special place in my heart.

6. **Chester Crown Court** – this is another former castle, which boasts two of the most wonderfully ornate courtrooms you could

ever wish to see. One of which saw the trial of the Moors Murderers, something the local bar will tell you every time you happen to go there.

7.   **Liverpool Crown Court** – in particular the corridor just outside the Recorder of Liverpool's court (the Recorder is the Senior Judge), because the court- rooms themselves are modern and unspectacular, but the view across the city and River Mersey that is afforded by the massive windows outside this court is utterly spectacular. When I was there I got a bollocking for being late because I was stood outside, transfixed by the boats coming up and down the Mersey.

8.   **Shrewsbury Crown Court** – perhaps a bit of an unusual choice, but, as any lawyer who has been to Shrewsbury will tell you, the court building there has the most amazing café. I spent a week there and ate home-made cakes and pies every day for under £3, marvellous. And a rare treat, because believe it or not, these days many courts no longer have a café or restaurant, which is a shame in my book because if you're in court all day, you really need a cup of tea and a bun.

9.   **Minshull Street Crown Court, Manchester** – when I was sent to do a hearing in Manchester, the instructing solicitor, a rather lascivious man of a certain age, who was later done for VAT fraud, told me, 'Russ, you'll love it at Minshull Street, mate, the solicitors clerks are all gorgeous-looking birds.' I didn't believe him but damn it he was right – it was like being on the set of *Hollyoaks* – and, because of that, Minshull Street Manchester sneaks into my top ten.

10. **Snaresbrook Crown Court** – another beautifully ornate Crown Court with wonderful gardens and even a lake. Inside it's like Hogwarts, with its magnificent staircases, impressive turrets and mysterious locked doors. I have to admit that I always have a lovely warm feeling whenever I'm given a brief to go to Snaresbrook.

The Court of Appeal and the
case of R v J (a minor)

One of my more memorable cases at number one on that list, the Court of Appeal, was the case of R v J (a minor).

J was a fifteen-year-old lad called Josh. He had had sex with a thirteen-year-old girl. As such, in the eyes of the law, both were under the age of consent to have lawful sex. They had been caught when one of her friends posted about her mate's dalliance on, yes, you've guessed it, Facebook. The girl's parents discovered this and they weren't happy. When they questioned the girl, she intimated that she had been raped.

Josh was interviewed and accused of rape. His response, perhaps understandably given his immaturity and the seriousness of the allegation, was: 'Rape! She was mad for it.'

The girl was then interviewed again and admitted that it wasn't rape. Unfortunately for Josh, having made an admission to having sex with a thirteen-year-old girl, which is a criminal offence, he was charged with sexual activity with a child. And, in the Youth Court, having confessed to the charge, he had little option but to plead guilty.

After entering his plea, his solicitor started to wonder whether this was right and asked me what I thought. 'Because,' as he said, 'it doesn't seem fair, does it, that one kid under sixteen should be charged because he was a boy, and the girl who was also under sixteen, and therefore had also technically broken the law, wasn't charged at all.'

I saw the logic in this, so I tried to be clever and drafted grounds of appeal to challenge the decision to charge 'J'. I said that this was an unreasonable decision, and that the conviction should be quashed. I genuinely believed that I had made a smart legal point. I signed my grounds of appeal and argument and sent them off feeling pretty pleased with myself.

When it came to the hearing, I arrived at the Royal Courts of Justice with my blue bag slumped nervously over my shoulder and walked past the usual array of cameras and journalists, who were there for a much more newsworthy case involving a footballer. I then made my way through the massive oak doors, through security and into the marble-floored hall. As a barrister it is where you want to be, demonstrating your brain and wits in one of the highest courts of the land. The problem though, is that your wits and your brain are minuscule in comparison to the brain and wits of a High Court Judge. They are smarter than you, they know more than you, and they will take what *you* think is a clever point and destroy it. Unless, of course, it really is a clever point, in which case they will make you argue it and discuss every detail of it, until you are left pleading with them to stop. As my shoes clip-clopped across the forecourt, I was now starting to worry that my clever point was actually a bit shit.

I went down to the robing room and started to put my kit on. There is a different atmosphere in the robing room of the Royal Courts of Justice. The banter, mild bullying and overt misogyny of a typical Crown Court robing room gives way to gloom and fear. There is no conversation, no laughter, no smiles, just the grim features of lawyers busily losing all confidence in the arguments that they are about to proffer.

When I first started, the robing room at the Royal Courts of Justice had a lovely elderly attendant called Arthur who used to play Radio 3 on a transistor radio, and called everyone sir – sadly, Arthur's been retired off, and the sound of Radio 3 has been replaced with the grim silence of fear.

I was to be in front of Mr Justice McCoombe, Mr Justice Lacey and Lord Justice Swinton. I had been in front of Swinton once before. He asked me a question which I answered in such a garbled way that he never bothered asking me another one.

I made my way into the court and sat on the Counsel's row; my heart was pounding and a strange nervous pulse had developed inside my wig. I no longer had any confidence whatsoever in my clever point.

I listened to the two cases that were heard before mine. Both were appeals against sentence. One of them involved an armed robbery; a rather old, tired-looking barrister with a Northern accent was sluggishly suggesting that the sentence of six years was manifestly excessive.

Suddenly, Mr Justice McCoombe turned on him. 'Mr Leaman,' he said, 'your client pointed a sawn-off shotgun into the face of a totally innocent Post Office cashier.'

'Ah,' said Leaman, pointing a hoary old finger in the direction of the Judge, 'but at least he didn't pull the trigger, My Lord.' The appeal was dismissed.

By the time they got to me, my confidence had completely evaporated. I stood up, a complete bag of nerves. I opened my mouth and hoped that words would follow in the form of vaguely coherent sentences.

'My Lords,' I began, 'this appeal concerns the inherent wrong that, in my respectful submission, befell my client.'

They seemed disinterested but at least no one had shouted at me. I continued tentatively, like a mouse tip-toeing through a minefield. Initially it was going quite well, until I got to my – increasingly less clever – point: 'After all,' I said, 'the Sex Offenders Act was not meant to be a stick to beat errant teenage boys with.'

At this they took it in turns to kick me, metaphorically, around the court.

'Mr Winnock, isn't it designed to protect teenagers?' asked Lacey.

'Yes, of course, My Lord,' I said.

'Then why shouldn't it protect the thirteen-year-old girl your client had sex with?'

'It should, My Lord.'

'So what is the point of your appeal?'

'It's just unfair and unreasonable, My Lord.'

Lord Justice Swinton now joined in. 'Unreasonable to protect children, Mr Winnock? Unfair to protect thirteen-year-old girls? Really?'

'No, My Lord.'

'Because that is what you want us to find, isn't it?'

'Not at all, My Lords.'

'But you accept that if we find in favour of your client, that is, that it was unreasonable to prosecute him for having sex with a thirteen-year-old girl contrary to the law as passed by Parliament, then we would be saying that it was wrong to protect thirteen-year-old girls from having sex with men?'

'I don't think that's what I'm saying, My Lord.'

At this stage I no longer knew what I was saying, my mind had taken on a cabbage-like quality. He was absolutely right. My point was totally garbage. Complete crap. I had tried to be clever and had come up before people far cleverer than me.

'Is that what you want public policy to be, Mr Winnock?' added Mr Justice McCoombe. 'Some kind of green light for everyone to have sex with thirteen-year-old girls?'

I stood there and made a noise that I imagine was not dissimilar to the sound of air coming out of a dead person.

'Do you have anything else to put to us, Mr Winnock?'

Only that I wanted to run away and hide. 'No,' I said.

And with that, the appeal of 'J' (a minor) was dismissed. I left court truly humbled I had tried to be clever, and I wouldn't be trying again any time soon.

The case against Tasha Roux

The case of the Crown versus Tasha Roux consisted of exactly 933 pages, which from a business point of view was pretty good.

It took me two days and two nights to read it all. This was the story according to the prosecution papers:

Tasha Roux was a 23-year-old woman living in a tower block in London Bridge called Tarvin House. Her mother was a white Londoner, her father a black South African who had fled to London in the 1980s to escape apartheid. He had left her mother when Tasha was still a baby. She had not seen him since. His whereabouts were unknown.

When she was eight, her mother put Tasha into care because she couldn't cope with her and the five other children she had. By the time she was fourteen, Tasha was abusing drugs and committing some petty crimes. She had stopped going to school. There was a suggestion that she was also working as a prostitute, though she denies this and there are no convictions recorded against her for soliciting sex or similar offences.

When she was fifteen she had a baby who was herself taken into care and adopted, because, at the time, it was feared that Tasha would be an unsuitable mother.

Then, when she was seventeen she met Gary Dickinson, a bodybuilder and doorman from South East London.

Dickinson was ten years older than Tasha and had already amassed a lengthy list of convictions for drugs, violence and fraud.

Tasha moved into her flat in Tarvin House on the sixth floor. A one-bedroom flat in a high-rise full of lonely one-bedroom flats. Dickinson would live there some of the time, but his main address was with his mother in Lewisham.

Tasha worked in various jobs: in a nightclub as a waitress, in a factory that sorted out old clothes for recycling, in a call-centre, as an assistant in a nursery. All the jobs were short-lived and most ended badly through absenteeism or suspicions about her being under the influence of drugs or drink.

In the five years before Dickinson's death, the police were called out a total of sixteen times because of disturbances at the address. Some of the calls were made by Tasha, but most were made by her neighbours.

One neighbour, Mrs Pauline Adamson, recalls hearing screaming and arguing on a regular basis. She claims loud music was often played, but she could still hear the arguments over the music. She describes lots of young men coming in and out of the flat in the middle of the night.

Another neighbour, Mr Rick O'Rourke, recalls being awoken one night by the sound of Mr Dickinson banging on the door of the flat, begging Tasha to let him in. His opinion of Miss Roux is that she often appeared drunk.

On the night of the killing, Tasha went out to a bar called Nomads in Elephant and Castle, then to a nightclub nearby called Rendezvouz. CCTV showed her returning home alone at around 4am. About twenty minutes later Dickinson can be seen entering the flats and taking the lift up to her floor.

At 5am neighbours report hearing noises from the flat; a Mrs Hussain (number 41b) describes hearing the sound of raised voices, and a Miss Adams (49c) recalls hearing the words, 'You do it every fucking time, Tasha,' being repeated over and over again.

Doors could then be heard slamming and neighbours became aware of a female crying in the hallway outside the flat.

At this point, Mr O'Rourke opened the door of his own flat, but accepts that his view was partially obscured as he was too nervous to open the door the whole way. He saw Miss Roux and Mr Dickinson square up to one another, then saw Mr Dickinson move away towards the stairwell. He then saw Miss Roux rush towards the stairwell as well. The next thing he heard was a scream from Miss Roux, followed by a thud. He called the police but stayed in his flat.

Miss Adams did come out of her flat and found Miss Roux sat against the wall with her face in her hands. She asked her what had happened and recalls Miss Roux said, 'He just fell, he just fell.'

When the police arrived they found Mr Dickinson slumped partially over the banister on the second floor, it was clear that he had received massive injuries to his head and was dead.

They also found Miss Roux by the stairwell. A PC Whitby asked Miss Roux what had happened and she said, 'I fucking killed him, he just kept pushing me and pushing me.'

The story of Tasha's life, just like so many of the others I deal with, had its own predictable narrative arc: a difficult start to life when nothing much was expected of her, a middle, when, if different decisions had been made, it could have turned out better, and finally a tragic conclusion.

Like so many of the defendants who I represent or prosecute, Tasha Roux had no stability as a child. I'm not saying that every child who comes from a broken home is doomed, nor am I saying that every stable family unit gives rise to stable well-adjusted adults, but background plays a big part in shaping a person's adult life.

I sometimes think of myself when I was a child and contrast how lucky I was, how my path of normality and relative success was already written out for me through the fluke of being born into a stable family. I remember being eight years old and having a fight with my brother. He wouldn't let me in the house so I picked up a broom and in temper smashed the kitchen window. I don't know who was more shocked, me or my brother, as the glass erupted into tiny fragments all over him and the kitchen.

When my dad got home he exploded with anger and ordered me to my room, where I sat and stewed for about an hour before he came up. His eyes incandescent with fury, he pointed at me as he spoke. 'Everything you do has consequences, Russell,' he told me, 'every decision you take, everything. And if you spend your life doing stupid things and bad things, then nothing good will ever happen to you.'

Then he stood and looked at me. The eyes boring into me were not the normal warm Dad eyes, but serious, 'you've got to listen to this and never forget it' eyes. 'Do you understand, Russell?' he said.

I nodded.

'Good,' he said, 'now the consequences of what you did are that you'll have no pocket money and no football for a month, and if you ever break a window or lose your temper like that again, me and your mother will call the police and you'll go to jail.'

I waited for about two days before he hugged me. And that was the most important hug ever after what felt like the two longest days of my life.

Have I made bad decisions since? Yes, of course I have. But the difference is that I've been lucky enough to grow up knowing that there were people around me who cared about my decisions, who would tell me off if I made the wrong ones, but hug me later. Tasha Roux never had that. Nor do most of the other people who enter our courts ravaged by drugs and in awful dead-end lives.

Am I advocating the 'traditional family unit'? No, that's not my place. Am I criticising errant fathers and pregnant teenagers? No, I don't hold a brief to do that either. All I'm saying is that life is a hell of a lot easier if you're born with people who care about you enough to stick around.

Girls

'Aunty Margaret wants to know if you'll be taking anyone to Lucy's wedding?' my mum said over the phone one night.

'Mum, I've told you already, if I go at all, I'll be on my own.'

'You've got to go.'

I sighed, 'Okay, if I can I'll come. But I'll be on my own.'

'Surely there is a nice barrister you can bring?'

'Well, I could bring my roommate Amir if you like, but that might cause a bit of gossip though. You know what Uncle Arthur's like – "they're all queers down south".'

She scolded me for being facetious.

This is my mum's favourite subject: my love life. I have reached an age where she wants to marry me off and she has this image of me meeting a lovely female barrister – probably getting hitched in Gray's Inn Chapel, before settling down to a lovely life making little barristers.

Which brings me on to the subject of female barristers.

How can I write this without sounding like either a raving sexist dinosaur, the type of man who emits a Sid James type 'phwoar' every time a woman comes into view, or a rampant neo-feminist who will not rest until there is equality and harmony between the sexes.

I am neither. But, I do feel sorry for women at the Bar. Especially the Criminal Bar. It's not easy. The odds are stacked against them.

First they have to deal with the robing room. Robing rooms are bastions of machismo. They are stacked with extremely confident males, many of whom have come from fairly privileged backgrounds, often from all-boys schools where they learned much about many things, but absolutely nothing about women. The atmosphere in the robing room can be boorish, gladiatorial, boastful and ungallant, though, I hasten to add, it can also be gentle, helpful, genuinely funny and collegiate. You have to be confident and thick-skinned to survive and survival is a hell of a lot easier if you're a bloke. As a baby barrister, I was sent up to a court in the Midlands, to make an application to vacate a trial. I searched for my opponent and when I eventually found him and told him that I was applying to adjourn our case he just took one look at me and told me to 'fuck off'.

Then there is the overt sexism. And I mean proper 1970s *Carry On Up the Khyber* sexism. Conversations, in which male barristers will discuss whether a juror, or a witness, or a WPC or another barrister is 'fit', are commonplace. And there have been occasions when I have watched as young female barristers walking into a robing room are looked up and down by the men who are clearly making an assessment of their looks rather than their ability.

To survive this, female barristers often become even more masculine than the men. They might not be able to demonstrate the same instinctive boorishness, so they show their 'machismo' in court. Some female barristers are the most steely, ballsy operators I know. They will eat you up and spit you out in court because that is how they have been forced to demand respect. They will develop a stare or a pout that they use to put errant Judges in their place and obtain what they want for their clients. It can be incredibly impressive, and a little scary, to see them in action.

Of course, I'm generalising, but only slightly. After all, females were only allowed to practise in the 1930s and there are still far fewer female Judges than there should be.

Am I proud of the fact that my profession is inherently sexist and has forced some women to suppress their femininity? No, I'm bloody not. Do I want it to change? Well, I'm not sure about that either. At least not entirely. Barristers, both male and female are, by definition, a bit odd. There needs to be characters, there needs to be big Silverback gorillas with massive personalities and even bigger egos charging around, because without them, the courts, and I would argue the justice system, would be far more anodyne and much less effective. And, just as importantly, there needs to be the fierce female advocates, because the culture has led to the creation of some truly amazing women barristers – though hopefully over time, as the robing rooms and courts become less chauvinistic, women can be themselves and get on with the job without being hindered by the gender.

But do I want to marry a female barrister?

No, I bloody don't. The idea of coming home every day to find myself immediately thrust into an argument, which I will lose, about whose turn it is to do the washing up, or to be cross-examined within an inch of my life as to why I leave the toilet seat up, is my idea of hell.

I love my learned female colleagues, and yes, there are actually quite a few I fancy, but I've never gone out with one and I don't plan to change that any time soon. I planned to go to my cousin Lucy's wedding on my own.

Touting and solicitor's wars

Now let me put this into context – a man's got to eat. And, if you are in the business of providing for yourself and your family or whoever, by working in the Criminal Justice System, then every person who requires legal representation because they have been daft enough or unfortunate enough to get themselves accused of a crime is, potentially, a source of income.

That is why solicitors firms do everything that they can to get clients. I understand that, after all it's why I count my pages so carefully. I understand why solicitors clamour to get onto the police station duty rotas that determine which solicitor will be called out to represent someone in the nick. It's because that usually means that if they are subsequently charged, they will be given the legal aid certificate or Representation Order, which means that they will be paid for their work. Representation Orders therefore are the key to everything. Without a 'Rep Order' the Legal Services Commission will not pay out. And in a murder case, the 'Rep Order' is the most lucrative of all – it's like Willy Wonka's Golden Ticket.

Most solicitors firms have an official police station accredited lawyer, which means that lawyer's name is on a list held in various police stations, and their phone number will be called if they are the duty solicitor at the time when someone is brought into a police station. That firm then holds the golden ticket to represent that client throughout the proceedings; and at the end of proceedings they will cash it in with the Legal Services Department so that they can pay their staff, and everyone eats.

There was a time when this whole process of 'finders keepers' was accepted in a rather gentlemanly and dignified way, but those days have gone. Things are now decidedly dog-eat-dog – and, for me, that is a change for the worse.

And the reason for this state of conflagration is because there are some circumstances in which a Representation Order can be transferred from one firm to another. This transfer can only be granted by a Judge on application by an advocate who will tell the Judge that, for whatever reason, the defendant no longer wishes to be represented by his current solicitor but wants to transfer his Representation Order somewhere else. Judges won't do it willingly, they have to be satisfied that there has been either incompetence or a total breakdown in the relationship between the client and the lawyer.

In recent years the whole process has become more aggressive because the large firms know that the only way they can survive is if they acquire as many legal aid Representation Orders as possible. Unfortunately touting is now widespread. It normally takes place in prison, where a defendant on remand will sit in their cell worrying about their case. In these circumstances they are easy prey to unscrupulous elements. They will be visited by other solicitors who will often bring them gifts – new trainers or phone cards are particularly popular gifts. After all, what's a 50 quid pair of trainers if that person is potentially worth many thousands in legal aid money?

There are even rumours of solicitors entering into agreements with certain criminals that involve the exchange of money back to the client. So, in other words, a client would effectively be paid by the state for committing a crime – which is a horrendous prospect. But, as I say, I've no proof that this goes on, it may be nothing more than a rumour.

What annoys me most of all though is the making of false promises. And this happens a lot. Typically, if one advocate has tried and failed to get the client bail, the next day that same remanded defendant will invariably be visited by some stoatish, weaselly solicitor who will say to him, 'Don't you worry, you transfer your legal aid to me and I'll get you bail.' It's a promise that won't be kept.

Blatant tapping-up like this was the cause of my single biggest explosion of anger in a court building. I was instructed to represent an Irishman called Brian Turner. Mr Turner had been accused of stealing lead and copper piping. It wasn't the biggest case in the world, there weren't many hundreds of pages of evidence, but I had read the evidence and I had prepared myself to look after him as best I could.

On the day of his plea hearing I turned up to the cells to meet Mr Turner for the first time and was met by a woman in a sharp suit with big heels and massive, confident hair.

She introduced herself, told me she was from Harmsworth's Solicitors and said that she had been to see Mr Turner and that he wanted to transfer legal aid from the firm instructing me, to them.

I started to shake with rage. I tried to contain myself.

'What,' I said, my voice trembling, 'you've been to see my client without my permission?'

'Yes,' she said, and thrust towards me a letter that purported to come from Mr Turner authorising the application to transfer solicitors. I ignored her jutting hand.

'You've,' I repeated, 'been to see my client, without my permission?'

'Yes,' she said again, 'and here's his letter explaining the reasons why he no longer wishes to instruct you.'

Again, I ignored her letter.

'How. Dare. You,' I exploded, sounding a bit too much like Frankie Howerd as I tried to suppress my outrage. Now it was my turn to jut a finger. 'Don't you ever, ever, ever, go and see one of my clients without my permission unless a Judge says so.'

Miss Confident Hair didn't give a toss. 'Here's the application,' she said, 'here's his letter. I'll see you in court.' With that she flounced off.

I read the letter, it clearly hadn't been written by Brian Turner. It stated that he wanted to transfer legal aid because he no longer had any confidence in his legal team and wasn't happy with the way they'd represented him in court.

My innards screamed with rage. I went into the cells and plonked myself down in front of Brian Turner. I dispensed with my usual friendly compassionate matey spiel.

'Are you Brian Turner?' I said gruffly.

'I don't want to speak to you,' he said, 'I want to speak to my new lawyer.'

I repeated slowly, 'Are you Brian Turner?'

'I am.'

'You've never met me before, have you, Mr Turner?'

He looked at me, trying to think of something clever to say, before answering, 'No.'

'Then how can you write a letter saying you have no confidence in me?'

He turned away and I threw the letter down on the table.

'What did they give you, Mr Turner?' I continued. 'A phone card? A pair of Nikes? A few quid?'

He continued to look at the wall and repeated, 'I only want to speak to my new solicitor.'

'You didn't write this letter did you, Mr Turner?'

He started to whistle as he ignored my question. I got up and left him. It wasn't that I was desperate to represent him, it wasn't the money either, it wasn't a big case, it was the principle. It was the fact that some nameless, faceless solicitor from some massive firm had felt able to write a letter from a client I had never met, telling a Judge that this client had no confidence in *me* – that's what made me so angry.

The case according to Tasha Roux

A week after I had failed to secure Tasha Roux bail I went to see her again. It was time now for me to hear her side of the story. She sat across from me and Kelly in a visitors' room at Holloway Prison and started to tell me about Gary Dickinson. I stopped her, I didn't want to know about Dickinson yet, I wanted to know more about her. I wanted to find out more about the person who had done this – I felt that I would then have a better chance of gauging whether or not she was telling me the truth and how she might fare in a courtroom.

'I tell you what,' I said, 'I'll ask you some questions; some of them might be a little personal, but not too personal, and some of them might be a bit painful. I'm sorry, but trust me, every question I ask you, I ask you for a reason.'

She nodded.

'Okay, how old are you?'

I knew that answer, but I wanted to hear everything from her own mouth.

'I'm 23,' she told me, then she continued to answer my questions about her childhood, about her mother having difficulties with drink and drugs and how she had five brothers and sisters, and that they were all taken into care when she was about eight years old.

'Eight is a really shit age for that,' she told me, 'because you understand enough when you're eight, you know how to feel abandoned and you know that it isn't right.'

She tried to skip over her teenage years, so I stopped her and asked her specific questions. She had got into the wrong crowd, she told me, 'Everyone was doing pills and smoking weed, so I just went along with it.'

I had heard this story a lot. Drugs and the culture of drugs were part of modern life. It would have been a greater surprise if she had managed to get to the age of 23 without some relationship with them. We moved from drugs to an even darker place. This was trickier. I composed my questions carefully in my head.

'Look,' I said, 'there's no easy way to ask this next question, but there is a suggestion in the papers that you were being used by men for sex?'

She looked down, then nodded. 'It didn't go on for very long,' she said, 'it started as a laugh, when I was about fifteen, me and some mates being taken out to clubs and that, then it got worse and we were expected to provide . . .' she paused, now she was picking the right words, words that wouldn't cause too much pain '. . . services,' she said. 'We were expected to provide certain services.'

'How did it end?'

She fidgeted with the plastic coffee cup in front of her.

'I got pregnant,' she said, 'and the baby was taken away.'

At this point a large perfect tear started to roll in silence down her cheek.

We moved on.

She described meeting Gary Dickinson. 'He was alright at first,' she said, 'he would look after me.' Then her eyes narrowed and a sense of urgency crossed her face. 'You do realise that he was up to all sorts?' she said.

'Oh, yes,' I told her, 'don't worry.'

She told me how she suspected him of having a few women living in various flats around the area, but she wasn't sure.

'He sold drugs,' she said, 'steroids and cocaine, M-Cat, speed, anything. And he had this licence to be a doorman,' she continued, her mouth sneering as she spoke, 'he was dead proud of this licence and how it meant that he hadn't been caught beating anyone up or selling drugs for three years, and he used to tell me it was because he knew where every CCTV camera was in all the clubs he worked.'

'Did he ever beat you?'

She nodded, then looked away. For a few seconds she said nothing, I knew she was composing herself. She continued, 'But he was clever,' she told me, 'he would never hurt my face. He had this thing that he did, he would clench both of his fists and bring them down on either side of my head, here.' She used both of her hands to point to her temples. 'His knuckles would be sticking out.' She demonstrated, bashing her fists together.

'It killed. Sometimes, if he did it, it hurt so much I passed out – but it never left a mark. I thought it might kill me. You hear don't you, of being hit in certain parts of your head and dying.'

'How often would he do that?'

'All the time.'

'How many times? Ten? Twenty?'

'More like fifty,' she said.

'What else did he do to you?' I asked.

'He used to take my benefit money. He said that I owed him it for drugs. But I didn't.'

'Do you still use drugs?' I asked her, adding quickly, 'Don't worry if you do, I'm not here to judge you about any of that, okay, it's just better if I know.'

She nodded. 'A bit of charlie,' she said, 'that's all really.'

I knew that she was probably understating her drug use, most drug users did.

'Did he ever do anything else?' I asked. 'What about using you for sex?'

She went quiet again. 'He kept badgering me to go out with these fellas he knew. I only did it a couple of times.'

'What fellas?'

'There was a guy called Tony, and another guy, a Pakistani guy called Salam, he kept telling me that it was okay if I fancied them, if I wanted to have sex with them, but I didn't fancy them. I knew what he meant though, I knew what he was trying to do. They were all involved in drugs, Gary was trying to get favours off blokes. The Pakistani guy asked me if I was like Gary's other girlfriends and kept trying to kiss me and feel me up.'

I nodded.

'I knew what was happening though,' she continued, 'I wasn't fifteen no more.'

She told me all of this. She told me about how he would control every part of her life and how her only moments of freedom and happiness were when she could meet up with Shandra. 'Shandra was like my mum,' she told me, 'that's why I trust her when she says that you're a really good barrister.'

I frowned. 'I'm not sure about that,' I said, 'there are loads better than me.'

Kelly scowled at me when I said this, but I wasn't going to start boasting about skills I wasn't sure I had, not sat here, listening to this story, not yet.

'So,' I said, 'what about the night when this happened, tell me about that.'

She took a deep breath.

'I'd been out, I went to Rendezvouz club in Lewisham. I was supposed to have met one of Gary's friends, a bloke called Rio, but, for some reason, I never met him. It wasn't my fault.' She paused. 'You see, I wanted to have a baby, Gary's baby, I didn't want to get involved in all of that. It sounds stupid now. But I thought that that would sort everything out, make everything normal. Like a family.'

I was desperately trying to empathise with and understand everything that she was telling me. It wasn't easy. You can't just place yourself into someone else's tragedy.

'Did you meet him at all?'

'No. I went home. Then Gary arrives back at mine and he's shouting at me for not meeting this Rio geezer and I'm shouting back and then he leaves saying that he's going to get this Rio now, and a load of other lads and they were going to come back to the flat to do me. That's what he kept saying, that I was worthless and that I needed to be shagged by loads of different blokes. And he leaves the flat, so I lock the door. And then he's banging on the door saying that I had to open it, and that it wouldn't matter because he had a key in his car anyway. And he did. He did have a key. And I knew that he was going to get it, so I opened the door and I saw him standing there.'

She paused before repeating, 'I saw him standing there by the banister.'

I knew now that the next few words were going to be crucial, what she told me now would mean the difference between her having a defence or not.

'Yes,' I said, 'take your time. What happened next?'

'I went towards him, he seemed to have relaxed his shoulders, as though he was no longer angry, you know. I thought, he's not going to get these lads, he's not going to do it, so I went towards him, I wanted to hug him, it sounds fucking pathetic, I wanted to thank him for not getting his friends to come round and rape me. In that instant, at that moment, I was so happy. I went towards him.'

She paused again, her eyes looking upwards, tears streaming down her face.

'I went towards him,' she continued, 'I went to hug him, I know I'm stupid, but I want to have a baby, I wanted to have a baby, with him.'

She stopped, trying to control her sobbing voice and rubbing away the tears in her eyes.

'You're not stupid,' I told her.

'But as I did,' she continued, making her voice as strong as she could, 'as I went towards him, he formed two fists, and I knew that he was going to hammer them down on my temples, I knew he was going to do it, outside by these banisters, in front of the neighbours, he had his fists like this.' She showed me two shaking fists formed with the knuckle of the index finger protruding outwards.

'I knew it was going to hurt. Mr Winnock, I can't tell you how much it hurts.'

She was sobbing now as everything came back to her, images and feelings and emotions.

'So what did you do, Tasha?' I asked quietly.

'I pushed him,' she said, even quieter.

'What part of him did you push?'

She shrugged. 'I had my eyes closed and my head sort of cocked, because I was just expecting to feel the pain of his fists against my temple, so I'm not sure, I just pushed as hard as I could.'

I nodded. 'What happened to him?'

'He fell backwards and I screamed. I just screamed. I didn't know what to do. I just screamed.'

I looked at Kelly who had stopped making her notes for a second. I sort of hoped that Kelly would do something sympathetic, give her a handkerchief or a cuddle or something, but she was just listening, a look of absolute concentration on her face. I knew that she'd never heard anything like this either.

'Okay,' I said, as gently as I could, 'it'll all be okay. There's just one more question I need to ask you, Tasha.'

And she nodded without saying anything.

'Why did you push him?'

Now it was her turn to look me in the eye, to beseech me, to implore me to believe her, to trust her. 'Because I thought he was going to hurt me,' she said.

And I nodded. A gentle smile crossed my lips. That was the answer I wanted. 'Tasha,' I said, 'look, from what you've told me, you're not guilty of murder – you acted in self-defence because you thought that Gary Dickinson was going to hurt you. You weren't to know that by pushing him he was going to fall over the banister. Do you understand all that?'

'Yes,' she said.

I smiled more broadly at her now, then told her that I would draft her defence statement, which is the short statement that is given to the Judge and the prosecution saying why someone is not guilty of the charge.

'I can't guarantee anything,' I said, 'but I'll do my best for you.'

Self-defence and politicians

Amir was in full flow. 'Right,' he said, 'my claimant wants to sue a company who organise paintball competitions because he got shot in the bollocks from short range and subsequently had one of his gonads go septic on him. Sadly the gonad never made it; they had to chop it off.'

A chambers pupil, a rather austere young woman by the name of Emily, who, rumour has it, is a born-again Christian, was grinning uncomfortably as Jenny Catrell-Jones responded by telling Amir and Angus that if someone was responsible for destroying one of her balls, she'd want revenge in the traditional, Old Testament way. 'A bollock for a bollock,' she was shouting.

I though, wasn't thinking about Amir's case, I was thinking about self-defence. Now there are a lot of words spoken about self-defence, it's one of those subjects on which journalists, politicians and blokes down the pub all have an opinion, and, for two out of three of those groups, it is nearly always wrong.

For journalists – and when I say journalists, I'm talking about certain types of journalists from certain types of newspapers – self-defence is an excuse for a cheap story, usually involving an old-age pensioner (preferably with wartime experience), who will have taken the law into his own hands after being terrorised by 'local youths', and is then, surprise, surprise, shock horror, prosecuted for his efforts.

We all know the type of story, it usually comes with a picture of the sad-looking or occasionally angry-looking pensioner with his medals, and another photograph of an anonymous ferocious-looking hoodie-wearing youth.

And then of course the politicians will line up to get a few cheap votes on the back of this by calling for a change in the law.

Well, the law on self-defence doesn't need changing: it works perfectly well.

So what is the law on self-defence?

It's this: if any one of us honestly and reasonably believes that we are about to be attacked, then we can use reasonable and proportionate force to defend ourselves. Similarly, we can use reasonable force to defend our property and others in the event of them being attacked.

And that's got to be right, hasn't it? Every one of us has the right to defend ourselves or our stuff, or another person, if we honestly believe that there is an imminent threat of danger, just as long as we do so with reasonable force. I mean, if someone comes at us with clenched fists and gritted teeth then there is, of course, nothing wrong with giving them a dig. It might be different if the person comes at us with clenched fists and gritted teeth and we repeatedly brutally stab them about the body, leaving them lying on the ground in a motionless bloody mess.

There is therefore a fine line between using reasonable and proportionate force and revenge or retaliation.

Take the case of Archie Whelan. Archie was my very own have-a go hero. A Falklands veteran, he lived on an estate where kids sniffed glue in bus shelters and jumped on the top of cars after the sun went down.

He slept with an army surplus bayonet knife under his pillow.

One day, someone tried to burgle Archie's house. Archie immediately retrieved his bayonet and ran downstairs to confront two young tracksuit-wearing lads who were trying to nick his telly.

Now, at this point, Archie was probably within the law when he held up the massive knife and told them to 'get the fuck out of my house'.

The reality is that most burglars are drug addicts who have no interest whatsoever in any kind of confrontation, as was the case with the two muppets in Archie's front room. Because, not surprisingly, when they were confronted by Archie and his massive knife, they ran away.

Alas, Archie ran after them; even more troubling for Archie was that he managed to catch one of them and, upon catching him, he decided to stick the bayonet up the arse of one of the would-be burglars, who had to have seventeen stitches to a wound to his anus and lost five litres of blood.

Now Archie's problem was that when he used force he was not under attack, the lads were running away, they were no longer a threat to him. It was retaliation. It wasn't reasonable self-defence.

To be fair to him, he accepted this, pleaded guilty and was given a suspended sentence by a very lenient Judge.

The local newspaper, however, thought otherwise, they published a photograph in the local paper of Archie holding his Falklands medals and his bayonet. But neither the local newspaper who championed his cause nor Archie – to be fair to him – could complain, because if it was lawful to act in this way, then our nation would cease to be an organised and lawful place, but a crazed vigilante-riddled free-for-all, where chasing people with knives and guns was commonplace and tolerated. And I can't see the press or your average politician being too happy with that either.

Contrast Archie's story with the story of Elsa Sharp, who I

prosecuted. Elsa was being stalked by an ex-boyfriend who couldn't understand why, after she had caught him rummaging through her handbag looking for the passwords to her Facebook account, she had decided to dump him. After a couple of years of increasingly menacing messages and phone calls, he started to threaten her with the most grotesque violence. One day, he followed her into a pub and confronted her. She responded by grabbing the nearest thing, which happened to be a bottle of alco-pop, and bashing him over the head. He lost part of his ear.

I was sceptical when I received the instructions to prosecute Miss Sharp. I didn't think for one second that a jury would convict her, but the CPS told me to bat on, so I did. And, I suppose they were right, the victim may have been an arsehole, but he was unarmed when he confronted her.

Her barrister told the jury that she had honestly believed, given all the letters he had sent to her, and all the things that he had said, that he was going to attack her, and I couldn't really disagree with that either. The issue for the jury was whether her use of a bottle was proportionate given that he was unarmed. I argued, as I was instructed to, that it wasn't. My opponent argued that it was, as the victim was much bigger than her, and that she didn't know what he might have in his pockets. He also made the point that she only hit him once with the bottle, which suggested that she didn't intend him serious injury but just wanted to defend herself.

The jury deliberated for six hours before coming back and finding Miss Sharp not guilty. This was the proper verdict. The jury had understood the law, applied it to the facts and come up with the right conclusion.

As I considered self-defence, the banter in my room continued.

'So,' said Jenny Catrell-Jones to the pupil, 'come on, Emily, if someone cut one of your bollocks off, how much money would you want in compensation?'

This was a big moment for Emily. An inability to join in chambers banter could cost her dearly when the decision was being taken whether or not to offer her tenancy. 'Well,' she said, 'depends: if, Jenny, I had bollocks as big as yours, then I could probably function perfectly well after losing one.'

Jenny grinned. Everyone laughed.

Emily was going to go far.

Consent

Jenny Catrell-Jones was sitting at her desk in front of a massive chocolate cake, in her hand was a bottle of something, the contents of which she was pouring into a mug which had the words, 'Office Tart' written on it.

'Ah, Russ,' she said, 'thank god you're here, I need someone to help me with this cake and this bottle of Prosecco.' She motioned towards the bottle. 'Courtesy of Mr Matthew Courtney. The chocolate cake's not bad, but after saving his sorry arse from fifteen years in Pentonville, you'd have thought he might have stretched to a proper bottle of Champagne rather than this fizzy wine.'

'Oh go on then,' I said, and picked up a rather dirty pint glass from a shelf, gave its rim a quick rub then passed it to Jenny.

She looked a bit forlorn.

I asked her what was wrong and she smiled awkwardly.

'I suppose, I'm feeling that awkward guilt that we sometimes get when we win a case.'

'Rape?' I asked her and she nodded.

Jenny was one of the best defenders of those charged with rape in the country. Most of her practice consisted of sexual offences, which was a result of some defendants and solicitors believing, rightly or wrongly, that having a woman cross-examine another woman on the issue of whether they were consenting to sex, is somehow an advantage. Perhaps it is – because she has an impressive strike rate.

'Don't tell me,' I said, 'Mr Cake and Wine met up with an ex in a club, they both got drunk and went back to his place, where she had sex that she couldn't really remember, but regretted the next morning.'

'Something like that.'

'She then spoke to her mates, and told one of them that her no-good ex had been round and tried it on, and her friend had said that she should go to the police because it sounded like rape.'

'You're unbelievably close. Were you listening in the back of court to my closing speech?'

I smiled. 'Only to get some tips from the master.'

It was a plausible scenario, because it happens a lot, when couples have drunken, regrettable sex. It is an extremely tricky area and it infuriates me when I hear politicians talk about rape as though it is a single entity with the same homogenous set of facts in every single case. True, there are some cases when some horrible dangerous masked man drags a poor defenceless woman into the bushes and commits rape, and of course, there are other awful cases where an ex or current partner decides to ignore the fact that it is every woman's right to say no. Of course, when those facts are presented to a jury they usually convict and the defendant gets a massive sentence and quite bloody right too.

But there are other situations, where people do have drunken sex and the issue of consent is not easy to determine. Don't get me wrong, every woman (and man), regardless of whether they are sober or not, has the right to say no, of course they do. But, if the person can't really remember saying no, or believes that they may have said no after willingly going back to someone's flat and having a right good snog, then the jury, faced with this confusion, quite often acquit. And we shouldn't be surprised about this. After all, in a scenario like this, there is hardly ever any evidence to support the allegation: there won't be any witnesses or CCTV because it happens in the bedroom; whilst the presence of DNA or sperm doesn't help because the issue is not 'Did it happen?' but 'Did they agree to it?' The fact that juries are not sure in cases like this shouldn't be something that makes us doubt our system nor should it be something that makes us fear that the system is inherently biased against the victims of rape. For all crimes, the prosecution bring the charge and they must prove it so that a jury are sure, beyond reasonable doubt. If the jury can't be sure, because a witness herself isn't sure, then the jury can't be criticised, and the system cannot be accused of being broken.

And barristers like Jenny Catrell-Jones will continue to do their job properly and effectively by pointing out to a jury that, actually, on the evidence they've heard, they can't be sure. Whilst a jury will continue to do its job properly and effectively if it determines every case on the facts.

Rape is a particularly emotive crime. There is something profoundly awful, something brutal, about a person who violates another in this base way, but, whether we like it or not, the issue of consent is not always as clear-cut as we'd like it to be, and whilst those convicted of rape should always be harshly punished, we should resist the temptation to rush to convict someone just because another person accuses them of rape. Rape, like every crime, should be considered in a temperate and fair way.

Jenny filled her mug with a bit more cheap fizzy wine and looked glumly into the middle distance. 'Sometimes,' she said, 'I hate this bloody job.' And I nodded, because I got that, most barristers get that feeling from time to time, when you realise that you are actually dealing with some of society's horriblest people doing the most horrible things.

'Come on,' I said, 'let's have a proper drink in a proper glass at the Erskine.'

Domestic violence and the case of Carl and Leanne Stafford

All barristers hate domestic violence cases.

Take the case of Carl Stafford. Apart from anything, it is memorable to me as it is one of the handful of cases in which I've been against my mate, Johnny Richardson.

Johnny was on the side of righteousness as the prosecutor, and me, well, I was representing Carl Stafford, a total bastard who would help to crystallise the image I have in my head of those who are accused of violence against their partners.

Carl was in his forties when I met him. He was a warehouse supervisor, overweight, and drunk most nights on supermarket lager.

His wife was Leanne.

Before the trial, Johnny had described Leanne to me: she was small, quiet, and had once been very pretty. The type of girl who had the best figure in the whole school, but now just looked defeated, controlled, scared and tired – tired of being scared, I suppose.

Carl Stafford was neither scared nor controlled; he was loud and abrasive, the type of guy who insisted on being the centre of attention wherever he went. People knew him, but few knew him well. He wasn't the type of bloke who went out with mates to the pub or to the football, he went to functions, he went to parties and gatherings. There seemed to be a lot of christenings and social events in the upstairs rooms of pubs, which Carl would insist on attending with Leanne. He would place her with the benign female friends he wasn't threatened by, whilst he took his place by the bar giving everyone who had the misfortune of being anywhere near him the benefit of his opinion on whatever was being discussed. He would try to dominate everything and everybody.

I have no doubt that his opinions were odious.

At the end of these nights, he and Leanne would get a taxi home, and this is where the problems would start. This is when Carl's inadequacies would race round his head chased by lager and self-loathing. He would remember the conversations he'd had, the reactions of his audience. Of how Mike, his sister's bloke, hadn't responded properly when he was giving some kind of anecdote; or how Brian, who worked with him, hadn't laughed at a joke, and then he would remember that there had been a man wearing a denim jacket stood at the bar who may have been looking at Leanne. Fucking Leanne, she was the source of his problems, she was laughing at him too. She was laughing at him and flirting with the bloke in the denim jacket, he bloody well knew this, and his concerns about Mike and Brian and all the other men he was threatened by would dissipate and be replaced by his rage towards his wife, who had done nothing wrong.

And that is when he would beat her.

And beat her.

And beat her.

The police had been called a few times, but Leanne had never pressed charges; she had always believed him when he said that he would change, when he told her that he loved her, when he told her that without him she would be nothing.

After a works quiz night at the Swallow's Arms, he meted out a particularly savage beating. Leanne had run out of her house wearing only her underwear and had been helped by a neighbour who had tended to the cut under her eye and the bruises to her body, and telephoned the police.

PC Simeonson had been outstanding. She had taken Leanne to her mother's and had carefully written down a statement in which Leanne Stafford had outlined everything that had happened to her over fourteen years. A fourteen-page statement as vicious and as desperate as any novel or gritty TV drama, except this was Leanne Stafford's real story, her real life.

Stafford had been arrested, charged and bailed not to go anywhere near her. Predictably, because it was against every fibre of his being to relinquish control, he had breached the terms of his bail by turning up at her mum's, pissed, and shouting an incoherent mix of how much he loved her and how she was a slag who had started it all. The police arrested him again and this time he was remanded into custody.

And that is when I met him – in a cell, as a remand prisoner.

His first words to me were 'Why the fuck am I in here? This is a fucking disgrace. I've got my fucking rights.'

I told him that he was in prison because he was accused of beating his wife with a dumbbell.

'It's all bollocks,' he told me.

'Okay,' I said, 'what about her injuries? How can you account for them?'

'I hardly fucking touched her,' he said, unable to meet my gaze.

The coward.

In his mind it was all her fault. In his mind she had driven him to it. I listened to him tell me about what a great dad he was, how he was missing his kids, how hard he worked for his family and how he planned to take them all to Florida next summer, and with every word, he sounded increasingly pathetic.

'You better get me bail,' he told me, and I shrugged my shoulders. 'I'll do my best, but it's not likely, not in a case like this.'

The next week he pleaded not guilty to GBH; the Judge looked at me. 'What is his defence, Mr Winnock?'

'He never caused her any injury,' I said.

'Well who did?' asked the Judge.

'Not him,' I answered. And I hated that Carl Stafford would have enjoyed the spectacle of my nonchalance in the face of the Judge's questions.

Later, in the cells, Carl Stafford told me that she wouldn't turn up for the trial. 'I know for a fact,' he said, 'she won't turn up.' Guilty men know a lot of things for a fact.

I nodded and warned him that the police would bring her to court.

He was right. At the first trial, Leanne Stafford didn't turn up.

Johnny had applied for an adjournment and the Judge had tutted. 'Is there any prospect of this lady turning up next time?' he asked.

And Johnny had assured him that there was. And Carl Stafford had smirked – because he knew better.

But at the next trial, Leanne *did* turn up.

Johnny had told me gleefully that she was in the witness care suite, reading through her statement.

I went to see Stafford.

'Your wife is here,' I told him.

And he looked at me, his face an ugly scowl, incredulous, disbelieving.

'It means you have to decide if you want to run this to trial.' I told him, 'And if we're having a trial you have to give me some instructions as to how she came about her injuries.'

'I never hit her with a dumbbell,' he said, 'I might have slapped her, but she kept goading me.' He paused. 'She ripped my clothes up once,' he said, as though this justified everything. 'She probably did most of the injuries to herself, to make things worse.'

Now it was my turn to scowl at him.

'You do realise,' I said, 'that if you have a trial, I will have to cross-examine your wife, and I will have to put it to her that she's lying and that she caused some of her injuries herself? You understand that don't you?'

He nodded.

And that's what I would do, I would put my wig on my head and my cape around my shoulders and I would put my client's case to the witness, just as I am trained to do. He was a coward and a bastard and I was an accessory. I took solace in the fact that it was a rubbish defence that was bound to fail and that Carl Stafford would end up serving even more time in prison. Should I confess this? Probably not, but it's true, and if a barrister tells you that there has never been a time when he wanted his client to lose, then he's probably not being truthful.

Johnny opened the case to the jury, who listened, probably grimacing inwardly at the thought of the bloated thug in the dock beating up his wife of fourteen years.

Johnny turned to the Judge. 'I call the first witness for the Crown, Your Honour, Leanne Stafford.'

But Leanne Stafford didn't appear through the door of the court. Instead an usher rushed in and whispered something in Johnny's ear. I knew exactly what was happening. It was all depressingly predictable. Johnny told me later that Leanne had been left in the witness care room, shaking with fear, crying at the worthlessness of her existence, and decided that she couldn't give evidence. She had asked to go to the toilet and run away.

The Judge wouldn't allow Johnny another chance. 'I'm afraid,

Mr Richardson,' he said, 'that enough taxpayers' money has been wasted on this already, you've had your chance.'

Taxpayers' money. He couldn't have put it in a more callous way.

Twenty minutes later Carl Stafford was released. I didn't stick around to shake his hand. I hated him and felt no pride in securing an acquittal for my client.

Bradley Edwards and the 'Furry Fuckers'

A common fear amongst barristers who are dependent upon legal aid money is that we will become stuck in a sort of timeless career which is difficult to get out of. It is harder to become a Judge, which is one traditional way out; harder to retire, because our pensions, if we have one, are worth very little; and pointless becoming a QC, because there's not much money in that either. I'm not moaning, but it's a fact that the Criminal Bar will probably shrink as fewer and fewer people become barristers, and as such we fear that eventually there will be a small rump of ageing men and women who cling to their wigs and gowns, customs and traditions and occasionally get wheeled out in front of a court to present some case or other.

Bradley Edwards is a sort of ghost of the future, who haunts various courts around London, showing us what might come to pass.

Bradley is extremely old. Estimates have him at 84 years old, though there is a fair bit of speculation that he could even be a couple of years older than that. Legend has it that once upon a time, Bradley was a fine advocate, a great lawyer who was destined for the highest position. But, sadly, he was passed over for both the Judicial bench and Queen's Counsel. My old pupil-master Ronnie Sherman suggested that he been caught messing around with the wife of the Master of the Rolls at a Lincoln's Inn dinner back in the 1960s, but other stories of whatever misdemeanour befell Bradley range from a predilection for schoolboys to a rather public brush with Communism at Cambridge in the 1950s. For whatever reason though, Bradley Edwards never really progressed, but nor has he ever retired, instead he stalks the corridors of the Bailey and other courts, clutching the odd rather limited brief to represent some minor felon or other.

I first met him in the flesh during my first ever appearance at the Old Bailey. I was due to mitigate in a sentence in a case where a man had deliberately knocked someone off his bike by London Bridge.

I was young and nervous, awed by my surroundings, and at first paid little attention to the Counsel, who had quietly sidled in by my side.

Then, when that Counsel started to make strange wheezing noises I looked to my left and saw Bradley Edwards. I knew it must be him, I'd already heard the stories. He sat with his mouth open and his eyes fixed in the middle distance, as some other barrister in another case made submissions to the Judge. He smelled of something rotten, as though one of his body parts had died and had yet to inform the rest of him. His wig was a strange shade of nicotine yellow and his gown was coated in a grey crusty ash-type substance, the source of which was a mystery.

After a few minutes listening to what was going on, or appearing to, he turned to me – 'Have the Furry Fuckers been in yet?' His voice boomed over the hapless brief, who was on his feet, and caused the Judge to stop and look in his direction.

Bradley Edwards didn't give a monkey's about this though. At the age of 80 whatever, he was far beyond any judicial admonishment and would speak as loud as he thought he had to, regardless of whether he was in court or not.

'Sorry?' I whispered.

'The Furry Fuckers,' he repeated, 'have they arrived yet?'

I shrugged. I hadn't a clue what he was talking about. He looked at me with a degree of concern.

'Is this your first time at the Bailey?'

I nodded, moving uncomfortably in my seat as I did, in a vain attempt to try to distance myself from anything that might possibly irritate the Judge.

At this point Bradley rather loudly cleared his throat, re-arranging 84 years of phlegm and the dust of a thousand visits to the Old Bailey from his chest to his larynx.

'I can't believe no one's warned you about the Furry Fuckers,' he continued, to my excruciating embarrassment. 'You see any minute now, there'll be a knock on that door to the Judge's left, and when it's opened you'll see an old man in a fur coat and hat, bowing like a fucking imbecile at the court.'

I wanted the ground to swallow me up there and then, I wanted to shout out across the courtroom, 'I'm not with this decrepit old fart, he's nothing to do with me.' But, of course, I couldn't.

'They're the Aldermen of the City,' continued Edwards, 'and in order to get a free lunch, they have to earn it. Now we can't let them anywhere near the courts, so we pretend by making them dress up in their furry best and nod at us. That's why they're the Furry Fuckers, they always bloody turn up when you least want them to.'

I thought he was mad.

I thought he was mad right up until the moment when there was a knock on the door and the court rose as one to acknowledge the man in the fur coat and hat.

'See,' said Edwards, 'I told you.'

He was absolutely right. He stayed by my side for the rest of the morning, I wasn't sure if he actually had a case or was just wandering around for something to do. He listened to the prosecutor opening the case against my client, and then leaned towards me. 'If I were you,' he said, trying his hardest, but failing miserably, to whisper, 'in front of this Judge, I'd tell him about your client's excellent work record.'

On a whim, I decided to do just that. I changed my initial speech in mitigation and told the Judge about the fact that my client after years of being homeless and unemployed had now obtained work, and was doing well.

It worked. My client was given a suspended sentence and left the court a very happy man.

By the time I had finished, though, Bradley had already got up, coughed a bit, swore audibly about something and waddled out of the courtroom.

You don't see him too much now. Perhaps he's still wandering the corridors of some Crown Court or other, clutching a flimsy brief in his hand and passing on the lessons from his years of experience to some other young barrister, fresh from law school. I hope so.

The story of Charlie Parkman QC

I had only spoken to Charlie Parkman twice in my ten years in chambers, once at a chambers drinks do to commemorate the appointment of Tim Belton to Silk and another time when I happened across him in the chambers kitchen making coffee. I think on the first occasion he made a few polite comments about chambers doing very well; and on the second, he mentioned how he was resisting the urge to have a chocolate HobNob, because he was putting weight on, which precipitated a brief conversation about the merits of HobNobs as opposed to Gingers or Chocolate Digestives.

He wasn't one of those barristers who immediately demanded attention when he entered a room.

There were stories about him and not all of them were good.

As soon as I'd been given permission to instruct leading Counsel, I arranged for us to meet in chambers library.

I was nervous. I sent him copies of all the papers in the case together with my typed-up notes from the conference with Tasha and some of my own thoughts about tactics for the trial.

Before our scheduled meeting, I ventured into the chambers common room, which is a sort of communal area, ostensibly for barristers to meet and have a chat, though in reality it has become a dumping ground for old briefs and out-of-date law books.

To my surprise, sitting there quietly reading the newspaper was Edward Grieve. Eddie Grieve is our most senior Chancery and Civil barrister. Rumour has it that he is the top earner in chambers and has refused to take Silk or a judicial appointment because he's earning more as a junior barrister. He's also a very nice guy, the type of bloke who overflows with helpful wisdom.

He looked up when I entered the room and greeted me warmly.

'Ah, young Mr Winnock,' he said, 'what are you up to?'

'I'm meeting Charlie Parkman,' I told him. 'He's going to lead me in a case.'

'Oh, I didn't realise you did family work.'

'No, it's a criminal case,' I told him and watched as Eddie's expression turned from one of surprise to one of interest.

'How well do you know Charlie?' he asked me, his eyes scrunching slightly in contemplation.

'Not well at all.'

'Do you know about the case of Mark Griffin?'

'No,' I said, though the name rang a quiet bell somewhere in the part of my brain that stored the stuff I'd learned at Law School.

Eddie continued, 'Charlie was a brilliant junior, you know,' he said, 'he was a Silk after fifteen years call, he couldn't have been much more than about 38.'

'Gosh.'

'He did a lot of crime then: prosecution and defence.'

I nodded.

'He was junior in the case involving the maid who'd been stealing from the Queen.'

Again, another faint bell rang, this time from my childhood.

'Then, not long into Silk, he was instructed in a case involving a dispute over the turning off of a life support machine for a young lad who'd been in a car accident. The boy was only thirteen. Terrible business. He was diagnosed as being in a vegetative state.

'The mum wanted to keep the life support machine on, the dad wanted to turn it off. Charlie was for the dad. Alan Harper was for the mother, or Mr Justice Harper as he now is.'

I nodded again.

'Harper, as you know, is a brilliant lawyer. He used everything he could to persuade the court to keep the machine on. They spent about a month arguing before the High Court, a month in which Charlie was arguing just as vociferously in favour of bringing to an end the life of a thirteen-year-old boy.'

'Did he win?' I asked.

'Yes,' said Eddie, 'he won and the life support machine was turned off, but Charlie was never really the same again. He stopped doing any criminal cases, stopped doing cases involving children, and has, as far as I know, spent the last twenty years doing high-end divorces.'

'So why change now?' I asked. 'I don't really get it.'

Eddie shrugged. 'Perhaps he feels stronger, perhaps he needs a new challenge, I don't know. I don't think it's about the money though, he'd get far more for his divorce work than he would for a legal aid case. What is your case about?'

'Murder,' I said, 'and the Crown have got Roger Fish, and he's slippery, clever and battle-hardened. I don't want to lose.'

Eddie pondered this. 'Well, my advice is to trust him and help him as best you can, because he might just come up trumps for you.'

'Thanks.'

Somehow this story made me feel more confident about my leader.

A little while later I went into the library for our meeting. Charlie Parkman was already sitting at the table. He was a slight man of about 60, who was well served by his still dark and thick hair, which gave the impression he was about ten years younger than he was. Spread out on the table in front of him were the papers in the case of R v Roux. Behind him were the packed library shelves containing the dark and brooding law books that have been collected by chambers for over a hundred years: the All-England Law Reports, the Weekly Law Reports, the Legal Review, Halsbury's Laws. These books contain words written by long-dead Judges and politicians; the judgements of Lord Denning, Lord Lane, Lord Upjohn and numerous forgotten Masters of the Rolls; the Acts drafted by Privy Counsellors and Government Ministers. The brains who decided the cases and drafted the statutes which frame all of our lives, tell us what we can and can't do; the words that determine the parameters of our relations with our fellow citizens – written down and recorded in these dusty books is the law.

And sitting quietly in front of them was the man who had argued every day for a month that, in law, a dying boy's life should be ended. I felt the massive weight of all their words and the ghosts of the men who had written them.

How would I have coped with such an argument?

Could I have done it? Just put my wig on and taken a side in a dispute in which neither side would ever be happy with the outcome? I wasn't sure.

But I was sure that a case as tragic as that of Mark Griffin gave Charlie Parkman a humanity that I liked.

He stood up when I entered and shook me warmly by the hand. 'Ah Russell,' he said, 'how nice to see you again.'

For a brief moment I was confused, I didn't know whether to shake his hand or not. You see, barristers don't normally shake hands, we are supposed to trust one another implicitly without the need to shake hands. Parkman's gesture, though, was natural, instinctive and warm. I grasped his proffered hand and shook it firmly.

'Yes,' I said, 'brilliant. What do you think about the case then?'

'Well,' he said, 'first, I'm delighted that you've asked me to lead you.'

'Pleasure.' Obviously, I didn't tell him that I didn't so much as select him as have him selected for me.

'I know you'll be concerned that I haven't done a great deal of crime in the last few years.'

'No,' I lied, 'I'm not bothered at all.' Then added, 'What do they say about footballers – form is temporary, class is permanent.'

As soon as I said it, I realised I'd taken the rule about telling your leader how good they are to an Olympic level of sycophancy within the first five minutes of meeting him. Charlie looked embarrassed. 'I'm not sure about that,' he said, and we both cringed silently for a couple of seconds.

After that, and for the next twenty minutes, we sat there in the library talking about the case. He spoke in an informed way about the law and the evidence and how he proposed to deal with each of the witnesses. He *was* impressive.

I watched and nodded and chipped in with my own views when they were invited. I noticed that he had small nimble hands that moved around his papers with a strategic expertise.

'This Dickinson sounds like a real piece of work,' he said, 'and I agree with you that our problem is the Irishman who says he saw Miss Roux run towards Dickinson. My view,' he continued, 'is that we have to cast as much doubt as we can on that evidence, whilst painting a picture of our girl as a victim. We want to make it as easy as we can for the jury to acquit her.'

I nodded, I was becoming increasingly excited by the presence of my leader.

'You say that Tasha told you that he may have been seeing other women?'

'Yes,' I said, 'she was very clear about that.'

'I wonder what they think about this? I wonder if he was doing to them the type of things he was doing to Miss Roux?'

I nodded as Charlie smiled at me. 'I can't see any harm in tracking one or two of these girls down, what do you think?'

'Yes,' I said, effusively, 'absolutely.'

'Okay,' he said, 'well, can I leave that to you?'

'Absolutely,' I repeated, 'leave that to me.'

'Great.'

We agreed to visit Tasha together, and to meet again in a week or so. I left the library enthused and excited. I walked away from the law books, I walked away from the dusty ghosts of Judges and politicians, and went back into the real world.

I was pleased with Charlie Parkman QC. Of course, I was yet to see how he was in court, but I realised that he cared about his clients and that he would come to care about Tasha and that was good enough for me.

The queue at HMP Stoneywood and the case of Sam Wheldon

Stoneywood is a modern prison, set in the middle of nowhere, that caters for young prisoners, remand prisoners and lowest category prisoners. If it wasn't for the barbed-wire fences, you could easily take HMP Stoneywood as a call centre or a factory, making high-end computer equipment. The inmates call it Butlins because they are allowed games consoles in their cells and they aren't banged up for twenty hours a day, which is the case in higher security prisons.

Oddly, some of the old lags hate it; they can't cope with such a liberal regime. They prefer bars and screws and the quickening of the pulse when it's your turn to shower. I suppose they prefer a pecking order and a prison in which they know their place.

I arrived at Stoneywood at 8.30 in the morning for a conference at nine and took myself to the visitors centre to go through the rigmarole of security. It was a freezing cold, grey and damp morning but already there was a long line of young women dressed as though they were queuing to get into a nightclub: a long line of short skirts, massive heels, fake tan and lipgloss. Lurid colours against the dim, gloomy morning. Some pushed prams, some laughed and joked with newly made friends, some looked lonely and pissed off as they shivered in the morning mist. These are the

'Mrs', the girls left behind whilst their errant boyfriends and partners do their time.

I felt sorry for them, they are under massive pressure. They have to turn up looking happy, but not so happy that their bloke thinks that they are up to no good; they have to look concerned, but not so concerned that their bloke thinks that they are unable to cope without them; they have to put aside the problems they have about paying the bills, and looking after the kids and putting up with his bloody mother, who keeps coming round pestering them; and, they have to look drop dead gorgeous and give the impression that they are desperate to shag them, even in the least romantic environment known to man that is the visiting room of a prison.

Interspersed amongst the line of 'Mrs' are the mothers. These are the hard-faced women who turn up week after week to show solidarity with their daft offspring who've managed to get themselves locked up. The mothers eye the 'Mrs' with suspicion.

The mothers don't look quite so glamorous.

And to cap it all, there are always a couple of uncontrollable toddlers charging around like it's playtime. It always amazes me how easily they take to the environment, how they find getting strip searched, and sniffed by a dog, just another fun part of their lives.

As a legal visit, I'm allowed to the front of the queue, which doesn't, as you might imagine, provoke a torrent of abuse and cat-calls from those freezing in the queue behind me, which makes me wonder if some of the girls are happier gossiping in the queue than they are having to endure the hour-long visit inside.

I was taken to a booth where my client, Sam Wheldon, would be waiting for me. I was accompanied by a rather nervous trainee solicitor called Brian Simmonds. We made our way through the security barriers and up the endless disinfected corridors towards the bay reserved for legal visits – our footsteps squeaky against the linoleum floor.

'Fair bit of flesh on show in the queue today, Brian, eh?' I ventured with a wink.

He smiled weakly. This is clearly one of his first visits to a prison and he is far too petrified to contemplate the visitors in the queue.

'Do you know if they've organised a DVD player?' I asked.

'I hope so,' he said, 'I've telephoned a few times to remind them.'

Thankfully, when we arrived at our designated booth, there was a DVD player and a client.

'Good morning Mr Wheldon,' I said.

The client nodded back at me.

'I'm Russell Winnock, I'm the barrister who's going to look after you. This is Mr Simmonds, he's from your solicitors.'

I then told Sam Wheldon what I tell all my clients – that it is their case and I'll do what they tell me, but I will be honest and straight with them when I go through the evidence that they face.

Sam Wheldon nodded at this and I could tell that this was going to be one of those forgettable cases.

Sam Wheldon faced an allegation of affray – he's committed one of the most common crimes known to young British males. He, together with about five of his mates, have got themselves completely pissed in various pubs in the suburban town where they live; they have then gone out into the streets and for some reason managed to get into a massive fight with a gang of similarly pissed lads, after one of them made a comment about a girl who happened to be with them.

The fight was caught in splendid technicolor by the increasingly effective CCTV cameras that patrol our streets.

Now for those of you who don't know, it's very very easy to

be guilty of affray. If you go up to someone in a pub or on a street, and you raise your fist or throw a punch whilst shouting the odds, and this causes, or might cause, someone to fear violence, then that's enough, you have committed an affray. Which means that for a generation of young lads, like Sam Wheldon, who've grown up causing mayhem on our streets, CCTV has made it very difficult for them *not* to be guilty of an affray pretty much every time they leave the house.

'Now, Mr Wheldon,' I continued, 'you've been charged with an affray, following the ruckus outside Wetherpools Pub.'

'I wasn't involved,' he said immediately and with confidence, 'I wasn't there that night, I was at home with the Mrs.'

'Okay,' I responded as brightly as I could, 'in that case, you have a potential alibi and potential defence and we'll have a trial.'

He seemed pleased with this. 'But,' I added, 'I have here a DVD of the CCTV taken on the night. Now the police have said that the man wearing a distinctive stripy yellow and green jersey trying to hit someone over the head with some scaffolding is you. Okay?'

He nodded and I placed the DVD into the machine. The three of us sat and watched it in silence.

We watched as the camera zoomed in on the Essex street where this took place. At first everything was quiet. Then the camera panned towards a couple who were having a rather full-on snog in a bus stop. Then, as the couple suddenly stopped snogging and looked up the street, the CCTV followed their gaze and we saw the man in the yellow and green stripy top leading his mates into battle. They strutted like young baboons towards the camera, which zoomed in on one of them, who had his mouth open and was clearly shouting the battle cry of choice for this generation – *'come and have a go if you think you're hard enough.'*

The camera then panned back up the road to the recipient of the threat, introducing us to the rival gang, who were making their way up the street with similar haste and intent. We then went back to the other gang and there was a close-up of the man in the stripy top who had now armed himself with a scaffolding pole.

'I'm going to stop the DVD here,' I said and I pressed the pause button. 'Have a look at this person carrying the scaffolding pole.'

'Okay,' said Sam Wheldon.

'Now,' I ventured carefully, 'I've got to be honest with you, Sam, that person looks uncannily like you.'

Wheldon looked at me with a rather blank defiance as I pointed this out to him.

'And, the fellas who have also been arrested are all your mates.'

I looked at him closely now, I was aware that one of my eyebrows had managed to raise itself.

'And, when the police arrested you at your house a couple of hours later, you were described as wearing a yellow and green stripy top, by not just one, but six police officers.'

'What are you trying to say, Mr Winnock?' asked Wheldon.

'I'm saying that you're going to find it very difficult to win a trial, Sam.'

Wheldon sighed. 'But I can't go to prison, Mr Winnock, my Mrs will leave me.'

'Okay,' I said, 'I understand that. But, well, you already are in prison.'

'Yes, but I could be out if I get a not guilty, couldn't I?'

Now it was my turn to sigh. 'That's not going to happen, Sam, not with that CCTV. All a jury have to do to find you guilty is to consider firstly, is that Sam Wheldon in that stripy top? And secondly, if I saw that person running around with that scaffolding post shouting "have this, you fucker", would I be scared? Now Sam, let's be realistic. What's the likely answer to those questions going to be?'

Wheldon looked down, he looked downhearted.

'What am I likely to get?' he asked quietly.

'Eighteen months tops,' I said, 'you'll be out in nine months, you've already done six weeks on remand, so that'll come off. You'll be back to your Mrs in no time.'

'She wants to have a baby,' he said, looking forlornly at me.

'Well I can't help there can I,' I smiled, I was trying to be warm, not flippant.

And Wheldon gave me that resigned smile that young men do when they realise that they're going to have to plead guilty to the charge.

I walked back with Brian Simmonds, by now the glamorous girls were making their way out of the visiting hall. There was a chorus of 'Love you babes' and 'Say bye to Daddy,' as they tottered towards the exit.

A couple of them immediately pulled jumpers out of their bags as they emerged from the building and braced themselves against the cold, ready for another week on their own.

Disclosure

The queue to the Women's Prison in Holloway was decidedly different. Sure, there was a consternation of mothers, but they didn't look quite so hard, just forlorn. There were a few 'Mrs' I suppose, but they didn't look quite so glamorous, and the children queued in grim and unhappy silence. This wasn't a happy weekly visit to see their exciting Dad, no, this was a horrible reminder of their absent mother.

I was there to visit Tasha. It was her first conference with myself, Kelly and her QC, Charlie Parkman.

Charlie came with no papers and no pens – he didn't need them. With incredible precision he spoke gently to her about her case for over an hour. Clearly every fact and detail was now in his head.

The jealousy that I had expected to feel when another, more experienced barrister came into my case had completely dissipated, giving way to a feeling of contentment and confidence: Tasha was happy and impressed and that was good enough for me.

She gave her account to Charlie in exactly the same way she had given it to me – and he listened and nodded and looked softly at her and told her that we would do all we could for her. I was happy with the use of the collective noun 'we', it made me feel part of everything. *We* were a team.

Before we parted, Charlie gave us all our tasks: Kelly and I were to deal with disclosure, track down witnesses, especially Gary Dickinson's ex-girlfriends, draft a bad character application, and deal with the interviews.

I reacted like a tail-wagging Labrador each time Charlie gave me something new to do.

The next day I eagerly started to deal with the issue of disclosure.

If you get the chance, look up the poster for the 1994 Demi Moore and Michael Douglas 'gripping courtroom drama' *Disclosure* – tag line: 'Sex Is Power'. It shows Demi Moore, skirt hitched up to her waist, in mid-clinch with Michael Douglas. Well, I can tell you that this does not in any shape or form reflect the reality that is disclosure.

Disclosure is not sexy, but, in every legal case, it is crucial.

Let me tell you how it works in criminal cases.

The police investigate a crime and in the course of their investigation they take statements and accumulate evidence. They then send their file to the Crown Prosecution Service who decide whether or not to prosecute. The test for the CPS is whether it is in the public interest to prosecute and whether, on the evidence, there is a realistic chance of a conviction. They are therefore not allowed to prosecute hopeless or pointless cases.

Once they've made their decision to charge, they carry out what is known as primary disclosure. This is when they serve on the defence all the statements and exhibits that they are relying on to prove the charge.

After primary disclosure, if the defendant is contesting the charge, he must serve something called the defence statement, which says why he is not guilty.

The prosecution then respond by serving the items of evidence that they haven't yet disclosed, which will either assist the defence or undermine the prosecution. And that is an important test, because it relies on the integrity and intelligence of a disclosure officer.

They also serve upon the defence a list of all the statements and documents that they have which they are not relying upon, this is called the schedule of unused material, which the defence must go through carefully to see if there is anything else that, in their opinion, assists them, or undermines the prosecution's case.

See I told you – nothing to do with sex or power or Demi Moore in a short skirt.

Now, I'll be honest, in most of the minor cases that I do, the issue of disclosure is fairly straightforward. Most of the material is disclosed and anything that is held back is usually completely uncontroversial (for example, a statement from a police officer describing how they disposed of their protective gloves after they'd seized some drugs from the anus of a drug mule doesn't really assist the defence or undermine the prosecution). But there have been cases when a failure to disclose has been potentially catastrophic for my clients.

Take the case of Abdul Ramzi. Abdul was the owner of a curry house in the East End. He was a family man and well-respected member of his community. Alas for Abdul, he also had a penchant for young men, particularly rough young white men, preferably with tattoos.

And after one liaison with a nineteen-year-old man from Dagenham, he was accused of rape. The complainant claimed that he had met Abdul in a gay bar. They had chatted and then shared a taxi because they were going in the same direction, before Abdul ordered the taxi to stop by some waste ground where he was alleged to have raped the young man in some bushes.

At first, Abdul denied any knowledge of the Dagenham boy – 'This is ridiculous,' he told me, 'I am a married man. I am 100 per cent straight. I have never met this man.'

The one flaw in Abdul's assertion that he had never met the man was that his DNA and sperm was all over the complainant's underwear and body.

I met him in chambers for a conference. He was shaking as he told me how this was all a total set-up and how he was not gay.

'That's fine,' I told him, 'no one is suggesting that you are gay. But, if you want me to help you, then you are going to have to tell me everything, because the evidence in the case shows, over-whelmingly, that you have had some kind of contact with the complainant.'

After a couple of months of total denial, just before the trial, a very contrite Abdul finally made the decision to tell me every-thing. He told me that he had met the man in a pub, they had kissed in the pub, had some jiggy-jiggy in the pub toilets and left together in a taxi, going on to have consensual sex in a disused bus station.

This was massively important. As soon as I heard Abdul's proper account, I knew that there was potentially evidence to corroborate his story. You see, you can't cop off with anyone in a pub and expect it to remain a secret: CCTV is everywhere.

I scoured the schedule of unused material for reference to the CCTV footage of the pub. It was inconceivable that the police wouldn't have seized it in a case like this. But, amazingly, there was no mention of it. Nothing, not a sausage.

I asked my solicitor to get in touch with the police and the CPS and ask them to have a look for it, and the answer came back that it didn't exist.

I didn't believe them.

I asked again, and got the same message back: 'There is no

further material that either undermines the prosecution case or assists the defence.'

I went before a Judge and made a big fuss. The Judge agreed that there must be something and suggested that a failure to seize the CCTV footage was a serious flaw in the investigation.

Lo and behold, a few days later I received a brown envelope containing a CCTV disc. On it, clear as day, was Abdul and a young blonde man sitting at a table in Flumes Club in Basildon, then Abdul and the young blonde man kissing in Flumes Club, then Abdul and the man disappearing to the toilets, then Abdul and the, seemingly very happy, content young man walking out of the club, hand in hand, towards a taxi.

The Crown dropped the case against him a short while later. After this, they knew that there was no longer a reasonable prospect of a conviction.

Now, in the case of Tasha Roux, the schedule of unused material ran to many pages. I scoured it. There was very little that was of interest: a few things about Gary Dickinson's previous convictions (which were not insubstantial, but, alas, nothing for violence against women), lots of unhelpful briefings and some statements from other people in the flats who said that they hadn't seen very much. Not surprisingly, there was nothing about any of Dickinson's other girlfriends.

I reached the end of the schedule and sighed. I was desperate to establish something that showed that Gary Dickinson was capable of hitting women in the way that Tasha described. I knew that there must, somewhere, be an ex-girlfriend who could give evidence about Dickinson and what he was capable of. I needed at least one other girl, especially one who had never met Tasha and had no reason to just back her up. It might make the difference between a jury believing or disbelieving her account.

Tasha had been certain that there was a girl from a club in Deptford called the Purple Velvet Club, who Dickinson had been seeing behind her back. Lilly, Tasha had said.

It was time for me to find Lilly.

Goodbye to Johnny Richardson and hello to Lilly Spencer

Johnny Richardson's leaving party was in an upstairs room in a pub in Shoreditch.

Bless 'em, some of the people from his chambers had tried to create a bit of a Middle Eastern theme by getting hold of a couple of blow-up camels and building a rather elaborate pyramid. There was a banner that read 'Good Luck Johnny!' with some pictures of playing cards on it to symbolise his new career as a croupier in a Dubai hotel.

I looked at the banner and the camels and the pyramids and felt like weeping. It all seemed so unfair, such a waste.

I got myself a pint and found my old university and flatmate, Ed Douglas, who was talking with a group of his Chancery pals. Predictably, they were talking about a case. One of them, who had thick glasses and acne that any thirteen-year-old boy would be proud of, was chastising another for trying to obtain an injunction in relation to some assets which were being hidden. 'But if you don't even know what country the assets are in,' he was saying, 'how can you make such an application?'

'Easy,' I said, butting in.

They all looked at me. 'Well it's all there, isn't it, in the case of,' I paused, 'Bradley versus Tompkinson.'

'What?' They stared at me, as Ed Douglas' face broke out into a big grin. 'Is that the case about the ship that went down killing the cargo of puppies?' he asked, playing along with my joke.

'They were kittens,' I answered. Still none of the Chancery boys realised we were taking the piss.

'Ah, yes,' responded Ed, 'the case where Mr Justice Foreskin ruled that no knowledge of the unknowable assets accrued by the benefactors of the third party could be injuncted, if the rule in Stoppard, Stoppard and Pintglass was invoked before 10 o'clock on a Thursday?'

I burst out laughing. Ed burst out laughing. The Chancery boys said nothing and carried on with their conversation.

I ushered Ed to the bar where Johnny Richardson was holding court wearing an Arab headdress.

'Is that what you're going to be wearing in Dubai?' I asked. 'You're going all that way to swap one ridiculous costume for another?'

'Ah,' said Johnny, suddenly becoming wistful, 'the costume is about the only thing I'm going to miss.'

We drank some beer and reminisced about girls we had known at university and the things we'd got up to when we first came down to London.

Then we drank some more beer, and a small Scottish barrister called Harvey Johnstone joined us and started to talk about the barristers who were no longer working. He reeled off a list of names. 'Pete Ashton,' he said, 'went to become a teacher. Ernie Haselhurst, you know, with the lisp, he left to become an antiques dealer or something. Andy Renshaw has become a golfing instructor. Graham Lloyd-Smith joined the army. And little Tommy Conrad, well, who knows what happened to him, he just disappeared: he made a bail application in a burglary case, left court, and no one saw him again.'

It was a list of the fallen: barristers who had worked at the

Criminal and Family Bar who could no longer work because of the cuts to legal aid and the changes to the way we get our work. Now our mate Johnny was about to join their ranks, leaving the profession he had spent five years studying to join, to go and work in a hotel. I felt sad as I remembered the pride on the faces of his parents and his little sister when they came to his graduation.

'Will you come back to the Bar?' I asked him.

He shrugged. 'Not unless things change. I'm sick of the debt. It's not a profession for the likes of us any more. It's a job for the sons and daughters of the rich.'

It was difficult to stand and listen to the negativity, to have another conversation about how defeated we were, how we were all doomed, how the promise of a lovely secure professional way of life we had assumed was ours, was going to crash around our heads. They may be right, but I wasn't giving up. Not yet.

We drank more, toasted Johnny, drank some more, then hugged him and wished him well.

Eventually, just after Harvey Johnstone had completed his third toast in the style of Rab Burns, I looked at the time, it was just after midnight. I turned to Ed Douglas. 'Look Ed, will you do me a favour?'

'Sure.'

'I need to go to a club in Deptford. Will you come with me?'

'A club in Deptford?'

'Yes.'

'Christ, Russ, haven't you suffered enough listening to the voices of doom in here?'

'I need to find a girl,' I told him, adding quickly, 'Not like that. It's for a case I'm doing – for my murder. It's the club where the deceased used to work.'

'What, you want us to go to a nightclub in Deptford, where the person your client is accused of murdering used to work, to find a girl?'

'Yes.'

Ed smiled. 'You're completely mad.'

Ten minutes later we were in a taxi rushing through the twinkling London night towards the Purple Velvet Club, Deptford.

It is an old-fashioned nightclub, the Purple Velvet, one that probably saw its heyday in the 1980s. Now, though, it looked very quiet. I was nervous. The beer was starting to wear off and I was seriously questioning whether this was the right thing to do. It was the first time I had ever chased a witness, in fact it was the first time I had ever taken one of my cases into the real world. Normally my cases existed in the form of statements and photographs and the odd bit of CCTV. They would only come alive for me in my room and in my head, where they would be properly penned in by the confines of the law and my position as a barrister – the two things that protect me.

I had now entered the world of Tasha Roux and Gary Dickinson and I was an imposter, I wasn't meant to be there.

My pupil-master had told me that I should never get too close to a case, yet here I was in the club where the deceased had worked, trying to find one of his girlfriends. It was utter madness. If I had been sober I'm pretty sure that I would have turned around, got back into the taxi and got as far away from the Purple Velvet Club as I could.

Ed looked at me, sensing my reticence. 'Look, we're here now, we might as well have a drink.'

I nodded, and we entered without any problem.

The club was quiet. There was a bar on the right-hand side and a deserted dance floor that was pulsing with disco lights.

I followed Ed to the bar. 'Right,' he said, shouting above the music, 'what does this girl look like?'

'I've no idea,' I said.

'Well, what's her name then?'

'Lilly.'

'Okay, watch this,' said Ed and turned towards the bar where a barmaid came to serve him. What happened next left me stunned. The ordinarily bookish and shy Ed Douglas suddenly started to flirt outrageously with the barmaid. The barmaid was a rather portly girl with dyed jet-black hair and a nose ring. I knew straight away that she would have never been involved with Gary Dickinson, this girl wasn't his type. Ed ordered us both a drink, then bought one for the barmaid before declaring with incredible and unexpected confidence, 'You must be Lilly then?'

The barmaid looked confused. 'Er, no.'

'Oh,' said Ed, 'I'm really sorry, I thought you were. Is Lilly working tonight?'

'Lilly Spencer?' asked the goth girl.

'Yes,' said Ed.

The girl looked at her watch. 'She's in the upstairs bar. You'd better hurry though, she's about to finish her shift.'

Ed winked at me, and I rushed upstairs, ignoring the voice in my head that told me I was being a complete idiot.

At the top of the stairs was a set of double doors. As I reached them they opened and there stood two women wearing coats and looking as though they were ready to get off home. One of the girls was Hispanic-looking and the other, who was slightly older, had fair hair.

'Hi,' I said, panting. They looked at me, alarmed, instantly dismissing me as a pissed-up bloke on the pull. 'Sorry,' I continued, 'but I'm trying to find Lilly. Are either of you Lilly?'

The Hispanic girl glanced towards the fair-haired girl. Bingo.

'Why?' she said.

'I'm a barrister,' I continued, as though this made being drunk, sweaty, out of breath and a bit embarrassing, somehow more acceptable.

'I need to speak to her in relation to a case I'm doing.'

The blonde girl immediately looked down, as the Hispanic girl came to her defence. 'If it's about Gary then she doesn't want anything to do with you,' she said.

'Please,' I said, 'I just want five minutes. That's all.'

The two of them started to push past me on the way down the stairs. I turned and followed them.

'Please,' I repeated, sounding desperate now, 'a young girl is in danger of spending the next twenty years of her life in prison.'

'Well she shouldn't have done it then,' hissed the Hispanic girl.

'But, that's just it, she didn't do it.'

By now the two girls were moving away from me, and one of the bouncers was making his way up the stairs in my direction.

'Lilly,' I shouted, 'Lilly, please.'

But it was too late. With an incredible deftness of touch, the bouncer grabbed my arm, and effortlessly placed me in a shoulder lock. A few seconds later, I was dispatched through a back door and into a back alley, ending up on my arse.

I sat there in the dark and deserted alley, the walls were damp and slimy with dubious history. This was a place where crimes were committed. This was a place where men had brandished knives and used their feet to kick, this was a place where women had been raped and drugs had been exchanged for money.

This was real.

I felt stupid. I shouldn't have done this.

Bad character

I woke up the next morning with a tongue as dry as a camel-herder's sandal and a massive grey cloud of guilt and self-loathing sitting uncomfortably above me.

What was I thinking? Going to the Purple Velvet Club in search of a witness, after having a skinful of beer was possibly the stupidest thing that I had ever done.

And then getting myself chucked out. I groaned to myself as the awful reality of what had happened came back to me.

It got worse. I checked my phone and saw that at some point I had sent a series of text messages to Kelly Backworth. The first, cockily proclaiming my decision to go to the Purple Velvet Club in search of Lilly, to which she had replied, with incisive prescience, 'Do you really think that's a good idea Russ?'

Then twenty minutes later, a rather pathetic drunken message that read 'bin checked out of the Purple Club.'

To which she replied with a single word – 'Tit'.

I limped into chambers, drinking Lucozade and eating bananas and extra strong mints (my age-old, tried and trusted hangover cure), and decided to carry out the next task on the list of things that Charlie Parkman wanted me to do: draft the application to adduce the bad character of Gary Dickinson.

Bad character is a tricky issue, though on balance it's probably slightly more interesting than disclosure.

I'll tell you about it.

Bad character is, as you'd expect, the generic term to describe whether someone has ever been in trouble before. To put it simply, if you have no previous convictions, cautions or reprimands, then you are entitled to call yourself a person of good character. If you have a list of form as long as your arm, or even a single conviction, then you are not – you have bad character.

How much a jury should know about your character has been debated by lawyers, Judges and clever people for as long as there has been trial by jury.

And it can be massively significant. If you are charged with, say, the offence of indecent assault, and in the past you have been convicted of possessing indecent images of children, then as soon as the jury hear about that previous conviction, the chances of you being acquitted pretty much disappear, regardless of the evidence. Because, understandably you might think, if there is one thing that juries hate, it's child pornography. And of course, it doesn't just apply to sex offences. In any case, as soon as the jury hear that someone has broken the law in the past, the task of making them like that person becomes that little bit harder.

Most defence lawyers want to keep their client's bad character as far away from a jury as possible, but will be quite happy to bandy around the bad character of the complainant or a witness who is adverse to them.

Now, in the old days bad character really only went before a jury if, either someone had previously committed a crime which was 'strikingly similar' to the one with which he was now charged, or if he had cast aspersions on the character of someone else – which is called losing your shield.

That situation worked well for years, so, of course, they decided to change it. So now the issue of character and whether a jury should find out about someone's antecedent history is extremely complicated, both in terms of law and in terms of judgement. The defence or the prosecution can make an application to bring someone's form before a jury if they think that it will help a jury to decide an important issue in the case or that it will establish that the defendant has a propensity to commit the crime he is charged with.

It can be a massively devastating piece of information for a juror, and a Judge has to think long and hard before allowing it in.

Take the following two cases.

I once prosecuted a case in which an Albanian man had been charged with raping a sixteen-year-old girl. The prosecution case was weakened because the girl had waited for a week before complaining and then had admitted that she had gone back to the Albanian fella's flat voluntarily because he had promised her lager.

I knew that he had a conviction in his homeland for what was termed in Albania as 'serious sexual violence', which I took to mean rape. Sadly, I didn't have any of the details of his offence. I applied to the Judge for the conviction to go before a jury, saying that it showed that the man had a propensity to commit offences of a sexual nature, which, as he was denying it, was an important matter in the case. The Judge asked me what 'serious sexual violence' meant. I had to confess that, not being entirely au fait with the Albanian criminal justice system, I wasn't sure.

'Well, Mr Winnock,' said the Judge, with a great deal of reluctance, 'how can I allow a conviction before a jury, when neither of us are quite sure what it means?'

And, reluctantly, I had to agree, the Judge was right. It would be unfair.

The Albanian man was acquitted of everything apart from stealing beer. An acquittal that made me feel sick to the stomach.

After they had returned their verdicts I read out to the jury the defendant's previous convictions. When I said that he had a conviction for 'serious sexual violence', collectively, their hands went up to their mouths. It was obvious that they felt that they should have known about it – but, would that have been fair? Would it have been fair to prejudice a jury with the knowledge of an offence that I wasn't even sure I understood?

I don't know the answer to that.

Then take another occasion – the exact opposite. My client was a young lad, Ashley Hunt, who'd got into a fight in a nightclub with a squaddie (alas, squaddies get into fights with a depressing regularity). Ashley told me that the squaddie was a known thug with previous convictions. Unfortunately for Ashley, he too had a load of previous convictions, including a rather nasty one involving a spade.

'If I ask the Judge to allow me to cross-examine the squaddie's previous convictions, then he'll let the prosecutor put yours in,' I told him. But Ashley was adamant, he wanted them in.

The Judge looked at me. 'Are you sure, Mr Winnock?'

'Those are my instructions, Your Honour,' I said, which is code for: I think my client is completely daft for making me do this, but, hey-ho, it's his funeral.

'So be it,' said the Judge, and I was duly given leave to cross-examine Private Matt Davis about an assault in a pub a few years ago.

It was a disaster.

'So, Mr Davis,' I began, 'this isn't the first time you've been involved in a fight in a pub, is it?'

'No, sir,' said Private Davis, then he turned to the jury with doleful eyes. 'After I came home from Iraq, I was in a bad place, having witnessed two of my colleagues killed in an ambush by insurgents. I admit, sir, that I went off the rails a bit after that. Since then I've received counselling and help with my anger from the army.'

Ouch.

Ashley Hunt on the other hand, wasn't quite so attractive a witness, in fact he was awful. He stood there in the witness box looking every inch the thug he was. The prosecutor was an experienced old brief called Roger Cairns. As Cairns got up to cross-examine my client, I wondered how he would deal with his previous convictions.

'Are you a violent man, Mr Hunt?' he asked.

I cringed, I knew what was coming. Ashley Hunt shrugged and muttered something that sounded a bit like, 'No.'

'I see,' said Cairns. 'What about the time you hit someone over the head with a garden shovel?'

Ouch again.

It took the jury twenty minutes to convict Ashley Hunt.

In the case of Tasha Roux, the issue of character was going to be absolutely vital, we wanted the jury to know that Gary Dickinson was a bastard. We wanted them to know that he was a man who had a temper and would resort to his fists. But, at the same time, we knew that this would probably mean that Tasha's, albeit limited, convictions would also go in. But that wasn't what bothered us. What bothered us was the possibility that the jury might think we were unnecessarily tarnishing a man who couldn't defend himself because our client had chucked him over a banister.

It was a difficult call. If the jury didn't like Tasha, then they wouldn't like us resorting to tactics like this, and that was why it was so crucial that we tracked down a witness who might be able to give proper evidence about what Dickinson was really like. I was convinced that Lilly Spencer could provide that evidence, which is why I had been so desperate to speak to her.

I finished the bad character application and emailed it to Charlie Parkman with a little note telling him that we were doing everything we could to find a corroborating witness but that it was proving to be tricky.

Then I put my head on my desk and waited for my hangover to subside.

The trial of Tasha Roux day one – the robing room bullies

I strode into the robing room on the first day of the trial of Tasha Roux like a colossus. It felt great. I was in a murder trial and I wanted everyone to know about it.

'Hi Russ, you're not prosecuting a two-handed robbery are you?'

'No, I'm in the murder case.'

'Russ, what are you up to today? Could you cover a bench warrant in court four?'

'No, sorry, I'm in the murder case.'

Yes, I don't mind admitting it, that morning I swanned into the robing room like I was the biggest hunter-gatherer in the pack.

Roger Fish and Josh Benedict-Brown were sitting down by a desk on the far side of the robing room. With them were a couple of the young and beautiful clerks from Extempar Chambers who were unloading the case papers from some fancy wheeled suitcases with the logo: Extempar Chambers, 'We Don't Judge, We Just Care' emblazoned on them. Normally, that would have annoyed me, but not today. I wasn't bothered that I had my papers in a couple of Asda bags, hell, that morning, I even carried my blue bag of shame with a swagger.

I confidently went over to them. 'Hi Roger,' I said, making sure that everyone knew that I, Russell Winnock, was in a case with Roger Fish, the Fishmeister.

Roger was sitting impassively, reading through some documents, making efficient notations with his rather expensive fountain pen.

He looked up at me. 'Good morning, Russell,' he said, 'I'm afraid I've got some late additional evidence for you. Sorry that's it's come to light on the morning of trial. You know how these things are in a case like this.'

That was the problem, I didn't know, I'd never done a case like this before. I didn't know how I was supposed to react: should I make a fuss? Should I stamp my feet at this eleventh-hour service of new material?

I didn't know.

In the end I just sort of grinned and murmured something about how I was sure it would be okay.

Josh Benedict-Brown smirked. 'It's not good for you, old boy,' he said. 'We've just had the phone records back from the mobile phone specialist. There are a few messages on there that you might want to have a look at.'

He then handed me two copies of the same document. 'One for you and one for Charlie Parkman,' he said. 'Where is your leader by the way?' he added. 'I hope for your sake he's going to turn up. Don't suppose you'll want to do this solo.'

Cocky bastard. And who uses the phrase 'old boy' for crying out loud.

By now Kelly had arrived. She was taking her coat off.

I went over to her and told her about the new evidence.

'Bastards,' she said, 'they've had her phone for ages, it's outrageous that they've only got round to serving it today. What did you say to Fish? I hope you gave him what for?'

I decided to lie, I didn't want Kelly thinking I was a pushover.

'I told him that we weren't very happy.'

She scowled.

'Where's Charlie Parkman?'

This was now starting to bother me. I had spoken to Charlie the previous day, when he had told me that he would see me in court.

'He'll be here any second,' I assured her, 'probably held up in traffic.'

She scowled again.

I sat down and started to read the new document. It was a list of the text messages that had been sent to and from Gary Dickinson's phone that were recorded on Tasha Roux's phone.

Kelly was right, they'd had Tasha's phone and Dickinson's phone since the night of the incident, there was no reasonable excuse for them serving this evidence on the first day of the trial. This was wrong. But even worse was the fact that Josh bloody Benedict-Brown was right – the messages were damning. My eyes fell on the very first one.

4pm, Saturday 5th March: 'Gary I mean it, if u do that again I'll fuckin kill u.'

5.15pm, Saturday 5th March: 'U R a bastard! I hate U.'

Then on the night Dickinson was killed: 'I don't ever wanna C U again. U come near me I'll kill U.'

I sighed. This wasn't good.

And where was my bloody leader?

I tried phoning him but received an answerphone voice telling me to leave my message after the beep.

I read more of the messages.

2.13pm, Friday 15th April: 'You don't scare me Gary – I mean it.'

Together with the odd. 'I love U XXXX' and 'I can't wait to hold you again! U R my man Gary!'

It didn't read like a woman who was in any way scared of the man she had killed. I needed to talk to my leader about these. I felt myself becoming frantic. I knew I shouldn't have instructed a family lawyer, I knew he'd bottle it. He was probably at Gatwick airport or Dover getting the first plane or ferry out of here, leaving me to pick up the bloody pieces and try to defend a woman who had killed the man who one minute she wanted to hold and the next she wanted to kill. Fuck.

'Any sign?' asked Kelly.

I frowned. 'Not a bloody sausage.'

Josh Benedict-Brown had now appeared behind me. 'So what do you want to do about the telephone material?' he asked.

I scowled at him. 'I'm going to take instructions,' I said, adding quietly under my breath, 'just as soon as my bloody leader shows up.'

'Perhaps he's outside the courtroom already?' said Kelly.

We went to find him. We looked outside court three, which was where we were listed. There was no sign of him.

I went to the security queue: there was no sign of him.

I looked in the lobby and up the corridors: nothing.

He'd bottled it. He couldn't handle the pressure. I felt myself wanting to scream in fear, anger and exasperation, but mainly fear.

Finally we tried the public canteen, which was about the last place most barristers go, as it invariably means bumping into clients, or worse, clients' families. But, lo and behold, there he was. Charlie Parkman QC, sitting having a cup of coffee, and with him was Shandra Whithurst.

She had both his hands in her own and was clearly talking to him in impassioned tones. Charlie was nodding at her and occasionally smiling, kind, gentle smiles. As I got closer I could hear what she was saying. 'You must help her, Mr Parkman, she is a good girl.'

'Well,' said Charlie, 'perhaps we can help her together. Now you know what you've got to do?'

Shandra sucked in her lips as if fortifying herself for whatever it was Charlie had told her to do. 'I understand,' she said, and with that, she got up and walked away, giving me a wave as she did.

'Charlie,' I said, 'you're here.'

'Yes,' he said, 'I prefer it in here. I can get some peace and quiet away from the robing room bullies.'

'Well,' I said, 'you're going to love this.' I handed him the new telephone material.

He looked at it for a short while, then looked up at me. 'When did we get this?'

'Just now.'

'That's a bit sneaky isn't it?'

'I thought so.'

Charlie sighed then took a final swig from his cup of coffee. 'Right,' he said, 'let's go and make acquaintance with Mr Fish.'

We made our way back upstairs to the robing room where Fish and Benedict-Brown, now minus the beautiful Extempar clerks, were sitting down robed and ready for action.

Parkman went over. 'Good morning Roger,' he said, then without waiting for a response, he added tersely, 'now what's this new evidence that you've served on me this morning?'

'Telephone evidence,' replied Fish, before adding with snake-like smoothness, 'very sorry, I realise that you should have had it a few weeks ago but I'm afraid that these things do happen in the Crown Court.'

'Not in this trial,' replied Parkman, 'I'm not having this type of caper. If you've got any more surprises I want to know about them now.'

I stood behind Parkman, my chest heaving with pride as he stood up to the formidable Roger Fish.

'Steady on, old chap,' replied Fish, 'I'm just the messenger.'

'Well, you can give a message to the Judge that we can't start today, because the defence need another day to deal with this new evidence that has been served weeks late.'

And with that my new hero Charlie Parkman turned on his heels and walked out of the robing room, with me, star-struck, in awe and half tempted to blow a raspberry at Josh Benedict-Brown, following in his wake.

It was only when I got outside into the corridor that I realised that Charlie was shaking slightly and that beads of sweat had formed on his brow. 'I can't be doing with this kind of slippery nonsense, but more significantly, we've got a problem, those text messages don't help us at all.'

We went to see Tasha. We sat across from her. It was no longer time for soft, cuddly avuncular lawyers, now was the time to prepare her for the roasting that she was going to get from the prosecutor.

'Why did you send a text message telling Gary Dickinson you were going to kill him?' asked Charlie. Tasha was taken aback by his tone.

'Because he was a bastard,' she replied.

'A bastard who deserved to die?' continued Charlie. 'A bastard who you were quite happy to throw over a banister?'

'No.'

'Because you knew that if you managed to get him over that banister he'd be seriously injured didn't you?'

'I didn't mean to hurt him.'

'Then why send him the message saying you were going to kill him?'

'I didn't mean that.'

'Well what did you mean?'

Charlie grilled her and grilled her. We went through every message, over and over again.

'Did you love him?'

'Yes.'

'Then you weren't scared of him, were you?'

'Not always.'

Tasha struggled and I sat there silently watching her struggle. I listened to her as she tried to explain why she had sent a particular message at a particular time. It wasn't easy. None of us send texts that we think will come back and haunt us, but often they do. Of course Tasha hadn't planned to kill him, of course those messages were idle threats. If Tasha had planned to kill him she would have done it with a weapon, a knife probably, she wouldn't have tried to throw him over a bloody banister. I knew that, but I also knew that the Crown would take those messages and use them to goad her and provoke her, to try to get under her skin in order to try to prove to the jury that she intended to hurt this man, that she wasn't scared of him and that he was no threat to her.

By the time we left, Tasha was tired and tearful and under no illusions that this was going to be tough. Charlie was tired as well. The slight tremor to his hand had returned and he looked drained, his face lined and grey.

'Are you okay?' I asked him.

'Absolutely fine,' he said, 'tomorrow we'll get the jury sworn.'

I walked back to chambers with Kelly.

'What do you think of Charlie?' I asked her.

'I think he's going to find this tough,' she said, 'he's good, but he's fragile. I just hope he makes it to the end.'

'So do I,' I said, 'otherwise I'll be stepping into the breach.'

'Yep,' she said, 'and we don't want that do we?'

Which wasn't exactly the response I was looking for.

The trial of Tasha Roux day two – the jury

Our Judge was Mr Justice Vernon, a gruff Lancastrian with a rather no-nonsense approach and a wonderful gift for the crushing look of disapproval, something he had demonstrated the previous day, when Fish had to concede that he had served a load of new evidence on the defence at the last minute, and that we were not going to be able to start the trial.

The next morning, the Judge looked witheringly at Roger Fish. 'No more surprises for Mr Parkman today then?'

'No, My Lord,' said Fish (and you'll note he used the proper My Lord way to address a High Court Judge, as opposed to Your Honour, which is the way one addresses a Circuit Judge. I'm telling you this, just in case you ever have to appear in front of a court).

'Good.'

We were ready to start.

And the first part of any trial process involves the swearing in of the jury.

'Can we empanel a jury?' asked the Judge.

'Yes, My Lord.'

We then waited for about five minutes until the door that led to the jury room opened and into the light of the courtroom traipsed twenty or so nervous-looking individuals.

At this moment, none of them have the faintest idea what the trial is going to be about. It is still an adventure. I have often looked over at a jury if a rather trivial charge is read out and watched as their faces express either relief or disappointment; and, conversely, if the charge involves a sexual offence or violence against a woman, I have seen a look closely resembling fear or horror.

This was my first murder, so I watched the jury closely. Some of them were impassive as the word 'murder' left the lips of the Court Clerk, others glanced towards the dock where Tasha sat. Poor Tasha. Kelly had purchased her a smart skirt and blouse – she looked like a temp, a scared temp. She sat facing forward towards the Court Clerk, her eyes were wide and no doubt her heart was beating as fast as it had ever done. I felt sorry for her.

In America, there is a tradition of challenging jurors, indeed, if you believe John Grisham – and I've no reason to doubt him – there are even specialist jury lawyers whose sole job is to vet potential jurors to make sure that any who might conceivably be prejudiced against their client are removed.

Thankfully, we have nothing like that in the UK. In the UK, just as long as someone has never met the defendant or any of the witnesses and is compos mentis enough to utter the oath (they don't even have to read it), then they're in.

This doesn't stop some very senior lawyers, or very stupid lawyers, trying occasionally to wheedle out those who they think might be biased. In one famous case a Silk asked the Judge to exclude anyone who was from an ethnic background from sitting on the jury of a man accused of sending racist letter-bombs.

'Those are my instructions,' said the old Silk.

'Well your instructions are a load of cobblers,' said the Judge.

Then there was a quite recent case, when another very senior and well-paid Silk tried to prevent anyone who was a member of a trade union from sitting on the jury of the former editor of the *News of the World*. You'd have to have some front to make that application – again, the Judge wasn't having any of it.

For me, the most controversial thing I have ever had to cope with in terms of juries is when, two days into a trial, a very attractive female juror (there is almost always one) declared that one of her fellow jurors had been taking photos of her on the sly with his mobile phone.

'What do you want me to do?' the Judge asked me.

And I have to admit, I hadn't a clue. It wasn't a very nice thing to do, it was certainly a creepy thing to do, but did it prevent either juror from carrying out their role properly? I didn't know. I think it came down to the age-old test of whether the Judge liked the cut of the juror's jib. He didn't, and so the creepy juror was discharged and told to behave himself in future.

Tasha Roux's jury was the usual mixture. The initial panel of twenty was whittled down by ballot to twelve. Twelve men good and true – or in Tasha's case, seven women and five men.

I listened intently as each of them took the oath and started to ask myself questions that I couldn't possibly answer: was having more women than men a good thing? Possibly, because women might feel compassion towards another woman, but then, possibly not, as they might feel sorry for the deceased, they might be mothers with sons or have brothers or boyfriends who they wouldn't like to see being pushed over a banister.

Was it a good thing if someone affirmed rather than swore on the Bible? Again, traditionally it was believed to be a good thing to have a few 'affirmers' as it was once thought that 'affirmers' were more liberal and therefore would be more likely to go soft on the defendant; but these days it is thought that perhaps an 'affirmer' might be more attuned to the evidence, and less likely to reach a verdict on a hunch – which might be bad.

These were the imponderables. These were the pointless questions I couldn't possibly hope to answer.

I looked at the men and wondered whether they were the type who might go for a pint down their local and want to bring back hanging, or the type who would vote Liberal Democrat and listen to Radio 4. I watched and listened and I made pointless generalisations and suppositions about twelve of my fellow human beings based solely on what they looked like and how they spoke. It was as pointless as it was stupid, yet most barristers do exactly the same thing.

After the last of the twelve had been sworn, I turned to the dock and looked up at Tasha. 'Okay?' I mouthed.

She nodded without smiling, indeed without any change in her facial expression. The trial was about to start, and it would start with Roger Fish's opening.

Roger Fish's opening speech

Just as Roger Fish was about to open the case for the Crown, just as all eyes turned on him, he did something unusual – he picked up his pens and very calmly and slowly placed them on the desk behind him. He then picked up his one single folder and placed that on top of the other folders that were already on the desk behind him; then, without any sense of urgency, he calmly poured a glass of water from the carafe in front of him, and took a sip from it.

Then, finally, he looked at the jury.

They were mesmerised. Each one of them had watched his every move. Spellbound. He looked at them, placed his hands on the lectern in front of him, and, quietly, but with absolute and compelling authority, he began. 'Miss Tasha Roux is in the dock.' He paused. 'She is in the dock because she pushed a man over the banister from a sixth-floor landing. That push caused him to fall to his death. You may look at her and her life at times during this trial and feel that she is deserving of your sympathy – but, you must also remember that the man she killed, her lover, Gary Dickinson, was not in any way deserving of death in that rather brutal manner.'

It was a tour de force, a brilliant opening speech that continued for about another forty minutes, as Roger Fish told the jury what the case was about, laying the seeds in their heads as to why Tasha was guilty.

It was now that I realised why Fish was held in such high regard, as he elegantly turned the courtroom into a theatre, and why those advocates who are able to stand up and demand everyone's attention, like great actors, are the ones who are truly brilliant.

Fish had control. Fish could command, he was a superb mix of Shakespearian actor and Roman Consul. Some sniffy lawyers with none of his stature or ability might disagree, they might call him overly theatrical, a bit hammy – they are wrong. I was enthralled, and petrified, by Roger Fish; everything seemed so effortless, so controlled, and over the next few days, the way in which he presented his case left me in awe.

Just before he ended his opening speech he looked at the jury in such a way that he seemed to focus, in one magical moment, in one mesmeric instant, a gaze upon each of them both collectively and individually, and said, '*You* will decide this case, ladies and gentlemen, not me, not His Lordship the Judge and not Mr Parkman who represents Miss Roux, *you* – and you will do so, ladies and gentlemen, not because you feel sorry for someone, or because you are revolted by someone else, but on the evidence. *That* is all I ask.'

Then he sat down. It sent a shiver through me that started somewhere near my feet and ended up in my wig. It was bloody magnificent.

The witnesses for the Crown

Roger Fish called his first witness: Mrs Shamilia Hussain.

The jury waited and Mrs Hussain was brought into the courtroom.

It's a funny thing, being a witness. Unless you are a police officer or an expert, being a witness is almost always about fate: the fact that you happened to be somewhere at a particular time, the fact that you happened to be looking in a particular direction at a given moment, the fact that you happened to hear a conversation that wasn't meant for your ears.

Mrs Hussain happened to have been a neighbour of Tasha Roux and, as fortune would have it, was awake when Tasha and Gary Dickinson were arguing; she could have done nothing, but she didn't, she opened the door, looked out and had seen parts of what had been going on. Because of this twist of fate, she was a witness in a Crown Court in a murder trial, and her words, just like the other witnesses in the case, had the potential to lead to a lifetime of imprisonment for Tasha Roux.

A single nuance here, a slight fib there, a half-remembered memory turning into an unequivocal assertion could see my client convicted of murder.

I have to say that the thought of capital cases, when someone might end up getting hung on the words and memory and ability to articulate those memories of another person, sends a shiver of revulsion right through me – I don't think I could be a lawyer in a system where the state is allowed to kill people.

Mrs Hussain is quite a fair witness.

Fish takes her through her story:

She didn't know the defendant very well, just to say hello to, and she had never had a conversation with the deceased; in the past, she had heard shouting and arguments coming from the defendant's flat.

She remembered the night of the death because she was annoyed at being awoken by the sound of slamming doors and raised voices. She then heard a voice that she thought was a man's voice shouting, 'You do this every time, Tasha, you do this every time.'

'What was the tone of that voice?' asked Fish.

Mrs Hussain thought for a second, then added, 'Annoyed, he sounded annoyed.'

'What happened next?' asked Fish.

'There was a pause,' said Mrs Hussain, 'then I heard like a growl, as though someone was charging.'

'What did you hear next?'

'Next I heard more screaming, followed by sobbing.'

'Thank you,' said the Fishmeister, who then smiled, perhaps a bit too sweetly, to ensure that the jury knew he was happy with the way the witness had given her evidence.

Charlie got to his feet. I was sitting directly behind him, next to me was Kelly. I was conscious that he had not risen to his feet in a Crown Court for over fifteen years. He looked quite small.

He picked up Mrs Hussain's statement and pretended to look through it for a second. 'Mrs Hussain,' he said, his face contorted into an expression of perplexed confusion, 'I've got the statement that you made here, to the police on the morning when all this happened.'

Mrs Hussain nodded. Charlie continued, 'You made that statement at,' he paused for effect, 'six-thirty in the morning, so about an hour or so after the incident.'

Mrs Hussain nodded again.

'So when you made that statement, things would have been fairly fresh in your memory?'

'Yes.'

'Fresher than, say, today, six months later?'

Mrs Hussain didn't answer this question, as she was bright enough to know where this was leading.

'You see Mrs Hussain, today, six months later, you've told this court that you heard a growl like a charge, yet you made no mention of that to the police two hours after the event?'

Charlie looked up at her as he finished his question. It was the classic line of cross-examination that arises when a witness says something in court that they didn't say when they were interviewed by the police. It almost always confuses a witness.

'Any reason for that?'

'Sorry?'

Charlie raised his voice slightly. 'Any reason why suddenly, six months on, you've remembered a crucial fact that you didn't mention when you were first questioned about this by the police immediately after the event?'

The jury, as twelve, craned themselves slightly towards Mrs Hussain. She shrugged. 'Don't know.'

'Is it perhaps because you've been talking to others about this?'

'No.'

It was as good as we were going to get from Mrs Hussain. Of course, she was never going to crumble under cross-examination, we all knew that, she wasn't suddenly going to give evidence in a way that was helpful to us and our case. But I was pleased with Charlie – he had made the right points, and done so in a smooth and confident way. It was all I wanted in my Silk.

The next witness for the prosecution was Miss Lyra Adams. She was a young student nurse who, on the morning of Dickinson's death, had just returned home after a night shift. She was nice and smiley and well-spoken and utterly credible on every point. She was a prosecutor's dream witness and a nightmare for the defence. Thankfully, she hadn't seen the incident, so her evidence could only go so far.

She knew Tasha by sight and had seen Dickinson on a few occasions but had never spoken to him. She also described hearing raised voices and slammed doors, and could remember a male voice saying, 'You do this every fucking time, Tasha.'

She described the tone of the male voice as exasperated rather than angry. She also heard screaming and the sound of aggressive shouting coming from Tasha; she told the court that it was the screaming that made her come out of her flat. She then said that she could see Tasha sat against the wall sobbing. She cradled Tasha, who just repeated over and again, 'He just fell.'

'Which voice was the more aggressive, the female voice or the male voice?' asked Fish.

And young student nurse Lyra Adams thought about it, and the jury watched her think about it, and I watched her, and Kelly watched her, and, no doubt, Tasha watched her.

Lyra said, after what seemed like an age, 'It's hard to say, the female sounded frantic, the male just sounded fed up.'

Charlie rightfully decided to get her out of the way as quickly as possible. He realised that there was little point in asking a very good witness too many questions – because nothing could be gained by that. He simply reminded her that she hadn't actually seen these events, and therefore couldn't help the jury as to whether this had been an act of aggression by Tasha Roux or an attempt to defend herself.

'Yes,' she said, 'I agree with that, but,' she added with the force of a knife being thrust between Tasha Roux's shoulder blades, 'it didn't sound like the man was attacking her.'

Charlie now had to make a decision. Should he ask her how she had come to that conclusion and risk giving her the opportunity to expand on her answer, or should he just stop there and let her get on her way before she could do any more damage? I stared at the back of Charlie's neck as I waited for him to ask the next question. I knew what I would have done; I knew that if I had been the one on my feet, I would have said nothing more and sent her away, as far away from my case as possible. I wondered what Charlie would do. For a second he seemed to panic. For a second he turned a few pages in his notes, which was a giveaway sign that he had temporarily lost control. His head and face were turned downwards towards his notes rather than strong and straight towards the witness. This wasn't good – this was a sign of weakness.

Then, thankfully, he recovered.

'That, of course, Miss Adams, is supposition isn't it, you don't know for certain who was the aggressor as you weren't watching the events, you were still listening to them. Is that fair?'

'Yes,' said the nice nurse, 'that is fair.'

We adjourned for the day.

We traipsed back into the robing room. Joshua Benedict-Brown caught me up. I expected him to grin at me, make some kind of condescending remark, but, even worse, he tried to come over all pally. 'We don't want to get through this trial too fast,' he said, 'we'll be doing ourselves out of money. We need to drag this into a third week at least.'

'Yes,' I said. But I didn't want him to be all pally-chummy with me, I would rather he be horrible and superior, the whole experience would be easier if I could hate him.

'And I'll tell you another thing, old boy,' he said in a slightly hushed and lascivious tone, 'your instructing solicitor's a bit of alright isn't she?'

We both allowed our gaze to fall on Kelly Backworth who had just reached the robing room door about twenty feet in front of us, and was smiling at something that one of the ushers had said to her. I was in no mood for Benedict-Brown's attempt at a bit of blokey banter, it was even worse than his attempt to endear himself to me.

'I hadn't noticed,' I said, adding, 'I'm far too busy concentrating on this case.'

Josh smiled at me and winked. 'Of course you are.'

A short while later we found Charlie sitting quietly having a baked potato in the public canteen. Kelly and I joined him. He betrayed no sense of emotion at all.

'How do you think it's going?' I asked. I wanted Charlie to reassure me that everything was going to plan, that he had a cunning ruse up his sleeve and that it was all going to end in stunning forensic victory.

Instead he just smiled lamely and shrugged slightly. 'It's going exactly how I expected it. How do you think it's going?'

'The same,' I answered nervously, 'just as I thought it would.'

The reality was that I had no idea how I had expected it would go. Charlie went back to his food. 'Is there anything else you want me to do?' I asked.

Charlie looked up at me and Kelly. 'Yes,' he said, 'I'd like you both to go through the interviews and edit out anything that shouldn't be there.'

I nodded.

The next witness was the most difficult for us: Rick O'Rourke was the witness who had actually seen part of the incident. He emerged into court, his eyes scampering from side to side as he took in the sight of the Crown Court in full operation. He took the oath with a booming Northern Irish accent. I immediately feared the worst. I could sense that Mr O'Rourke was going to be one of those witnesses who believes, rightly or wrongly, that once they have become a witness for the prosecution, it is their mission to help secure a conviction. He took the oath, confident and unhesitating, promising to tell the truth, the whole truth and nothing but the truth.

Sometimes these types of witnesses can be helpful to the defence as their zeal causes them to exaggerate some of the facts, or become unnecessarily argumentative and unattractive. I hoped, in fact I prayed that O'Rourke's prosecutorial enthusiasm might annoy the jury.

'I'm going to ask you some questions about the defendant Tasha Roux,' said Roger Fish, to which the witness sucked in deeply and disdainfully, as though he was about to be asked questions about Adolf Hitler.

Rick O'Rourke then proceeded to tell the jury how in his opinion Tasha Roux was probably up to no good, as she was always having men and parties late at night, and her music was too loud.

'She was a bit of a party girl, if you know what I mean,' he said, 'probably up to all sorts.'

This was outrageous.

At this point I wanted Charlie to get up to his feet to object. I wanted to hear one of those American courtroom drama exclamations, 'I OBJECT!' Instead, and with far more subtlety and force, Charlie simply stood up and scowled at Roger Fish. 'My Lord,' he said, 'Mr Fish knows better than to allow his witness to say things like that.'

'Yes,' said Mr Justice Vernon, and he gently admonished Roger

Fish and the witness, 'Your view that the defendant was probably up to all sorts means nothing in a court of law, please confine yourself to what you actually know.'

O'Rourke's enthusiasm, however, remained undimmed. He continued to give evidence in a way that was entirely hostile to his erstwhile neighbour. It was emotive and brutal, unfair. I mean, what had Tasha Roux ever done to him?

'I was awoken by the sound of shouting and screaming coming from up my corridor,' he said, 'I knew immediately which flat it would be coming from, because there's regularly shouting coming from Miss Roux's flat.'

'Was this the usual type of shouting you heard?' asked Fish.

'Oh no sir,' said O'Rourke, 'I could tell that something terrible was about to happen.'

I wanted to stand up and shout, 'What a load of bollocks. How could you possibly tell what was about to happen, you daft Irish fool!' Of course, I didn't, I simply dug my biro into my notes and wrote with increasing venom my record of what Mr O'Rourke had said.

He continued in a similar vein, telling the jury how after about half an hour of slamming doors and shouting and screaming he opened his door and peered out.

'How much of the door was open?' asked Fish.

'Just enough for me to see out onto the landing but still keep the chain on,' replied O'Rourke.

'And what could you see?'

O'Rourke's face turned grave, he knew that he was about to impart some serious information on all of us.

'I saw the deceased, Mr Dickinson, banging on the door, sir, then I saw *her* open the door.'

'Did you hear any of the conversation at this point?'

'Yes, he was saying that he was sorry – I don't know what he was sorry for, he just kept repeating, I'm sorry, let me in.'

'Did she let him in?'

'They went in; then a couple of seconds later he came out and walked away. And then she came after him.'

'What was he like?'

'He was just trying to get away.'

'And what was she like?'

O'Rourke paused – 'She was wild, sir.'

'Go on.'

'They squared up to each other – she was shouting in his face, he was trying to get away.'

'Did he get away?'

'Yes, he made his way away from her towards the top of the stairs.'

'What happened then?'

'Well,' said O'Rourke carefully, 'at this point, I couldn't see him, only her, but I reckoned that he'd got as far as the banister at the top of the stairs.'

'Why?'

'Because in that time he couldn't have got much further away.'

'What did she do?'

'She rushed towards him.'

'What do you mean by rushed?'

'Her face changed, and she went towards him. And the next thing I heard was this almighty scream.'

'A man's scream or a woman's?'

'Both, sir.'

It wasn't good. Rick O'Rourke was describing Tasha rushing towards Dickinson in an aggressive way, and, if she was doing the rushing, if hers was the aggressive act, then she wasn't acting in self-defence.

Charlie got to his feet quickly – we needed to nullify O'Rourke as best we could. Charlie went on the attack.

'Had you been asleep?' he asked.

'I'm a light sleeper,' replied O'Rourke.

'But at five o'clock in the morning you weren't at your most awake were you?'

'I'm a light sleeper, what more can I say, I heard the noise and got up and went to the door.'

Damn, O'Rourke was good.

'You didn't see Miss Roux and Mr Dickinson coming together, did you?'

'No, that I didn't, sir.'

'Nor did you know what Mr Dickinson was doing to her immediately before he fell over the banister.'

'No.'

'For all you know, he could have had a knife in his hand at that moment.'

Fish got to his feet. 'Is My Learned Friend suggesting that Mr Dickinson had a knife in his hand at that point?'

'No,' said Charlie, 'My Learned Friend knows full well I'm not suggesting that, what I am suggesting is that in the moment immediately before Dickinson fell over the banister, anything could have happened, because Mr O'Rourke didn't see it.'

The rest of the cross-examination was bad-tempered and meandering.

Charlie tried to get out of Mr O'Rourke that he hadn't seen the facial expressions of either person, but O'Rourke was insistent that he had.

Charlie tried to suggest that the gap in his door was actually smaller than O'Rourke was saying, but O'Rourke simply invited him to come and measure it, reminding Charlie that he lived there and had done so since 1976.

It wasn't good.

If it had been a bullfight, with Charlie Parkman as the matador and Rick O'Rourke as the bull, the bull didn't have a single sword sticking out of his flank, and the matador was, well, the matador was on his knees.

We left court downbeat. Charlie looked exhausted. I think he'd forgotten how emotionally and intellectually tiring a day cross-examining witnesses in the Crown Court could be.

'I'll see you in the morning,' he said, then he turned to me. 'Do you think that there's anything else I could have done today, Russell?'

'No,' I said, dutifully, 'you were brilliant.'

He shot me a half-smile that suggested that he was grateful but didn't quite believe me, then took himself off, leaving me alone with Kelly.

'We're going to have to do these interviews,' I said.

She nodded. 'I know.'

I hadn't planned for the next sentence that was about to leave my mouth. 'Look,' I said, 'if you've got nothing on, I mean, no plans, I'm going to do the interviews tonight. Why don't you come round to mine and I can cook us a bit of dinner, you know, supper, a bit of food, nothing fancy. It's not a, you know, just a bit of food and we can do the interviews together.'

She smiled at me.

Brilliant.

'Okay,' she said.

Brilliant.

Dinner with Kelly Backworth

I hadn't planned to ask Kelly around for dinner. I wasn't even sure it was dinner, not a proper dinner. Not a change your underpants, put on your best aftershave and prepare a playlist for your iPod with hanky-panky in mind, dinner.

No, this was just a casual, come round for what posh people would term supper – that's all. And I wasn't going to get excited about it. I mean, she probably had no idea that I fancied her. And if she had thought that then she might have run a mile, suggested that we do the interviews back in chambers or in one of the conference rooms by the court, rather than put herself in my flat, with me, alone.

By the time I got home, I had temporarily forgotten about Tasha Roux and the problems that we were having and I was preparing myself for my night with Kelly Backworth.

I decided to cook that most staple of dishes known to single men: spag bol. I couldn't go wrong with spag bol. Unfortunately, when I checked my fridge, I found that I had precisely two cans of lager, one bottle of strange sauce that my parents had brought me back from a holiday to Peru two years earlier, half a bottle of milk and a bumper pack of yoghurts. This wasn't good.

I took myself off to the corner shop and got the ingredients.

I then considered what to wear.

I didn't want to look like a barrister, but at the same time, I didn't want to look like someone desperately trying not to look like a barrister.

Many barristers find dressing outside of court a huge challenge. The occasional chambers parties or away days are like a gathering of fashion criminals, as my colleagues mix red corduroy with brown brogues, pink v-neck jumpers with striped shirts, high-waisted jeans, and occasionally garish T-shirts which have clearly seen better days.

She was due at 8pm. I had a shower, prepared the food and dressed myself in a casual shirt and jeans. I was definitely better dressed than most barristers. Of that I had no doubt.

I then set about flossing and brushing my teeth.

This was important. One of the worst aspects of being a barrister is that occasionally, one is prone to 'court breath', a particularly pungent brand of halitosis that sets in if you have had about five cups of coffee and spent most of your day sitting in a courtroom without saying very much. The worst aspect of 'court breath' is that the sufferer may well have to turn and speak quietly and close up to a solicitor or opponent, which means invariably letting out death breath fumes directly into their face. It's awful and I wasn't taking any chances.

Just in case. I mean, you never know.

At 8.10, Kelly arrived at my door.

It was the first time I had seen her out of her dour grey and black suits. It was the first time I had had the chance to see her shape, unleashed and feminine and, as I had expected, she was gorgeous. She looked at me, and I could tell that she was a bit embarrassed and nervous.

'Hi,' I said, 'come in.'

She offered me a bottle of white wine, which I immediately put in the fridge.

'I didn't know if it was appropriate,' she said, 'you know, to have a glass of wine whilst we were working, but I thought after today, we both needed one.'

I smiled and thanked her. She looked different. Her hair was clean and springy, her face was softer and her lips seemed smooth, with a glistening quality.

It struck me that perhaps she thought this was a 'dinner' dinner. Shit, I started to wish I'd put together a suitable playlist now.

'I've just cooked spaghetti bolognese,' I said, adding nervously, 'is that alright?'

'That's great,' she said, adding, 'if I'd had to bet on the food you'd cook, I would have chosen spag bol.'

I wasn't sure if this was a compliment or not. I got the feeling not, or perhaps it was good that she was teasing me. Damn, it had been bloody ages since I'd done this. I was starting to realise that I'd spent too long being single, I was clueless, I couldn't read the signs that are particular to girls. She'd only been in my flat three minutes, and already I was confused.

We sat down and I opened the wine. And then we talked.

We talked about music. I told her about Neil Young, and she said she'd never heard anything by him, so I played her 'Ruby in the Dust', which she didn't seem too impressed by. But this was okay, I could work with this.

We talked about the law, and she told me which barristers she liked and which ones she hated. By now we'd had a drink and she was starting to relax and show an indiscreet funny side. She told me that she had liked my friend, Johnny Richardson, but she thought that Angus Tollman was a complete arse who was rubbish with clients. I'm not proud to say it, but this made me quite happy. She said that she was scared stiff of Jenny Catrell-Jones, so I told her that I was even more scared of her boss Mrs Murdoch.

I asked if I was still NIHWTLBOE, and she told me that I probably was.

And we both laughed.

Things were going well.

I liked having her in my kitchen. I liked looking at her face, I liked laughing with her. I started to wonder how I might move things along.

'Well, I suppose we'd better get down to it then,' she said.

And I burst out laughing. 'Yeah, but what about the interviews?'

She feigned shock. 'Russell!' she exclaimed, 'I'd get the sack for going anywhere near you. First rule of our firm, never shag barristers. Especially NIHWTLBOE ones.'

I felt my innards swoon, she was thinking about it, I knew she was. She'd used the word shag. I was in. Was I? I was. There was a pause, I looked at her. I leant over, and I kissed her.

There, I've said it. I've confessed, I've told you that I kissed Kelly Backworth, in my flat, in my kitchen, just before we edited the police interviews that had been carried out with Tasha Roux.

And it was bloody nice as well.

You don't need to know any more.

Tasha gives her evidence

The Crown's case continued for the next couple of days. Two days in which we had mostly uncontentious evidence: there was the pathologist's evidence, which was delivered by a strikingly handsome grey-haired bloke who looked as if he belonged on the TV. He told a riveted court that Gary Dickinson had died because of massive trauma to his head, which had caused a severe cerebral contusion to his lower cranium and a subarachnoid haemorrhage, which, in plain English, is having your head smashed in.

He had diagrams and reconstructions and told us that Gary Dickinson would have died within three minutes of landing.

This was a poignant piece of evidence. This is the exact moment when the gravity of the trial really hit home – three minutes from fall to death. Three minutes to have your physical existence here on earth ended. That resonated with all of us except, perhaps, the Judge and the Fishmeister, who had both heard it all before.

We then had the telephone reports which showed the dreaded text messages, and some toxicology reports which showed that Gary Dickinson had had a small amount of alcohol that night and, possibly, a small amount of cocaine. Whilst Tasha had had quite a lot of alcohol and was twice the legal drink drive limit (not that she had planned to go anywhere in a car) and had had a moderate amount of cocaine.

Then the interviews, which had been so painstakingly edited a couple of nights before, were read out, and that was it – the Crown's case was over.

'That is the case for the Crown,' said Roger Fish, and did a rather elaborate bow towards the jury.

I had been sitting next to Kelly throughout. Neither of us had mentioned the night at mine – well, not in detail. I wasn't sure if we'd do it again or if she just saw me as a bit of fun. I didn't know.

But now wasn't the time to think about that, now was the time to start our case, and that would start with Tasha.

Before she gave her evidence, we went to see her, to give her one last pep-talk, to make sure that she was as ready as she could be. And to tell her the bad news that we hadn't been able to track down anyone to back up her account of what Gary Dickinson had done to her.

I asked Charlie if he didn't mind if I said a few words to her. 'Of course,' he said, 'feel free.'

Tasha was quiet. She looked petrified. It was funny how her mood would transform her physical appearance. She would grow and harden when she was angry, then visibly appear to soften when she was sad or despondent. Now, she was petrified, and that seemed to make her smaller.

I sat down opposite her and smiled. 'Are you alright?' I asked, which, on reflection, was a monumentally dumb question.

She nodded, but we both knew that she was far from alright.

'It's your turn now, Tasha,' I began. 'You're the star now; because, whether we like it or not, the jury have been waiting all week to hear from you.'

She nodded again.

'And I know that nothing I can say is going to make you less nervous. You're petrified, I know that. Christ, I'm petrified for you. But you've got to remember three things, okay?'

I paused to make sure that she was listening to me, that my words were making their way into the emotional maelstrom that was her consciousness.

'First, you've got to tell the truth, just like you've always told me and Kelly – okay? No one can ask any more of you than that.'

She nodded and tried a little smile.

'Second,' I continued, 'don't forget that we're here to protect you. If the questioning becomes too personal or inadmissible, Charlie will get to his feet to stop it.'

She smiled painfully as Charlie looked on like an uncle.

'And, finally Tasha, you've got to remember that this is your chance to tell your side of the story. So go up there and do your best, okay? We're all behind you rooting for you.'

I wasn't sure if I was expecting whooping and high fives at the end of my talk, but I didn't get it. Instead Tasha looked nervously towards the floor then up at me, wiped her eyes and gave me a thin-lipped nod.

Her evidence was difficult.

I can put it no better than that. She struggled with some of the questions, particularly when we asked her about her childhood and her teenage years, when she was taking drugs and living a rather crazy existence.

She became emotional when she described how she had had a baby taken away from her and how, because of that, she had vowed never to have another child, until she met Gary.

'Did you love him?' asked Charlie.

'Yes,' she said.

Then we got to the night itself. She told us how she had been out and how she was supposed to have been meeting one of Gary Dickinson's friends, a man called Rio.

'For what reason?' asked Charlie, and Tasha did this sly smile before she answered, which I knew was a mixture of nerves and embarrassment, but came across as a bit suspicious. I worried about that. I worried how a jury would interpret her smile, how a little thing like that could give them a particular impression, an unfair impression, which would be her downfall.

'He wanted me to go with them,' she answered.

'What do you mean by that?' asked Charlie. And Tasha paused, then looked upwards with the shame, then answered, 'He wanted me to have sex with them.'

'How did you feel about that?'

'I felt dirty.'

Charlie paused. He knew that the rhythm of her evidence was important, he knew that he had to allow some of her answers to make their way into the minds of the jury.

He asked her about taking cocaine, and she admitted that she had – it was better that that particular detail came from his friendly questioning than the hostile cross-examination that would be coming via Roger Fish. Then he moved on to the actual incident.

'How did you feel?'

'Upset.'

'Why?'

'Because of what he had wanted me to do with his friends.'

'How was he with you?'

'He was angry with me – because I hadn't met up with them.'

He then asked her about the way in which he would hurt her – and the jury watched, enraptured, as she described what he used to do to her, the way he would form both his hands into fists and bring them down on both sides of her head. She showed the jury the way he did it, bashing her own fists against her temples.

'How did that feel?'

'It made me want to pass out with the pain.'

'Why did you rush towards him?'

'I wanted to hug him, I thought that he wanted me to hug him, I thought everything was going to be alright, that I was going to be safe.'

'When you rushed towards him what did he do?'

'He formed his hands into fists.'

'What did you think was about to happen?'

'He was going to hit me instead. He'd conned me.'

'So what did you do?'

'I pushed him hard on the chest with both my hands.'

'And what happened to him?'

Tasha started to sob as she answered this question.

'He fell,' she managed, 'he fell backwards over the banister.'

Roger Fish got up slowly to cross-examine her. He knew that this was a tricky exercise. He knew that if he went too hard on her, bullied her, shouted at her, then she would cry and the jury might feel some sympathy for her and antipathy towards him. He started carefully.

'It's an awful thing that he was making you do,' he said, his voice gentle and friendly.

Tasha nodded in response.

'You must have hated him?'

She nodded again. 'Sometimes I did, but mostly I loved him, he could be kind and generous when he wanted.'

'But not on that night.'

'Well . . .'

'Well, he wasn't, was he?' continued Fish. 'He was horrible to you that night, wasn't he?'

'Yes, he was.'

'You must have been angry.'

'I was upset more than angry.'

'Come now, you were angry – you screamed at him, didn't you?'

311

Tasha shrugged. 'Yes, I did scream at him, because I was so upset.'

'Okay,' said the Fishmeister, his voice never changing from its soft tone. 'You were upset. In fact you were so upset that you wanted to kill him.'

'No,' said Tasha. I knew what was coming next.

'Well,' said Fish, 'let's have a look at that text message you sent him that night.'

I groaned. Here it came.

'A couple of hours before you killed him, you sent Gary Dickinson a text message saying, "I don't ever wanna C U again, U come near me and I'll kill U".'

Tasha's lips thinned. The jury stared at her. They knew the importance of this, they stared at Tasha and Roger Fish, standing no more than ten metres from each other, locked in an intense exchange. Two people who would never ever converse again as long as they both lived but at that moment engaged in a deep, deep intimacy.

Fish repeated, 'You come near me and I'll kill you And that is exactly what you did, didn't you, Miss Roux? You killed him, just as you'd threatened.'

Tasha emitted a sound as though her soul was leaving her body, her eyes were red and tears started to roll down her cheeks.

The rest of Tasha's cross-examination was just as painful. She struggled with questions about drugs and drink and anger. At times she seemed evasive and at times she came over as rock-hard, streetwise, capable of violence. By the end Fish was mocking her for the fact that she had never mentioned to anyone the way in which she was now saying that Gary Dickinson hit her.

'So you're now saying that Gary Dickinson used to hit you like this?' he said, putting his two fists against his own head in a rather limp and unthreatening way.

'Yes, but it wasn't like that, it was much harder, he would pound me,' responded Tasha.

'Why didn't you say this to the police?' His voice less gentle now.

'Because I was just trying to blot it out of my mind. He did it all the time. I hated it. I thought that one day, he would kill me by doing that.'

'That's a lie isn't it, Miss Roux?'

'No,' she wailed. 'No.'

'You wanted him dead and as he stood there, vulnerable, by the side of that banister, you saw your chance. That's right isn't it?'

Tasha shook her head, sobbing uncontrollably now. Roger Fish sat down. As far as he was concerned his work was done, the witness was defeated.

The Judge looked at Charlie. 'Is that your case, Mr Parkman, or will you be calling any further evidence?'

Charlie sighed. 'Can I have five minutes, My Lord, before I formally close the case for the defence?'

'Very well.'

We traipsed out of the court. Dejected. I felt helpless, our grasp on the case weakened and tentative, everything slipping away from us. It was almost over.

And that's when I saw her. Striding purposefully down the corridor, past the courtrooms, past the busy barristers and lawyers, past the court attendants, witnesses, criminals, families and victims and all the people who come to the Crown Court: Shandra Whithurst, large and confident and looking straight at us. She smiled a massive sunny summer's day of a smile at Charlie.

'I've found them,' she said, her voice booming along the ancient stone and brickwork. And with that she motioned to two women who were walking a few yards behind her – the first I recognised immediately as Lilly Spencer, the second, I didn't know.

'This is Lilly and this is Taylor,' said Shandra.

And I felt my own face break out into a massive grin. I knew immediately that Shandra had tracked down not just one, but two of Gary's former girlfriends, and both were now here in court willing to give evidence.

By the time Lilly Spencer and Taylor Lumsden had finished giving their evidence, the case against Tasha Roux was very different.

Charlie examined both of them perfectly.

'Do you know Tasha Roux?' he asked them.

'No.'

'Have you ever met her?'

'No.'

This was vital. They were independent witnesses, they had no axe to grind, no cause to further, no wool to pull over anyone's eyes. They were here to simply tell the jury what they knew and both of them told the jury that they had been in relationships with Gary Dickinson. Both of them were able to describe how initially he had been loving and then had become controlling and aggressive.

Crucially though – bloody, bloody crucially – both Lilly Spencer and Taylor Lumsden described being assaulted by him, and both of them described the way he had done it: two fists, one knuckle extended, pounding against both sides of their heads. Taylor said it happened twice to her before she moved house to get away from him; but, for Lilly, it happened a lot – she cried as she described it. 'I felt like he might kill me,' she told the court, and the court shook with the resonance of that.

I listened, my whole body quivering with the joy that we had presented evidence to the jury to prove that Tasha Roux wasn't lying.

Later I would ask Shandra how she had found them and she

told me she, like me, had gone to the Purple Velvet Club to try to speak to Lilly Spencer.

'But how did you manage to persuade her?' I asked.

'Well I was sober for one thing, Mr Winnock,' she told me, then added, 'I'm not a fancy lawyer, you see, so I was able to tell Lilly that I was normal and that giving evidence to help another girl wasn't a bad or crazy thing to do, but a normal thing to do.'

I nodded. I got that.

'And how did you find the other girl, Taylor?' I asked.

'Facebook.'

I should have guessed. Bloody marvellous Facebook.

Charlie's speech

The next morning the jury heard speeches from Roger Fish and Charlie Parkman. The two Silks now in direct confrontation as they duelled for the affection of the jury.

Roger's was, as you would expect, polished and clever. He carefully built up his case, layer by layer. 'Tasha Roux had a motive to kill,' he said, 'she had the correct amount of anger to kill,' he said, 'and she had the opportunity to kill.'

I watched the jury to see if any of them nodded and occasionally one or two of them did as the Fishmeister's points struck home. I cursed them.

Then Charlie Parkman got to his feet.

He started slowly, holding on to the lectern, his body arched and small as though he was coiled, and then, as he unfurled his arguments, he unfurled his body. It was as though as his presence was growing, his arguments were growing, and the idea of reasonable doubt was growing, becoming something tangible that was moving about the jury and touching them gently, making them think again.

'Gary Dickinson did not deserve to die that night,' he told them. 'No one is saying that. Tasha Roux is not saying that, I'm not saying that. Gary Dickinson had a right to life – of course he did. It is a right we all have, each and every one of us. It means everything. But . . .' He continued emphatically, uncoiling himself, 'But. Each and every one of us also has the right to defend ourselves from attack from another person who intends to cause us pain. Tasha Roux had that right. And, whether we like it or not, Gary Dickinson was a man who caused her pain.'

Charlie expertly described the law of self-defence to the jury. He expertly dismissed the telephone text evidence, emphatically telling them that no one who was seriously planning to kill someone would actually be so stupid as to text them about it beforehand. And that pushing someone over a banister would not be the way that someone with a clear and settled intention to kill would do it. Then he reminded them of the two girls, Lilly and Taylor, who had come to court not to bat for a particular side, not to hoodwink them, the jury, into acquitting a friend or loved one, but to tell them what they knew, to help them reach the right verdict. 'And what they knew,' he said, 'was that Gary Dickinson was a man with a propensity for using violence in a particularly nasty and brutal way against women.' He then formed his fists and looked at the jury – 'Like this.'

The jury watched. Twelve pairs of eyes unable to move away from this man as he spoke to them.

'You promised to reach a true verdict according to the evidence,' he concluded, 'you made that promise to the court, to society, and to this young woman. Now I'm going to hold you to that promise, I'm going to ask you to find her not guilty.'

I wanted to stand up and cheer. I wanted to clap and whoop and hug my leader as he finished his speech, but of course I couldn't, I didn't. Instead I reached my hand out towards Kelly and gave her hand a little squeeze under the bench. She squeezed it back.

Tasha Roux was acquitted of murder.

She broke down in floods of tears as the foreman of the jury read out the verdict – then she mouthed, 'Thank you, thank you,' to them as they looked at her and no doubt shared her joy, but at the same time pondered whether they had done the right thing.

We waited for Tasha to be released. It took about twenty minutes. She arrived through a door by the cell area – free. There were hugs and smiles and tears as she thanked me and Kelly, then we let her disappear to her family and friends. Free. Free again.

I found Charlie sitting quietly in the robing room. Roger Fish was congratulating him on a job well done. Charlie smiled and said that it was nice to be back, but he'd forgotten how tiring it could be waiting for a jury.

And he did look tired. He looked as if every ounce of emotion had wrapped itself tightly around him, squeezing the life out of him.

'Well done,' I said.

'Ah Russell, thanks,' he replied wearily, adding, 'I've got something for you.'

And with that he pulled out a red bag with the initials RW embroidered on it in gold lettering. I held it. My red bag.

'I don't know what to say,' I said, 'this means an awful lot to me.'

'Well,' he said, 'this was my last case and I'm glad we won it.'

'Your last case?'

'Yes,' he told me, 'I've got a little part-time job doing some offshore work in the Turks and Caicos Islands. Trust law, boring stuff, but the climate will be nice. Semi-retirement for me and a long-suffering wife. That's why I wanted to do one last case in front of a jury before I slip away.'

I understood now what it had meant to him.

I watched as he packed his wig in his tin, and put his tin in his own red bag, given to him, no doubt, when he was a young, ambitious and enthusiastic junior barrister. I watched him tie the pink ribbon one last time around his last brief, put it all away in his case and walk slowly out of the robing room. The barrister who had his career scarred because he had been instructed to advocate in favour of the death of a young boy, and because he had followed his instructions to the letter. Done his job properly. A proper barrister.

Then I put my own wig tin in my new red bag, slung that over my shoulder and walked out and back to chambers.

Clem Wilson was waiting for me.

'Well done, sir,' he said, beaming proudly, 'a brilliant result.'

'Thanks,' I said coyly.

'Enjoy it,' he said, 'but don't celebrate too hard tonight.'

'Why?' I asked him.

'Because tomorrow you've got to go to Ipswich.'

'Ipswich?'

'Yes. Two sentences and a mention in a burglary. The papers are in your pigeonhole.'

Acknowledgements

I would like to thank all those at Friday Project for their help and perseverance, in particular Scott Pack for giving me the idea and Cicely Aspinall for making sense out of my tortured ramblings.

I'd also like to thank my agent, who knows who he is but can't be named, and my wife and children who put up with my long sessions behind my computer screen with a great deal of patience.

Finally, I'd like to acknowledge all of the lawyers, Judges, clients and court staff who make the job of being a barrister uniquely interesting and always challenging.